Trademark Acknowledgment

Credits

Authors
François Liger
Craig McQueen
Paul Wilton

Technical Reviewers
Mark Horner
Anthony Naylor
Phil Powers-DeGeorge
David Schultz
Erick Sgarbi
Imar Spaanjaars

Technical Editor
Nick Manning

Project Manager
Beckie Stones

Commissioning Editor
Andrew Polshaw

Managing Editor
Jan Kolasinski

Production Co-ordinator
Sarah Hall

Indexer
Bill Johncocks

Proof Reader
Chris Smith

Cover Design
Natalie O'Donnell

About the Authors

François Liger

François Liger is a program manager in the .NET Common Language Runtime group at Microsoft, specializing in the international aspects of the .NET Framework. Prior to this role, he had acquired extensive globalization and localization experience, working on MS-DOS, Windows 95, Internet Explorer, MSN, and Hotmail. He has been using Visual Basic since version 1.0, which he helped launch in France.

For Bérengère and Éloi.

Craig McQueen

Craig McQueen, is the Vice President, Software Development for M Systems Group. Craig has led the development of several major projects, such as Extranets and B2B Integration at Panasonic Canada, and Web Banking initiatives at TD Bank. He has a Masters degree in Computer Science from the University of Toronto and a Bachelor of Science degree in System Design Engineering from the University of Waterloo. Craig shares his knowledge through writing and speaking. He was a contributing author for six books and has written over twenty articles. Craig is also a frequent presenter at conferences in North America and Europe. He can be reached at cmcqueen@msystemsgroup.com.

Visual Basic .NET
Text Manipulation Handbook

® Wrox Press Ltd.

Visual Basic .NET Text Manipulation Handbook

© 2002 Wrox Press Ltd

First published June 2002

wrox

Published by Wrox Press Ltd,
Arden House, 1102 Warwick Road, Acocks Green,
Birmingham, B27 6BH
United Kingdom
Printed in the United States
ISBN 1-86100-730-2

Paul Wilton

After an initial start as a Visual Basic applications programmer at the Ministry of Defence in the UK, Paul found himself pulled into the 'Net. Having joined an Internet development company, he spent three years helping create various Internet solutions, including an e-commerce web site for a major British bank. He's currently working freelance and also busy trying to piece together the Microsoft .NET jigsaw.

Paul's main skills are in developing web front ends using DHTML, JavaScript, VBScript, and Visual Basic and back-end solutions with ASP, Visual Basic, and SQL Server.

Lots of love to my fiancée Catherine who ensures my sanity chip remains plugged in.

VB.NET

Text Manipulation

Handbook

Table of Contents

Table of Contents

VB.NET

Text Manipulation

Handbook

Introduction

Introduction

Text manipulation, as it has been defined at Wrox, is the process of dealing with text within your code. This doesn't just mean appending to, or replacing text in a string, it also covers the various different ways of storing text, in `Strings` or otherwise, and the various techniques used to convert between data types. Any application you create is likely to deal with text at some point in its execution, even if it is only to append the string representation of an integer to the text in a `Console.WriteLine()` statement. The .NET Framework has provided you, the developer, with numerous different data types and methods for manipulating text.

This book addresses exactly how the .NET Framework deals with text; the different ways it can be stored, what happens if a string is changed, why we need a separate `StringBuilder` class, and the implications of the Framework storing all text in Unicode. The book also covers implementation, explaining the various methods available and comparing their performance so that you can make an informed choice when deciding how to manipulate your text. VB6 used to store all text as variants, and gave you little control over how it would be dealt with, and so a very text-intensive Visual Basic application would often suffer in performance. Visual Basic .NET changes all that. Although not as complicated as when dealing with text in C++, for instance, more detail can be provided via the object-oriented framework as to how any text you use can be manipulated within code, and it is important that you understand how the .NET Framework is dealing with your text.

One of the most important new classes available to you for handling strings is `System.Text.RegularExpressions.Regex`. This provides all .NET developers with the ability to use the powerful pattern matching language that regular expressions provide. By "matching", we mean checking to see if a string follows a certain pattern and so contains the data we expect. This is usually more effective than trying to catch an exception from a method you might want to pass the string to (such as might happen when updating a database with invalid data). One of the barriers to Visual Basic developers using regular expressions has been their cryptic syntax, which to the layperson seems to bear little or no relation to the text you are trying to match. However, in Chapters 5-7 we guide you through the regular expression language, explaining what every component means, and instructing you on how to build up complex expressions for matching against even more complicated patterns in text.

Without regular expressions, performing even a simple check on whether an email address has been entered correctly could consume many lines of code. If we assume that the email address has been stored in the `myInput` variable, then a Boolean indicating whether a successful match has been made can be achieved with this line:

```
bIsMatch = Regex.IsMatch(myInput, _
   "^[a-z](\w|\d|[-.])+@([a-z\d-]+\.)+[a-z]{2,4}$", _
   RegexOptions.IgnoreCase)
```

This looks very arcane, but when you have read this book, you will see it as very straightforward. For brevity, this expression doesn't restrict `myInput` enough (although we will do this in Chapter 7), but it does specify the following pattern: The address must start with a letter, followed by one or more letters, underscores, numbers, hyphens or periods, or combinations thereof, followed by "@", followed by one or more patterns of a letter, followed by a possibly repeated pattern of one or more letters, numbers, or hyphens (followed by a period), and ending with a pattern of between 2 and 4 letters. This would match `support@wrox.com`, but not `support@wrox`.

If you are interested in discovering how to use this expression language with Visual Basic .NET code, then the authors will guide you through this pattern matching language as they have had much experience with it, as well as with Visual Basic itself.

Who Is This Book For?

All of the books in this series are targeted at practicing Visual Basic .NET developers, who need to learn more to complete a specific task. This book is no different and will prove useful for anyone who uses text in their applications; this means every developer. The code in this book assumes that the reader has a copy of Visual Basic .NET Standard Edition or above installed, but the code and concepts used apply to, and will work with, the .NET Framework SDK alone.

Book Outline

This book explains the various methods to handle text. Below is an overview of what the chapters contain.

Chapter 1 – How the System Deals with Text

This chapter explains how text is handled by the .NET Framework. It covers the various low-level details such as how strings are stored in memory. After explaining how text is stored, it will become clear why it is important to consider how you are going to be handling text. This chapter will look at some MSIL, but generally it is an overview of text, and a description of how memory and memory management (and so the duration for which strings consume memory) is handled in .NET.

Chapter 2 – String and StringBuilder

This chapter covers the `String` class in exhaustive detail, explaining how strings are implemented in .NET. It also explains how the `StringBuilder` class works and compares the different methods each of these objects have, to learn which methods are the fastest for certain operations. We also look at the Shared Source CLI implementation provided by Microsoft to try to gain some understanding of why different methods appear slower and faster than others, and so in what circumstances a seemingly slower method may be appropriate.

Chapter 3 – String Conversion

This chapter covers the issues behind converting strings to and from other data types. It discusses how different data types, such as numbers and dates/times are presented differently in different locales, and how to cope with this. We also cover some of the issues behind storing strings in arrays and collections and how to best manipulate strings stored in this way.

Chapter 4 – Internationalization

All text is stored in the .NET Framework in the 16-bit Unicode encoding. This chapter describes this to you and explains how to deal with the fact that string characters are now at least 16-bits wide. We cover locales in detail, and the various methods used to present text for different locales, as well as how to manipulate `Char` types, as in Unicode, a complete character could be made up of two 16-bit `Char` types. This chapter provides information on how you can prepare your text for presentation in different languages.

Chapter 5 – Introducing Regular Expressions

This chapter introduces you to the regular expression matching language, and how to use it to match patterns of text. First we teach you how to do the same jobs that can be done using `String` methods, but once you are more familiar with the syntax, then we cover the unique features that the language provides. We also walk you through the creation of a Regular Expression Tester that can prove very useful in testing your future expressions.

Chapter 6 – Advanced Regex Concepts

The previous chapter was an introduction to the matching language; here we ramp up the learning curve and as well as providing more examples of regexes, we describe groups, substitutions, and backreferences. Grouping allows the regular expression to attempt to match groups of text. These groups can be captured and given names. Backreferences can be used to pull out previous matches and can be used, for instance, to match an HTML close tag with its corresponding open tag.

Chapter 7 – Regular Expression Patterns

In this chapter we detail various regular expression patterns for matching specific types of common data, such as numbers, dates, etc. We describe how these patterns are formed, and so help you form your own patterns. One of the patterns used is an email address validator, which is a long and complex expression and apart from being useful in itself, its explanation will help explain how simple it is to build up expressions that match a variety of text patterns.

Appendices

There are four appendices; the first two contain tables listing the methods, properties, and constructors of the `String` and `StringBuilder` classes, whereas the third contains much of the regular expression syntax, options, and special characters for regular expressions. The last contains support and code download details for the book.

The Code Download

As with all Wrox books, the code contained within can be downloaded from the Wrox web site. However, to accompany the techniques described in this book, I have provided an assembly, called `Wrox.Text.dll`, which contains many of the useful methods, properties, and enumerations contained within this book that could be applied to your future projects. By importing this into your applications, you can immediately make use of many of the useful patterns and methods discussed in this book. All classes are contained within the `Wrox.Text` namespace.

Andrew Polshaw
Editor: Handbook Series, Wrox Press

VB.NET

Text Manipulation

Handbook

1

1

How the System Deals with Text

Text is the most used data type in computer applications. Manipulating and utilizing text effectively is vital for robust and maintainable applications. A robust and maintainable application is one that will perform well, use memory efficiently, and be easy to translate, if necessary. Used incorrectly, text processing can result in memory leaks, poor performance, memory exceptions, and difficulty porting an application to another language.

To provide an understanding of how text is used within MS Windows and the .NET Framework, the following issues will be addressed in this chapter:

- ❑ The .NET Framework
- ❑ Text as a data type
- ❑ Characters and strings
- ❑ How an operating system stores text
- ❑ Typical text operations
- ❑ Common text uses
- ❑ Internationalization and Localization

This chapter describes how text is used in a typical computer operating system. Specific descriptions are given of how text is used in Visual Basic .NET.

This chapter will show some examples to set the context of how text processing was performed before Visual Basic .NET and the .NET Framework. Within this chapter, the term "Visual Basic" refers to Visual Basic 6.0 and earlier. By the conclusion of the chapter, you will have an understanding of the underlying issues a computer application faces when processing text. We will also look at how .NET deals with string storage. The rest of the book will show how Visual Basic .NET specifically handles text processing.

The .NET Framework

To understand how the system processes text we need to understand particular portions of the system first. The .NET Framework represents a significant shift from the Win32 architecture and as such there are many new concepts.

The .NET Framework consists of an execution environment (a.k.a. runtime) and a class library. The execution environment is responsible for many of the core services required by a .NET application. This includes memory allocation and cleanup. Since strings require a lot of memory management, the implementation of the execution environment will have a significant impact on the performance of applications using string manipulation.

Common Language Runtime

The execution environment is generically called the **Common Language Infrastructure** (CLI). The CLI is a standard that Microsoft has submitted to **ECMA**, which is an organization dedicated to standardizing information and communication systems. The specific standard reference is ECMA-335.

The CLI defines a specification for executable code and the execution environment. The execution environment is also known as a **Virtual Execution System** (VES). Microsoft's implementation of the CLI is the **Common Language Runtime** (CLR). When discussing the Microsoft-specific implementation CLR is used. When discussing the standard which the CLR adheres to, CLI is used. In this book, CLR is used the majority of the time since it is the Microsoft implementation that we are using.

A core part of the CLI is the **Common Type System** (CTS). The CTS defines support for the types and operations found in many programming languages and will be covered in more detail later.

Related to the CTS is the **Common Language Specification** (CLS), which is a set of rules to promote language interoperability. A key goal of the .NET Framework is to enable you to write a program in any language you like and run it in .NET. Each language is supposed to be able to operate with any other. The CLS guides tool implementers to ensure the code that they write can move across languages as easily as possible.

The CLR can be thought of as the "manager" of an application written in .NET. The CLR makes sure the application adheres to security rules and provides resources to the application. An application written in .NET is called managed code since the CLR manages how the code runs.

Managed code is stored and transmitted through the **Common Intermediate Language** (CIL) and a file format. CIL is the instruction set that all source code languages are compiled to. So, if you are writing in Visual Basic .NET, C#, or any other .Net language, the compiler will convert the source code to CIL instructions. Microsoft's implementation of CIL is called MSIL.

Managed data is data allocated and released automatically by the CLR, and is stored in the managed heap. The automatic releasing is handled through garbage collection.

Managed Heap

The CLR provides automatic memory management, meaning that it takes care of memory allocation and de-allocation. This is a significant benefit for developers, since some of the most common and difficult-to-trace bugs in applications are memory leaks. A memory leak happens when a developer allocates memory and forgets to release it. Memory leaks also happen because it is sometimes not clear who is responsible for releasing the memory. For instance, if a component allocates some memory and returns the memory to the caller – who is supposed to release it and when?

Since strings usually have to be allocated, any memory management benefits translate to benefits for string use.

When an application first starts up, the CLR reserves a block of memory for use by the application. This memory block is the managed heap. All reference types are stored on the heap. As we will see later, a String is a reference type, so it is stored in the heap and treated like all other pieces of allocated memory.

Figure 1 illustrates what the heap looks like.

Figure 1

As you can see, the heap has a block of memory with a base memory address. The memory is contiguous and storage is allocated in a linear fashion. Since the heap memory is already allocated, the only thing the garbage collector has to do to return some allocated memory to the system is increment the next available address by the size of the memory being required. This makes for fast allocation of memory.

Allocation is straightforward; releasing memory is much more complicated. In fact, the term "garbage collection" really refers to releasing memory that is no longer being used. Computer scientists have studied various algorithms for performing garbage collection. The .NET documentation outlines the steps the garbage collector takes for releasing memory. They are not repeated here.

.NET Framework Class Library

The .NET Framework Class Library is a collection of types to support programming in the .NET Framework. A type includes classes, structures, and base types. For example, both the `System.Text.StringBuilder` class and the `Char` structure are considered types. The class library is quite extensive and includes classes for XML processing, file I/O, drawing, threading, and, of course, string manipulation to just name a few.

Within the `System` namespace there are two important classes:

❑ `Char` – This structure is a Unicode character that has methods for converting characters and categorizing characters, such as whitespace.

❑ `String` – This class is an immutable string of characters that has methods for manipulating the string. See Appendix A for a complete list of the constructors, properties, and methods of the `String` class.

The `System.Text` namespace contains the important `StringBuilder` class that can be used to incrementally construct strings (see Appendix B for a complete list of the constructors, properties, and methods of the `StringBuilder` class). The namespace also contains classes for converting one character encoding to another, such as `Encoding`, `ASCIIEncoding`, and `UnicodeEncoding`.

The `System.Text.RegularExpressions` namespace contains various classes for constructing and executing regular expressions, such as `Capture`, `CaptureCollection`, `Regex`, and `RegexCompilationInfo`.

To summarize, the following are the important points to remember out of this discussion.

❑ Text manipulation functionality is provided by .NET Framework Classes

❑ The CLR is responsible for application services including allocating and moving memory to support strings

❑ Memory management is implemented in the CLR as garbage collection

Next, let's look closer at what a data type really is.

Text as a Data Type

A data type in a programming language is data with predefined characteristics. The data type defines the rules regarding which values the data may take on. Most programming languages have some built-in data types. Examples of data types include integer, floating point, and string.

Strongly typed programming languages, such as the .NET languages, enforce these rules. If you try to assign a value that does not correspond to the data type, you will receive an error message. Typically these rules are enforced by the compiler, meaning that data type errors are caught early and do not make it to the run-time code.

In addition to the values it can take on, a data type is constrained by the operations that can be performed on it. For instance, using division on a string data type would not make any sense.

Text is a data type with minimal rules. Since there are minimal rules governing the values text can take on, it is used in situations where a programmer is unsure about the range of values in the data source, such as receiving data from an external source. However, this can cause problems as data may not be stored as efficiently as possible.

In some programming languages, the text data type has become awkward to handle. Visual C++ is an example. The following are some of the possible data type choices for storing text when using Visual C++.

Description	Examples
Character array	`char myString[32];`
Wide character array	`w_char myString[32];`
Standard C++ library	`std::string myString;`
MFC CString	`CStr myString;`
OLE Automation string	`BSTR myString;`
Class wrapper for BSTR	`CComBSTR myString;`

On top of that, there are functions to manipulate and convert between the different string types. There is no need to have this many ways to represent strings; they are a product of history only. Originally, characters were stored in one byte. As applications became more international, some situations required two bytes to represent all the characters in particular alphabets.

You will note that I started using the term string to represent text. I am not sure who originated the term 'string' for use in describing a programming language data type. However, it is obvious how it came about. Character string is the full terminology used and it represents a sequence (or string) of characters. For the rest of the chapter, the term string will be used instead of text.

Since .NET is a new software platform, there was an opportunity to define the `String` data type from scratch and avoid the mess that had evolved in some programming languages.

Visual Basic .NET Data Types

The types in Visual Basic .NET are built on the Common Type System (CTS). A goal of the .NET Framework is to give programmers the freedom to develop in a variety of .NET-compliant languages, yet still operate on the same underlying platform. The CTS defines the types that the .NET languages must implement.

Value Types and Reference Types

The two fundamental categories of data types in .NET are value types and reference types.

Value types include integers, enumerations, structures, and characters. Value types are stored directly on the stack, which is a contiguous area of memory set aside by the operating system for fast access to data. The CLR uses a virtual stack for each process that is running. Since the size of a value type is known, it can be stored on the stack. Value types are always accessed directly, never through a reference. When a value type is copied, the value is copied to another location.

Examples of reference types include classes, interfaces, arrays, and strings. Reference types are stored in the managed heap, which is an area of memory set aside for dynamic memory allocation where blocks of memory are allocated and freed in an arbitrary order. The sizes of reference types are not known until run time. This is why the heap is used for storing them.

Reference types are accessed through a reference to the storage (somewhat like a pointer). This allows the garbage collector to keep track of references and release storage when no more references remain. When reference variables are copied, the reference (which is the memory address) is copied, not the value itself.

Primitive Types

The .NET Framework class library is a collection of types that tightly integrate with the Common Language Runtime. The class library is object-oriented, meaning that all types have properties and methods. Some types are used so commonly that shortcuts are provided for describing them. These types are called primitive types.

Primitive types are identified through keywords, which are aliases for predefined types in the `System` namespace. A primitive type is indistinguishable from the structure type it aliases: writing the reserved word `Char` is the same as writing `System.Char`. Primitive types offer these additional operations over other types:

❑ All primitive types permit values to be created by writing literals. For example, `"A"c` is a literal of type `Char`.

❑ It is possible to declare constants using primitive types.

❑   When the operands of an expression are all primitive type constants, it is possible for the compiler to evaluate the expression at compile time. Such an expression is known as a constant expression.

The following are examples uses of primitive types declared in a Visual Basic .NET program:

```
Dim myChar As Char = "A"c
Dim myString As String = "My String!"
Dim myInt As Integer = 3
```

The String type is unique in that it is the only primitive type that is a reference and not a value type. This causes a flaw in logic; being a primitive type, strings can be declared constant. However, constants cannot be placed on the heap since the heap performs run-time allocation and constants are defined when the program is compiled. A constant string is a special situation and a process called interning is performed, which will be discussed later.

Before we look further into the string data type though, let's look at the fundamental unit of strings – the character data type.

Characters and Character Sets

A definition of a character can be found at http://whatis.techtarget.com. This web site defines a character as follows:

In information technology, a character is a printable symbol having phonetic or pictographic meaning and usually forming part of a word of text, depicting a numeral, or expressing grammatical punctuation. In information technology today, a character is generally one of a limited number of symbols, including the letters of a particular language's alphabet, the numerals in the decimal number system, and certain special symbols such as the ampersand (&) and "at sign" (@).

Several standards of computer encoding have been developed for characters. The most commonly used in personal computers is ASCII. IBM mainframe systems use EBCDIC. A new standard, Unicode, is supported by later Windows systems.

That is a good definition. It defines that a character represents a symbol to communicate information to computer users. The only addition is that since characters are historically represented by a byte, they are sometimes used to represent binary information. The definition also indicates there are standards for encoding characters.

ASCII is what PCs traditionally used to store characters. An ASCII character is stored as a 7-bit binary number. That means an ASCII character can take on one of 128 values. The ASCII format is quite old; it was originally developed for teletypes so some of the ASCII values are control characters for the teletype (for example, ASCII value 23, which represents "end of transmission block").

Since modern computers store information as bytes, each of which is 8 bits, one bit was wasted for each character. One bit may not sound like much but if all 8 bits are used instead of 7, twice as many characters values can be represented.

As computers evolved, programmers decided to make use of the extra bit and Extended ASCII was born. By using the extra bit, 128 more values could be added to the ASCII character set. These additional characters include accented characters, mathematical symbols, and graphics characters.

There are a few varying extended ASCII characters sets. If you are moving characters between platforms, for example from Windows to Macintosh, the extended ASCII characters may have different meanings. For example, the letter ç on Windows appears as Á on a Macintosh. Extended characters sets are also referred to as code pages.

If you intend to use the extended ASCII characters between platforms, you should identify the characters set by using a code page. With the Internet, HTML and XML tend to be the text documents that move between platforms. In HTML, you can specify the code page with the following:

```
<META HTTP-EQUIV="Content-Type"
       CONTENT="text/html; charset=ISO-8859-1">
```

In this example, the code page is ISO-8859-1, which is known as Latin1 and covers most West European languages, including English, French, German, Italian, and Spanish.

With XML, a processing instruction is used to represent the character encoding:

```
<?xml version="1.0" encoding="ISO-8859-1"?>
```

> It should be noted that the first 128 character codes of any of the ISO 8859 character sets are always identical to the ASCII character set.

In the late 1980s, a number of researchers tackled the problem of representing different languages with the same character set. Out of that research, the Unicode Consortium was born in the early 1990s. The Unicode Consortium is responsible for defining the behavior and relationships between Unicode characters, and providing technical information to implementers. Some of the members include Adobe, Apple, Microsoft, IBM, and Sun.

The Unicode Consortium states the following:

> Unicode provides a unique number for every character, no matter what the platform, no matter what the program and no matter what the language.

The Unicode standard defines codes for characters in most major languages written today. Examples of supported scripts include Latin, Greek, Cyrillic, Armenian, Hebrew, Arabic, Devanagari, Oriya, Tamil, and Braille. In addition to scripts, the standard includes punctuation marks, diacritics, mathematical symbols, technical symbols, arrows, and dingbats.

The Unicode Version 2.1 standard provides codes for nearly 39,000 characters from the world's alphabets, ideograph sets, and symbol collections. In addition, there are approximately 18,000 code values reserved for future use. The Unicode standard also contains 6,400 code values that software and hardware developers can assign internally for their own characters and symbols.

The Unicode standard manages to represent so many characters by using an extra byte. Unicode is a 2-byte encoding meaning it can represent 256*256 = 65,536 characters. However, what you get in flexibility you sacrifice with space. A Unicode text file is twice the size of an ASCII file, and the same applies to memory usage. As a result, if you are constrained for space, and are only using ASCII characters, you should consider how your programming language is representing the characters.

Alas, the original Unicode specification cannot handle all character requirements. The Chinese speaking community alone uses over 55,000 characters. To accommodate this problem, the Unicode Standard defines surrogates. A surrogate or surrogate pair is a pair of 16-bit Unicode code values that represent a single character. Using surrogates, Unicode can support over one million characters. This will be covered more in Chapter 4.

Characters in Visual Basic .NET

Visual Basic .NET stores characters as Unicode. A single Unicode characters is represented by the Char value type that maps to the System.Char structure. Since Unicode is represented by two bytes, a character can take on any value from hexadecimal 0x0000 to 0xFFFF.

One of the biggest differences between characters in .NET vs. those in previous languages is that characters are defined as objects, with members. This means that, instead of using functions that operate on a character, we use a character's methods. In addition, constants associated with the data type (such as a minimum value) are tied to the object itself, rather than a separate value listed elsewhere.

One of the more useful methods of the Char structure is GetUnicodeCategory(). This Shared method classifies the type of character passed to it into one of 30 categories. Example categories include UppercaseLetter, ParagraphSeparator, DashPunctuation, and CurrencySymbol.

The Char structure also has a number of methods to classify characters, such as IsDigit() and IsPunctuation(). Here's an example using these methods:

```
Dim band As String
band = "Led Zeppelin"

Console.WriteLine(Char.IsWhiteSpace(band, 3))    ' Output: "True"
Console.WriteLine(Char.IsPunctuation("A"c))      ' Output: "False"
```

Using the IsWhiteSpace() method, a test is performed to see if the fourth character in the string is a whitespace characters. The IsPunctuation() method tests if the letter "A" is punctuation. Note that the 'c' beside the "A" explicitly makes the value a character data type. See the .NET Framework documentation for all the methods supported by the Char structure.

You can obtain the character code (also known as code point) for a character using the Asc() method (the Unicode code point is returned using the AscW() method):

```
Dim intCharCode
intCharCode = Asc("A")    ' intCharCode is set to 65.
```

Similarly, the Chr() and ChrW() functions return the character represented by the given character code:

```
Dim myChar As Char
myChar = Chr(65)
Console.WriteLine(myChar)    ' myChar is set to A.
```

A good way to understand how characters are represented in memory is to write them to a file and then look at them with a binary editor. The bytes in the file are the same as those that get stored in memory. The following example opens a file and writes text to that file in three different encodings. The file extension is .bin to force the file to be opened with a binary editor:

```
Imports System
Imports System.IO
Imports System.Text

Public Class Binary

  Shared Sub Main()
    Dim fs As FileStream
    fs = New FileStream("text.bin", FileMode.OpenOrCreate)

    Dim t As StreamWriter
    t = New StreamWriter(fs, Encoding.UTF8)
    t.Write("This is in UTF8")
    t.Flush()

    Dim t2 As StreamWriter
    t2 = New StreamWriter(fs, Encoding.Unicode)
    t2.Write("This is in Unicode")
    t2.Flush()
```

```
        Dim t3 As StreamWriter
        t3 = New StreamWriter(fs, Encoding.ASCII)
        t3.Write("This is in ASCII")
        t3.Flush()

        fs.Close()

    End Sub
End Class
```

Using the binary editor built in to Visual Studio .NET, you can see that the data looks like the following.

```
Binary.vb  text.bin                                                ◁ ▷ ×
00000000   EF BB BF 54 68 69 73 20   69 73 20 69 6E 20 55 54   ...This is in UT
00000010   46 38 54 00 68 00 69 00   73 00 20 00 69 00 73 00   F8T.h.i.s. .i.s.
00000020   20 00 69 00 6E 00 20 00   55 00 6E 00 69 00 63 00    .i.n. .U.n.i.c.
00000030   6F 00 64 00 65 00 54 68   69 73 20 69 73 20 69 6E   o.d.e.This is in
00000040   20 41 53 43 49 49                                    ASCII
```

There are a few interesting points to notice. In all three encodings, the low bytes are the same. The low byte is the first sixteen bits of the value. For instance, the letter 'T' is represented by the value 0x54 in all cases. The Unicode encoding has an extra byte with each character that doubles the amount of space it requires compared to ASCII or UTF-8.

Now that we have covered characters individually, let us look at character strings.

String Data Type

As mentioned, a string is a series of characters. In fact, with the original version of C, strings could only be represented as an array of characters. The same functions for manipulating arrays of bytes were used to manipulate strings.

The .NET Framework uses a String class to implement the String data type. The following code shows declaration of a String and an array of Strings:

```
Dim myString As String = "My String!"
Dim arrString As String() = {"to", "the", "max"}
```

Strings can cause a lot of trouble. Strings are a unique data type in that they are the only primitive data type that is of variable length, and this can cause problems. Computers need to know how long data is so that space can be allocated for it. To understand how this issue has been approached let us look at how text is stored.

Text Storage

Storage of text is dependent on the programming language or software platform being used. To create a computer application, instructions are written in a programming language. The programming language may provide an implementation of these instructions itself or call on the services of an underlying software platform.

When compiled, for instance, a program written in C converts the instructions directly into machine code. Machine code does not know anything about strings; it only understands allocating memory and copying bytes. As a result, much of the work required to manipulate strings is part of the C programming language.

In the case of .NET, the CLR implements the functionality described within the program. Therefore, the CLR must understand how to do the text allocation and copying.

Text can be statically or dynamically allocated. If it is statically allocated, the operating system knows exactly how many characters (and thus how much space) will be required when the program is compiled. If it is dynamically allocated, then the operating system does not reserve any space for the string until run time.

There are two common methods for programming languages to keep track of how long a string is. They can either store the length of the string at its beginning or the string can contain a special character representing a terminator.

When the length of a string is stored at its beginning, it is often referred to as a **structured string** or a **Pascal string**. As you probably can guess, Pascal is one programming language that takes this approach. The first byte in a structured string is a length byte, which is the number of characters in the string. The actual characters themselves follow the length byte.

Since the length of the string is available immediately, string operations can be much faster. For instance, determining the length of a string is a matter of reading the first byte, whereas with a terminated string the entire string must be scanned to find the terminator. Consider the following pseudo-code:

```
For I = 1 to StrLen(myString)
    // do something
Next
```

If the string length were 1000, the number of operations for a Pascal string would be 1000. However, for a terminated string the number of operations would be calculated by the formula StrLen(myString)*StrLen(myString) = 1,000,000! This is an example of how, even though a programmer should be shielded from how a programming language implements operations, it is important to have an understanding of the implications of constructing code a certain way. A better way to implement the operation would be the following:

```
lenString = StrLen(myString)

For I = 1 to lenString
    // do something
Next
```

For a terminated string, this would reduce the number of operations back to a linear relationship rather than a quadratic.

Figure 2 shows how a Pascal string is stored in memory:

Figure 2

The alternative to prefixing the string with its length is to put a special character in the string indicating it is the end of the string. Often a null character of value 0x00 is used, as shown in Figure 3:

Figure 3

This approach has the flexibility of allowing strings to be any length, but it also has its problems. To determine the length of the string you have to go through every single character. In addition, as C programmers are already well aware, you can easily cause memory faults by forgetting to terminate the string, or overwriting the null character.

In both cases, programmers are encouraged to manipulate strings in a particular manner that is efficient for that type of string representation. However, the Pascal form of string manipulation is quite inefficient when used on null-terminated strings, as in C. Thus, code in one language that performs string manipulation cannot be directly translated to another language without introducing inefficiencies.

Since string manipulation is often expensive, software platform designers have often looked into techniques for improving performance. We'll take a look at some of those techniques now.

Caching

To minimize the amount of memory allocation that happens for strings, some systems implement a caching scheme. Microsoft Automation does this with Automation's representation of Unicode characters, also known as BSTRs (Binary Strings).

BSTRs are null-terminated; however, you can query a BSTR for its length rather than scan it, so it can contain embedded null characters. The length is stored as a 32-bit integer at the memory location preceding the data in the string. The theoretical maximum length of a BSTR is 4,294,967,296 characters, however, your operating system may grind to a halt long before this level depending upon available resources.

Automation may cache the space allocated for BSTRs. This speeds up the allocation and de-allocation sequence. For example, if the application allocates a BSTR and frees it, the free block of memory is put into the BSTR cache by Automation. If the application then allocates another BSTR, it can get the free block from the cache.

A null pointer is a valid value for a BSTR variable. By convention, it is always treated the same as a pointer to a BSTR that contains zero characters.

The Automation string cache is about 60K, so concatenations that fit in this size are optimized for performance. The cache is designed to operate on strings in an efficient way. Longer strings are heap-allocated and take considerably longer to be concatenated. The implication is that performance can be significantly increased by concatenating smaller strings first so that the cache is used.

For example, consider the following statement:

```
sLongString = sLongString & "." & vbCrLf
```

The chance that the cache is used will be increased by concentrating the smaller strings first:

```
sLongString = sLongString & ("." & vbCrLf)
```

Interning

Sometimes strings are continually reused in an application. Exploiting this characteristic can lead to substantial memory savings and performance gains and interning is a data structure and set of algorithms used to achieve these benefits.

Interning offers a performance advantage in the situation where the same strings are used repeatedly. It has some up-front resource cost, but once in place it supports efficient equality checking between strings, since it is comparing pooled objects rather than characters sequences.

The CLR automatically maintains a table, called the "intern pool", which contains a single instance of each unique literal string constant declared in a program, as well as any unique instance of the String class you create programmatically.

The intern pool is implemented as a hash table. Using a hash table means a string is represented by a single number or 'hash'. Comparing and searching for strings then becomes very efficient because, instead of comparing strings character for character, only the hash value has to be compared.

The intern pool conserves string storage. If you assign a literal string constant to several variables, each variable is set to reference the same constant in the intern pool, rather than reference several different instances of the String class that have identical values.

Strings created using the StringBuilder class can be manually added to the intern pool using the Intern() method. We shall see more about interning in Chapter 2.

Other Approaches

For specialized applications, there are algorithms and data structures for storing text efficiently. An example is a **trie**. A trie is a tree structure for storing strings and has been used to store large dictionaries of words for spell checking programming and natural language processing.

Let us look at a simple example of how a trie works. Consider the words "exposition" and "exposure". Stored individually, the total space occupied by these words is 18 characters. However, the first 5 characters are the same. A trie would store the common characters once and then have pointers to the other characters in the words. This reduces the number of characters stored to 13. When a large number of words are stored, the amount of memory saved can be substantial.

Certain programming APIs, such as **Xalan-Java 2,** implement a trie class. If the language does not support it natively, then the programmer would have to build the data structure.

The CLR implementation of the intern pool is as a hash table. However, it could also be implemented as a trie. With the CLI available as a shared source it would be possible for you to make that change as an academic exercise.

.NET Implementation

We have looked at various approaches to storing strings. Now let's use an example to demonstrate how .NET does it.

Consider the following simple Visual Basic .NET program that declares a string variable:

```
Module Module1
    Sub Main()
        Dim myString As String = "hello string"
    End Sub
End Module
```

When viewed with the ildasm command-line utility, the IL code that implements this source code looks like the following listing:

```
.method public static void  Main() cil managed
{
  .entrypoint
  .custom instance void [mscorlib]System.STAThreadAttribute::.ctor() =
( 01 00 00 00 )
  // Code size       9 (0x9)
  .maxstack  1
  .locals init ([0] string myString)
  IL_0000:  nop
  IL_0001:  ldstr      "hello string"
  IL_0006:  stloc.0
  IL_0007:  nop
  IL_0008:  ret
} // end of method Module1::Main
```

This is the extent to which the portable executable knows about loading a string. The IL code just knows that it is supposed to put the characters hello string into a string object. The actual work of doing this is up to the CLI implementation.

In the file string.cs of the Shared Source CLI we can see that the constructor is declared externally:

```
[MethodImplAttribute(MethodImplOptions.InternalCall)]
public extern String(char [] value);
```

To see the actual implementation, we have to switch from C# code to C++ code in the Virtual Machine. Within the code of COMString.cpp, we can find the code that implements the constructor:

```
STRINGREF COMString::NewString(const WCHAR *pwsz)
{
  THROWSCOMPLUSEXCEPTION();
```

```
       if (!pwsz)
       {
         return NULL;
       }
       else
       {
         DWORD nch = (DWORD)wcslen(pwsz);
         if (nch==0) {
           return GetEmptyString();
         }
         _ASSERTE(!g_pGCHeap->IsHeapPointer((BYTE *) pwsz) ||
                  !"pwsz can not point to GC Heap");
         STRINGREF pString = AllocateString( nch + 1);

         memcpyNoGCRefs(pString->GetBuffer(), pwsz, nch*sizeof(WCHAR));
         pString->SetStringLength(nch);
         _ASSERTE(pString->GetBuffer()[nch] == 0);
         return pString;
       }
     }
```

The AllocateString() call returns a pointer to a StringObject. The C++
StringObject class is the internal representation of a .NET String. A portion of the
StringObject implementation is listed below:

```
     class StringObject : public Object
     {
       friend class GCHeap;
       friend class JIT_TrialAlloc;

       private:
         DWORD   m_ArrayLength;
         DWORD   m_StringLength;
         WCHAR   m_Characters[0];
```

We have finally found where the data is stored. It is an array of WCHAR. A WCHAR is a
two-byte character. As you can see, an array length and string length are also stored.
The array length is the size of allocated memory measured in number of WCHAR's. The
string length is the number of WCHAR's in the string. The array length may be greater
than the string length, which means there is unused space in the string.

The m_StringLength has another responsibility as well. The two high bits of this
value indicate if the string has characters higher than 0x7F. If not, it means the
characters occupy the standard ASCII character set. If this is the case then the system
can use algorithms that process the string faster. The implication of this is that, if you
can keep the characters in a string to the ASCII standard character set, you may get
some performance optimizations from the system.

We have seen that ultimately a string is stored as an array of characters. Why not do
this to start with? The code would look like the following (the string was shortened to
make it more readable):

```vb
Sub Main()
    Dim myString As Char() = {"h", "e", "l", "l", "o"}
End Sub
```

The generated IL code looks like the following:

```
.method public static void  Main() cil managed
{
  .entrypoint
  .custom instance void [mscorlib]System.STAThreadAttribute::.ctor() =
( 01 00 00 00 )
  // Code size       37 (0x25)
  .maxstack  3
  .locals init ([0] char[] myString,
           [1] char[] _Vb_t_array_0)
  IL_0000:  nop
  IL_0001:  ldc.i4.5
  IL_0002:  newarr     [mscorlib]System.Char
  IL_0007:  stloc.1
  IL_0008:  ldloc.1
  IL_0009:  ldc.i4.0
  IL_000a:  ldc.i4.s   104
  IL_000c:  stelem.i2
  IL_000d:  ldloc.1
  IL_000e:  ldc.i4.1
  IL_000f:  ldc.i4.s   101
  IL_0011:  stelem.i2
  IL_0012:  ldloc.1
  IL_0013:  ldc.i4.2
  IL_0014:  ldc.i4.s   108
  IL_0016:  stelem.i2
  IL_0017:  ldloc.1
  IL_0018:  ldc.i4.3
  IL_0019:  ldc.i4.s   108
  IL_001b:  stelem.i2
  IL_001c:  ldloc.1
  IL_001d:  ldc.i4.4
  IL_001e:  ldc.i4.s   111
  IL_0020:  stelem.i2
  IL_0021:  ldloc.1
  IL_0022:  stloc.0
  IL_0023:  nop
  IL_0024:  ret
} // end of method Module1::Main
```

Yikes! That looks like a lot of instructions to initialize a string. Each individual character is loaded onto the stack and stored in an array location. It seems like an awkward way to initialize a string.

Alternatively, you can specify the character array explicitly as a string. This is more attractive to look at:

```
Sub Main()
    Dim myString As Char() = "hello world!"
End Sub
```

The IL code looks like the following:

```
.method public static void  Main() cil managed
{
  .entrypoint
  .custom instance void [mscorlib]System.STAThreadAttribute::.ctor() =
( 01 00 00 00 )
  // Code size        14 (0xe)
  .maxstack  1
  .locals init ([0] char[] myString)
  IL_0000:  nop
  IL_0001:  ldstr      "hello world!"
  IL_0006:  call       char[]
[Microsoft.VisualBasic]Microsoft.VisualBasic.CompilerServices.CharArra
yType::FromString(string)
  IL_000b:  stloc.0
  IL_000c:  nop
  IL_000d:  ret
} // end of method Module1::Main
```

There is a lot less IL code in this in case. Notice that a `String` object is created. This shifts more of the work from IL instructions to the CLR.

The methods used to manipulate arrays can also be used to manipulate strings. The following example demonstrates a few operations you can do:

```
Imports System

Public Class Methods

  Shared Sub Main()
    Dim myString As Char() = "hello string!"
    Dim i As Integer

    ' Display a substring
    Console.WriteLine(myString)
    For i = 6 To myString.GetLength(0) - 2
      Console.Write(myString(i))
    Next
    Console.WriteLine()

    ' Find the last 'l' in the string
    Console.WriteLine(Array.LastIndexOf(myString, "l"c))

    ' Reverse the string
    Array.Reverse(myString)
    Console.WriteLine(myString)
```

```
' Sort the characters in the string
    Array.Sort(myString)
    Console.WriteLine(myString)

    Console.ReadLine()

  End Sub
End Class
```

The following output will be displayed on the console:

```
hello string!
string
3
!gnirts olleh
 !eghillnorst
```

Some operations, such as `Sort()` and `Reverse()`, are not available as part of the `String` and `StringBuilder` classes, which makes a case for representing a string as an array of characters when the need arises.

String Operations

Operations on strings generally fall into the following five broad categories:

- ❑ Concatenating strings
- ❑ Extracting substrings from strings
- ❑ Comparing strings
- ❑ Converting strings
- ❑ Formatting strings

We will briefly look at these operations in this section, and then see how they combine for common text operations in the next section. The resource cost of the operations will be discussed in terms of performance (time to execute a task) and memory requirements.

Concatenation

Concatenation is probably the most used operation on strings. However, it is also probably the most expensive string operation since it demands substantial CPU resources to copy bytes. An application can really suffer from performance problems with string concatenation.

Let us look at a sample piece of code:

```
Dim str1
Dim str2
Dim str3

str1 = "abcde"
str2 = "fgh"
str3 = str1 & str2
```

Figure 4 represents the highlighted operation:

Figure 4

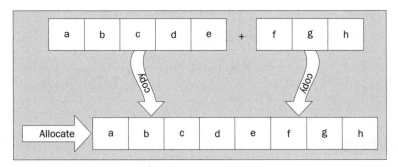

First, new memory has to be allocated to accommodate the new string. Then the characters have to be copied from the source strings to the destination string.

Unfortunately, the situation is even worse. String concatenation in legacy Visual Basic is such a performance killer that Microsoft released a knowledge base article. The article "*HOWTO: Improve String Concatenation Performance*" (*KB Q170964*) describes an alternative technique to normal concatenation that can improve performance for large strings by twenty times or more. Consider the following simple loop, which contains a concatenation operation in each iteration of the loop:

```
For i = 1 To N
   Dest = Dest & Source
Next
```

To execute this set of code, Visual Basic will execute the following steps.

1. Allocate temporary memory large enough to hold the result

2. Copy Dest to the start of the temporary area

3. Copy Source to the end of the temporary area

4. De-allocate the old copy of Dest

5. Allocate memory for Dest large enough to hold the result

6. Copy the temporary data to Dest

The following is the result Microsoft gives:

```
Using standard concatenation
 1000 concatenations took 2348 ticks
 2000 concatenations took 8954 ticks
 3000 concatenations took 20271 ticks
 4000 concatenations took 35103 ticks
 5000 concatenations took 54453 ticks

Using pre-allocated storage and pseudo-concatenation
 1000 pseudo-concatenations took 82 ticks
 2000 pseudo-concatenations took 124 ticks
 3000 pseudo-concatenations took 165 ticks
 4000 pseudo-concatenations took 247 ticks
 5000 pseudo-concatenations took 289 ticks
```

The implication is that good string design would use the "pre-allocated storage and pseudo-concatenation" technique. In Chapter 2, we will see how .NET addresses this problem with the StringBuilder class.

Substrings

Instead of making strings bigger with concatenation, we often want to make them smaller. The Trim() method in Visual Basic is used to remove leading or trailing white space and programmers often use this to clean up user-entered text.

Sometimes specific characters need to be extracted from the string. In Visual Basic, Right() and Mid() are examples of methods used to extract portions of a string. In reality, using a Trim() method is the same as extracting a sub-string; you are just relying on the function to determine where the sub-string should be taken. You can still use these methods in Visual Basic .NET.

In all cases, these functions consist of copying all or a subset of a string to another string. The specific steps are:

1. Determine the number of characters to copy

2. Allocate space for the characters

3. Copy the characters to the new string

Because of the memory allocation and copying operations involved, extracting sub-strings is also an expensive operation.

Comparing Strings

String comparison is a common operation. Often the user will have entered some text and the program needs to determine something about what the user has entered. Some string comparisons require an exact match. This is straightforward operation as it is simply a character-by-character comparison of the two strings. Visual Basic accomplishes this task with the StrComp() method. Since there is no memory allocation or copying involved, this operation is not as resource expensive.

Visual Basic defines two constants for comparing text; vbBinaryCompare and vbTextCompare. However, the naming is a little misleading. A binary comparison performs a case-sensitive comparison, whereas a text comparison performs a case-insensitive comparison. Instead of using constants, Visual Basic .NET takes a parameter to compare methods that specifies whether or not to compare case.

In many situations, string comparison is used for validation. Often the content is not what is important but rather the format of the data. Historically this has been tough to do with Visual Basic; for example, writing code to make sure a phone number is of the form XXX-XXX-XXXX where each X is a value between 0 and 9.

The best way to perform validation like this is to describe the pattern that it should represent and validate the text against the pattern. Pattern matching is implemented with regular expressions, which all .NET languages support through the System.Text.RegularExpressions namespace. Chapters 5 to 7 of this book are dedicated to them, since they provide such a powerful tool.

Conversion

Other data types that are not strings are represented in a form that is efficient for the operating system to store. In order to display them in a string, they need to be converted to characters.

.NET uses the ToString() method to return string representations of data types:

```
Dim myDate As DateTime
myDate = "March 6, 2002"    ' Assign a date.
Console.WriteLine(myDate.ToString)
```

This displays 3/6/2002 12:00:00 AM on a US-based system. However, it may be different depending on your locale's date format.

The steps to convert a data type to a string are as follows:

1. Select the conversion algorithm based on the source data type

2. Determine how big the resulting string will be

3. Allocate memory for the string

4. Execute the conversion algorithm to populate the string

The resource requirements for conversion will depend on the algorithm used. Conversion is an expensive operation since, in addition to the resource cost for the algorithm, there are also the requirements of determining the string length and memory allocation. Chapter 3 will provide more details on string conversion with VB.NET.

Formatting

It is common that various pieces of information are collected together into one string to pass to a user. In addition, often programmers want to control how the conversion from machine representation to character data takes place. This is known as formatting, which is similar to conversion, except that the programmer has more control over the algorithm used for the conversion.

Legacy Visual Basic is confusing when it comes to formatting. You can specify a formatting string or select from a list of formatting methods including `FormatCurrency()`, `FormatDateTime()`, `FormatNumber()`, and `FormatPercent()`.

In Visual Basic .NET, to implement a formatting string, you can use the `String.Format()` method. With the `Format()` method you can specify either a formatting expression or a named format. The result is that you have two ways to do the same thing leading to inconsistencies in coding style.

The difficulty with formatting in Visual Basic is that it only allows you to operate on one piece of data at a time. Programmers often want to put a number of pieces of data into one string. The formatting expression present in C is more powerful; it can format a string, perform conversion, and concatenate information at the same time. We will see in Chapter 2 how .NET brings formatting expression to VB.NET.

Formatting may vary, depending on user preferences or languages settings. For instance, forty dollars is represented as $40.00 with North American formatting and 40.00 $ with French formatting.

The resource cost for formatting is similar to conversion since an algorithm needs to be executed and a string needs to be allocated.

In summary, string operations that cause memory allocation and copying of bytes are resource intensive. String operations that scan strings for information are not as resource expensive. The resource costs can increase dramatically if the operations are performed in a loop. We will see examples of this problem in the next section.

String Uses

Text is used for many different purposes. Let's have a look at a few of them and think about what overhead is associated with each purpose.

Building Strings

One of the more common uses of strings is to build up some information to send off somewhere else. Examples include:

❑ Building a log entry to write to a text file

❑ Building an HTML page to send to a browser

❑ Building an XML document to place in a message queue

❑ Building a message for an automated email

❑ Building a SQL statement to pass to a database

With the popularity of the Web, HTML has become a widely used method of creating user interfaces. Since HTML is text-based, programmers use text operations and storage to build and manipulate it. A typical Active Server Page using VBScript looks like the following:

```
<%
  Dim strHTML

  strHTML = "<HTML><BODY>"
  strHTML = strHTML & "My name is: "
  strHTML = strHTML & Request.ServerVariables("SERVER_NAME")
  strHTML = strHTML & "</BODY></HTML>"

  Response.Write strHTML
%>
```

This approach is very easy to understand. You just keep appending information until you have everything you want, and then you send it to the client. However, this approach is not very efficient. When the strHTML variable is declared, the system has no idea how much memory needs to be reserved for it. Only when a value is assigned to the variable does it know how much memory to allocate. With each additional concatenation, the operating system has to allocate more memory and copy the characters. As we have already stated, memory allocation and copying takes time and resources.

The above code snippet potentially initiates four separate memory allocations, which may not seem like a big deal. However, since it is a web page, those allocations happen for each page request. Therefore, if the web page receives five requests per second, this translates to 20 memory allocations per second.

An alternative is to put all the string pieces in an array and use the Join() method:

```
<%
  Dim arrString(3)
  Dim strHTML

  arrString(0) = "<HTML><BODY>"
  arrString(1) = "My name is: "
  arrString(2) = Request.ServerVariables("SERVER_NAME")
  arrString(3)= "</BODY></HTML>"
```

```
strHTML = Join(arrString, "")
  Response.Write strHTML
%>
```

This will result in less memory allocations and fewer copies. If you have an inkling of how large the string will be before you create it, you can specifically allocate that memory. Let's look at an example that does this using the C language:

```
char strBuffer[256];

sprintf( strBuffer, "<HTML><BODY>My name is: %s </BODY></HTML>",
        strServerName );
```

In this case, when the string is declared (actually an array of characters), the amount of memory is fixed. This means that no memory allocations are necessary. However, a problem occurs if `strServerName` causes the entire string to be greater than 256 characters, as the memory will become corrupt.

To be safe and avoid wasting memory, the memory would have to be dynamically allocated:

```
char *pBuffer;

pBuffer = malloc( sizeof(char)*(sizeof(strServerName)+ 39 ) );

sprintf( strBuffer, "<HTML><BODY>My name is: %s </BODY></HTML>",
        strServerName );
```

This approach requires a memory allocation and is at risk of a memory leak. The programmer must remember to free the memory allocated to the string. This approach is not as intuitive to programmers when building strings either.

Parsing Strings

In addition to building strings, developers often have to take strings apart. This is commonly known as parsing. Parsing is breaking structured data into smaller pieces based on rules that describe the layout of the data. One of the most common problems a programmer faces is that of parsing a row of text separated by a delimiter, such as a comma.

In Visual Basic, you use the `Split()` method. This method takes a string and optionally a delimiter, the maximum number of strings to return, and the type of comparison to perform (text or binary).

Positional files are another type of text file that often needs parsing. In this case, instead of using a delimiter to separate fields, fields are given a fixed width. EDI transmission is an example of something similar to a positional file. Parsing positional files makes extensive use of the `Mid()` method, which can be expensive.

For both delimited and positional files, it is often better to use a specialized tool for parsing. The awk tool has been around for a long time in the UNIX environment and has been ported to many other operating systems, including Windows. It supports regular expressions, so it is also useful for search-and-replace operations.

There are other more complicated types of text that may need parsing. Examples include:

❏ Elements in an XML document

❏ Source code of a computer program

❏ Text in a word processing document

These types of parsing problems are beyond the domain of a programming language. Typically, tools are used to do the work of parsing these types of documents. These tools are specialized to perform optimally for the particular parsing problem they were designed to solve.

For example, XML documents can be parsed using an XML parser such as Microsoft's MSXML parser. XML parsers typically have had two approaches to parsing – DOM and SAX. The DOM will parse the text representing the XML document and store it as an object model in memory making it easy for programmers to access the information. SAX is another approach. Instead of having an object model representing the XML document, it informs the calling code when certain text elements have been parsed. These have their own advantages – DOM is necessary for writing XML data as you need a complete XML structure, whereas SAX is fast for locating and replacing data as it doesn't have to search the entire document.

The same approach can be taken for processing text files. If you need all the data in a text file you load the entire file into memory. However, if you are looking for a specific data item or can treat each line of data independently you only need to load one line of data into memory at a time. Also, as soon as the task is complete the processing can be halted instead of reading every line in the file.

Internationalization

The terms internationalization and localization are often used interchangeably but they have specific distinct meanings.

Internationalization is the process of planning and implementing products and services so that they can easily be adapted to specific local languages and cultures. The internationalization process is sometimes called localization enablement. Microsoft has adopted the term **world-ready** to mean internationalization. You may also come across Internationalization referred to as I18N, which is the first letter 'I', '18' to referring to the 18 middle characters, then the last letter 'N'.

Localization is the process of adapting an application to a particular language, culture, and desired local "look-and-feel". This includes translating the text of the application, and ensuring that formatting (of things such as currencies and dates) is correct for the specific culture.

A culture in .NET, is a specific language and region used to specify a language to use, and the various date, time, and number formatting options that region may have. For instance, en-US specifies that the language is English, and that the various data types should be formatted for the US. If en-GB is used, the language is the same, but the currency symbol is £, and dates are written as dd/mm/yyyy, as well as other regional differences.

Ideally, a product or service is developed so that localization is relatively easy to achieve. An internationalized product or service is therefore easier to localize. It is a programmer's job to ensure that the software is internationalized. When the software is to be made available in another language, the software is then usually handed to someone else who is a specialist in that area.

A core part of internalization is ensuring text from any language can be placed into the user interface. Certain simple guidelines should be followed when internationalizing text.

When things such as strings, characters, constants, screen positions, file names, and file paths are hard-coded, they can be difficult to track down and localize. It is much better to isolate all localizable items into resource files, and minimize compilation dependencies.

It is best not to declare buffers that are the exact size of a word or a sentence. The problem is that, when text is translated, the translated text may be of a greater size. For example, your application may declare a 2-byte buffer size for the word OK that could refer to the text in an OK button. However, in Spanish the word OK is translated as Aceptar, which would cause your application's buffer to overflow.

String composition should also be avoided. For example, consider translating wrong file and wrong directory into Italian. The results are file errato and cartella erratta, respectively. If you try to perform string composition using the syntax wrong%s, it is not going to work.

In addition to these recommendations for strings, character sets also need to be considered. We touched on character sets earlier in the chapter. The characters of a language need to be displayed in order to convey a user interface in that language. There has to be enough data space to accommodate multiple-byte character codes, such as Japanese Kanji. Some languages required more characters to represent concepts and therefore more space has to be accommodated in the user interface.

It is often important to put strings into a resource file. Since this resource file will most likely go to a translator it is also important not to put in resources that may confuse the translator. If you have achieved an internationalized application then localization should consist primarily of translating the user interface. This means the application's executable code should be separated from the text. To accomplish this, resource files are used.

.NET Resource Files

The .NET Framework provides three ways to create resource files: as text files, as XML files, or as binary resource files. Both text files and XML files end up as binary resource files by the time they are inserted in the application. The files are compiled into a resource file with the Resource File Generator (Resgen.exe) utility.

A text file can only be used if strings are the only resource to be stored. The text is stored as name-value pairs. Comments are allowed and demarked with a semicolon. The following is a sample text file:

```
[strings]
;prompts
promptAge = Please enter your age.

;error messages
msgNotFound = File not found.
msgNoRecords = No records were found for that query.
```

The advantage of using a text file is that it is straightforward to create and understand. A translator can edit the file in Notepad or any other text editor. The disadvantage is that if a syntax error is introduced into the file it won't be caught until the file is back in the hands of the developer.

The same resource file as XML could look like the following:

```xml
<?xml version="1.0" encoding="utf-8" ?>
<root>
  <xs:schema id="root" xmlns=""
             xmlns:xs="http://www.w3.org/2001/XMLSchema"
             xmlns:msdata="urn:schemas-microsoft-com:xml-msdata">
    <xs:element name="data">
      <xs:complexType>
        <xs:sequence>
          <xs:element name="value" type="xs:string" minOccurs="0"
                      msdata:Ordinal="2" />
        </xs:sequence>
        <xs:attribute name="name" type="xs:string" />
      </xs:complexType>
    </xs:element>
  </xs:schema>
  <data name="promptAge">
    <value>Please enter your age.</value>
  </data>
  <data name="msgNotFound">
    <value> File not found.</value>
  </data>
  <data name="msgNoRecords">
    <value> No records were found for that query.</value>
  </data>
</root>
```

The first section is a header that contains the schema for the actual content. A translator would only work with the content and not touch the header. Since XML is still a text file, it too can be edited in Notepad or any other text editor. Some specific tools can be used for editing the file. For instance, Visual Studio .NET has an XML editor built in, in which .resx files can be edited.

Any other XML editor can be used. Many XML editors (such as SoftQuad XMetal) are easy to use. Translators can focus on translating the text rather than worrying about preserving the syntax of the file. An additional advantage is that an XML editor will guarantee that the data written to the file is well-formed (and possibly valid) XML.

Summary

In this chapter, we have reviewed various aspects of using text within a computer application. Using text consists of working with individual characters and contiguous sets of characters – otherwise known as strings.

Many string operations are performance killers because of the memory allocations and character copies that take place. Proper string design is essential to ensure that programmers minimize causing this problem.

In the rest of this book, we will look at the various ways of manipulating text in Visual Basic .NET and advise you on how best to meet your goals.

VB.NET
Text Manipulation
Handbook
2

2

String and StringBuilder

The previous chapter outlined a number of issues for dealing with strings. In particular, since strings are a data type with variable length, there can be issues regarding performance and memory management. This chapter shows how the Microsoft .NET Framework addresses these string issues with the `String` and `StringBuilder` classes.

To gain an understanding of how text is used with Visual Basic .NET the following is addressed in this chapter:

❑   How to use the `String` class

❑   How to use the `StringBuilder` class

❑   Text operations with Visual Basic .NET

❑   Using the `String.Format` class

❑   Using text within Visual Basic .NET

As you will see, there are more ways than one to perform text operations within Visual Basic .NET. This chapter gives guidance on which methods are best for various situations, partially through the creation of performance testing applications in the latter half of the chapter.

Tools for this Chapter

To get a better understanding of the inner workings of the `String` and `StringBuilder` class, two sources of information have been used.

The first tool is the Microsoft Shared Source CLI (Common Language Infrastructure) implementation, also known as Rotor, available at: http://msdn.microsoft.com/library/default.asp?url=/library/en-us/dndotnet/html/mssharsourcecli.asp. You do not need to download the shared source, unless you are interested in pursuing the code yourself. Snippets of the code are shown in this chapter.

This is source code for a Microsoft .NET Framework implementation, but is not the same implementation that is the officially released .NET Framework. In fact, Microsoft states: "There are significant differences in implementation between this code and the code for Microsoft's commercial CLR implementation, both to facilitate portability and to make the code base more approachable." However, the source code can give much insight into how the String and StringBuilder classes may be implemented.

The second tool is the MSIL Disassembler (ildasm.exe) used in this chapter to show the Intermediate Language (IL) generated by the compiler. This tool is provided with the .NET Framework SDK. When compiling to code, the compiler translates the Visual Basic .NET code into Microsoft Intermediate Language (MSIL), for the CLR to compile to native code. This tool allows you to see the contents of the file before it is compiled to native code.

MSIL includes instructions for loading, storing, initializing, and calling methods on objects, as well as instructions for arithmetic and logical operations, control flow, direct memory access, exception handling, and all other operations the .NET Framework is capable of. Because MSIL is not native assembly code, it is quite easy to read and understand and so MSIL can give programmers insight into how code will perform, as it gives an underlying view of what the actual instructions are that will be executed.

Before code can be executed, it must be compiled to native code, and this happens through the use of a Just-in-Time (**JIT**) compiler – an implementation of one is provided as source with Rotor.

Text Architecture

One of the principal concerns introduced in Chapter 1 was the performance of string operations. This problem reduced to two principal components: memory allocation and byte copying. Therefore, by implementing strategies to minimize memory allocation and byte copying, performance should improve.

To reduce the number of memory reallocations and byte copying, you could allocate much more space than initially required. Then when the string grows, you can just copy the new characters into the space already allocated. This strategy is often used to improve performance. Of course, in this case you can often end up wasting memory. In addition, it is usually not possible to know how much memory you will need until run time. You can rarely be sure of whether the amount of memory allocated is enough, and therefore need a strategy for increasing the space available. In most cases, the developer should be focused on solving the business problem at hand, rather than being concerned about memory allocation. The memory allocation strategy should be integrated into the platform.

Both the Java and .NET platforms have taken similar approaches in text architecture. Both have a class that represents a string, and a class for building strings. The naming is very similar: Java uses `String` and `StringBuffer` whereas the .NET Framework uses `String` and `StringBuilder`. The namespace locations are similar as well. For .NET, `String` is located in the `System` namespace and `StringBuilder` is located in the `System.Text` namespace. For Java, both `String` and `StringBuffer` are located in the `java.lang` namespace (which contains the core Java classes).

The `String` type is immutable. That means that once a value is assigned to it, it cannot be changed. One benefit of it being immutable is that it is thread-safe. Since it cannot be changed, there is no concern of having a read/write or write/write conflict between threads (See the *Visual Basic .NET Threading Handbook*, ISBN: 1-86100-713-2 for more information).

When you do need to change a string, use `StringBuilder`. `StringBuilder` looks after the allocation and reallocation of memory for characters as any string operations demand it.

As mentioned in the first chapter, `String` is the only primitive data type that is a reference type. All the others are value types. Recall that a reference type only stores a pointer to data on the managed heap. In addition, when you are cloning an object of a reference type, you have a new reference but the data is the same. Cloning a value type results in a new set of data that has the same value.

By making `System.String` immutable, it can have value semantics, while still being a reference type. For example, consider the following code:

```
Dim str1 As String = "Rock"
Dim str2 As String = str1

str2 = str2.Replace("ck", "ll")
```

After the second line, both `str1` and `str2` point to the same set of data on the heap. After the third, they contain different references. If `str2` were not immutable, then both `str1` and `str2` would contain the value "Roll". This is because what would happen is that you would alter the contents of the heap and both `str1` and `str2` would point to this new data. Instead, what happens is the `Replace()` method creates a new string (set of data on the heap) and assigns to `str2` a reference to it. The original `str2` remains the same and thus `str1` does not change either. The contents of a string are never overwritten until after garbage collection explicitly frees the memory.

Visual Basic vs .NET Framework

The `String` and `StringBuilder` classes provide methods for comparing and manipulating strings. The Visual Basic 6 string functions are also still available, if you want them, so you do have a choice of functions that do the same string operations.

We strongly recommend that you don't use the Visual Basic 6 string functions, however. As discussed, the text classes in the .NET Framework were made to optimize performance. In addition, the class library is the same across all .NET languages. That makes porting the application much easier. A programmer using another .NET language (such as C#) would also be able to understand the code.

Indices

One of the most noticeable differences between strings in Visual Basic and Visual Basic .NET is that the methods for manipulating strings were one-indexed in VB 6, and they are zero-indexed in Visual Basic .NET, making them standard across all .NET Framework languages. The following code illustrates this point:

```
Dim str1 As String = "Dogs and cats"

' The following code displays True
Console.WriteLine(Mid(str1, 3, 3) = str1.SubString( 2, 3))
```

The second parameter of the Mid() function and the first parameter of the SubString() method is the starting position from which to extract the string. Therefore Console.WriteLine() outputs True.

This is particularly important when porting from Visual Basic 6 functions to .NET Framework methods. You will have to ensure that the indices are changed.

Nothing and Empty Strings

One of the key conceptual differences between VB6 and the .NET Framework is that Visual Basic provides functions to operate on data, whereas the .NET Framework has objects that have properties and methods. Here is an example of the difference:

```
Dim myString As String = "Cats and dogs"

' Explicitly set the string to Nothing.
myString = Nothing

' Displays 0.
Console.WriteLine(Len(myString))

' Causes an exception to be thrown.
Console.WriteLine(myString.Length)
```

An exception is thrown above because an attempt is made to call a method on an object that does not effectively exist. When you assign Nothing to a reference type, it contains a null pointer and so no longer points to the object on the heap, in this case a String. This means that myString cannot have a Length property, because it no longer points to any object. The best way to define a string as empty is to use the Empty shared property.

```
Dim myString As String = "Cats and dogs"

' Explicitly set the string to an empty string.
myString = String.Empty

' Displays 0.
Console.WriteLine(Len(myString))

' Displays 0.
Console.WriteLine(myString.Length)
```

String Class

System.String was introduced in Chapter 1 as a primitive reference type. The System namespace additionally contains all the core data types for .NET development. It includes fundamental classes and base classes that define commonly used value and reference data types. We will cover these in detail in the following sections.

The following table shows the public members of the String class that are covered in this chapter. The complete list can be found in Appendix A:

Member Name	Member Type	Member Description
Compare(String str1, String str2)	Shared Method	Performs a case-sensitive comparison of the two given strings according to the current culture.
Compare(String str1, String str2, Boolean ignoreCase)	Shared Method	Performs a comparison of the two given strings according to the current culture. If ignoreCase is True, a case-insensitive comparison is performed.
CompareOrdinal(String str1, _ String str2)	Shared Method	Performs a comparison of the two given strings without regard to the culture information.
CompareTo(String str)	Instance Method	Performs a case-sensitive, culturally aware comparison of the given string with the instance string.

Table continued on following page

Member Name	Member Type	Member Description
Copy(String str)	Shared Method	Returns a new string with the same value as the given string.
CopyTo(Integer sourceIndex, Char dest(), Integer destIndex, Integer count)	Method	Copies a sub-string from the instance string to the given destination string.
EndsWith(String str)	Method	Returns True if the instance string ends with the given string.
Equals(String str)	Method	Returns True if the instance string has the same value of the given object.
Format(IFormatProvider provider, String format, ParamArray args())	Method	Returns a string consisting of the format specification replaced by the argument array according to the given format provider.
Intern(String str)	Method	Returns a reference to the given string. If the string is not interned, this method will intern it.
Replace(String oldString, String newString)	Method	Replaces all occurrences of oldString with newString in the instance string.
Split(ParamArray separators())	Method	Splits the instance string according to the given character separators.
Substring (Integer startPos, Integer length)	Method	Returns a sub-string starting at the given position and for given length.
ToString()	Method	Returns a reference to the instance string.
ToString(IFormatProvider format)	Method	Returns a reference to the instance string.

Interning Strings

As mentioned in Chapter 1, the Common Language Runtime maintains an intern pool of strings. If you look at the shared source implementation of the CLI, there seems to be one intern pool per AppDomain.

To see an example of how string interning works, consider the following example:

```
Const s1 As String = "dog"

' Displays True if the string is interned.
Console.WriteLine(String.IsInterned(s1) <> Nothing)
```

You can see this illustrated in Figure 1:

Figure 1

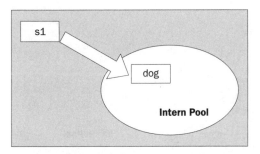

If a string is immutable, as it always is, and it is initialized to a value, then it is effectively the same as a constant. Let us see if the compiler interns it.

```
Dim s1 As String = "dog"

' Displays True if the string is interned.
Console.WriteLine(String.IsInterned(s1) <> Nothing)
```

When the code is executed, it displays True, indicating that the string has been interned. Let's try another example.

```
Dim s1 As String

s1 = "dog"

' Displays True if the string is interned.
Console.WriteLine(String.IsInterned(s1) <> Nothing)
```

The compiler can tell that the string will be fixed and therefore interns it. You might like to know when a string is not interned. Look at the following code:

```
Dim s1 As String = "Dog"

' The next line displays true.
Console.Writeline(String.IsInterned(s1) <> Nothing)

s1 = s1 + "s"

' The next line displays false.
Console.Writeline(String.IsInterned(s1) <> Nothing)
```

Here the string is tested twice but returns two different values. Remember that s1 is a reference to a string, not the actual value of the string. The String object is initialized to a value when it is declared. The compiler interns this string because it knows what it is at compile time. The new lines do not add an "s" to the previous string; they create a new string and assign the reference to the new string. Since this string was created at run time, it is not automatically interned.

Figure 2

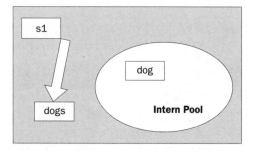

However, you could intern it programmatically:

```
Dim s1 As String = "Dog"

' The next line displays true.
Console.WriteLine(String.IsInterned(s1) <> Nothing)

s1 = s1 + "s"

String.Intern(s1)

' The next line displays true.
Console.WriteLine(String.IsInterned(s1) <> Nothing)
```

In summary, a string will be interned by the system if it knows at compile time what the characters in the string are. As we have seen, the interned string may or may not be a constant.

The other issue left for discussion is what happens to all the strings in the pool. It looks as though there would be memory lost due to non-referenced strings. The garbage collector can check which strings in the pool no longer have any references to them and remove them from the intern pool. For instance, once the s1 variable goes out of scope, there won't be any references to Dog anymore, as long as there is no other string variable in the application with the value Dog.

Construction

In Visual Basic .NET there are a number of ways to initialize a string. Consider the following.

```
Const str1 As String = "My string 1."
Dim str2 As String = "My string 2."
Dim str3 As New String("My string 3.")
```

Since strings are immutable, there are no functional differences between any of the declarations except that the compiler won't allow the str1 reference be changed in the code. In all three cases, once a string value is created in the heap, it cannot be changed. Recall that any perceived changes to a String object create a new String object and the reference contained within the variable then points to this object. In the above example, str1, str2, and str3 are all interned.

When three choices of instruction seem to do the same thing, you may want to know if there are any subtle differences between them. The IL shows us these differences. The code reduces to the following IL. Note that the IL may be slightly different for you since different compiler settings may create different IL code. Don't worry about the exact meaning of each of the IL instructions; what is of interest to us is how the source code is wrapped to IL. You can see the IL for the above code yourself by wrapping the code above within Module and Sub Main() lines, compiling it, and typing ildasm *filename*.

```
.locals init ([0] string str2,
          [1] string str3)
  IL_0000:  nop
  IL_0001:  ldstr      "My string 2."
  IL_0006:  stloc.0
  IL_0007:  ldstr      "My string 3."
  IL_000c:  call       char[]
[Microsoft.VisualBasic]Microsoft.VisualBasic.CompilerServices.CharArra
yType::FromString(string)
  IL_0011:  newobj     instance void
[mscorlib]System.String::.ctor(char[])
  IL_0016:  stloc.1
  IL_0017:  nop
  IL_0018:  ret
```

The first thing to notice is that "My string 1" has disappeared. A constant acts like a macro replacement. If it is not referenced, it will not be included in the IL code. If we change the code to use the constant, we will see the value in the IL code:

```
Const str1 As String = "My string 1."
Dim str2 As String = "My string 2."
Dim str3 As New String("My string 3.")
```

```
Console.WriteLine(str1)
```

The characters are loaded into a String object and the string is output to the console.

```
.locals init ([0] string str2,
         [1] string str3)
IL_0000:  nop
IL_0001:  ldstr      "My string 2."
IL_0006:  stloc.0
IL_0007:  ldstr      "My string 3."
IL_000c:  call       char[]
[Microsoft.VisualBasic]Microsoft.VisualBasic.CompilerServices.CharArra
yType::FromString(string)
IL_0011:  newobj     instance void
[mscorlib]System.String::.ctor(char[])
IL_0016:  stloc.1
IL_0017:  ldstr      "My string 1."
IL_001c:  call       void
[mscorlib]System.Console::WriteLine(string)
IL_0021:  nop
IL_0022:  nop
IL_0023:  ret
```

The next string, "My string 2.", is operated on with the ldstr operation. From the Common Language Infrastructure (CLI) document titled, *Partition III – CIL Instruction Set*:

> *"The **ldstr** instruction pushes a new string object representing the literal stored in the metadata as string (that must be a string literal).*

> *The **ldstr** instruction allocates memory and performs any format conversion required to convert from the form used in the file to the string format required at runtime. The CLI guarantees that the result of two ldstr instructions referring to two metadata tokens that have the same sequence of characters return precisely the same string object (a process known as "string interning")."*

It is saying that ldstr will take care of all the difficult work. Once the String object is created, it is then stored in the variable. Let us look again at what happens with "My string 3."

```
IL_0001:  ldstr      "My string 2."
IL_0006:  stloc.0
IL_0007:  ldstr      "My string 3."
IL_000c:  call       char[]
[Microsoft.VisualBasic]Microsoft.VisualBasic.CompilerServices.CharArra
yType::FromString(string)
IL_0011:  newobj     instance void
[mscorlib]System.String::.ctor(char[])
IL_0016:  stloc.1
```

In this particular case, the string is provided as a constructor. As you can see, more work has to be performed, compared with the "My string 2" string. The first two lines prepare the string to be passed as a parameter. The newobj instruction creates the new String object with the constructor. The String object is then stored as a local variable.

With that analysis, Const is shown to be the most efficient way to initialize a string, since it minimizes the number of IL instructions.

There are a couple cases when you would use the string constructor. One of the constructors allows you to populate the string with fixed characters. For instance, the following creates a string with four "D"s.

```
Dim myString As New String("D", 4)
```

In addition, you can create a string as a sub-string of another string. For example, the following code creates a sub-string three characters long starting at the tenth character.

```
Dim myString As New String("Cats and Dogs", 9, 3)
```

In this case, myString would point to a new value of "Dog".

Assigning Strings

As you know, some characters can be challenging to represent as a string. All string variables are assigned by enclosing them in a quotation mark, so the following code causes a syntax error.

```
Dim myString As String = "He said, "Dogs and cats.""
```

The compiler believes the string is "He said, " and then does not know what to do with the rest of the characters, returning a syntax error. Quotation marks have to be repeated in Visual Basic .NET to be properly represented:

```
Dim myString As String = "He said, ""Dogs and cats."""
```

Another option to perform the same output is as follows.

```
Dim myString As String = "He said, " & ControlChars.Quote & _
                         "Dogs and cats" & ControlChars.Quote
```

.NET offers control characters as part of an enumeration in the Microsoft.VisualBasic namespace. You can also use them to insert other characters such as tabs and carriage return/line feeds.

```
Dim myString As String = ControlChars.Tab & _
    "He said, ""Dogs and cats""" & ControlChars.CrLf
```

This is the preferred way of representing control characters, although it is possible to import `Microsoft.VisualBasic.Constants`, and use the old style of VB constants, such as vbCrLf.

The following table shows the constants that you may use in your application:

Constant	Unicode Value	Description
ControlChars.CrLf	x000D and x000A	Carriage Return/Line Feed
ControlChars.Cr	x000D	Carriage Return
ControlChars.Lf	x000A	Line Feed
ControlChars.NewLine	x000D and x000A	New line
ControlChars.NullChar	x0000	Character having value 0
ControlChars.Tab	x0009	Tab
ControlChars.Back	x0008	Backspace
ControlChars.Quote	x0022	Quotation mark

StringBuilder Class

As already discussed, the immutability characteristic of the `String` class allows it to be treated similarly to a value type rather than a reference type. However, this causes it to have the side effect of a new `String` object being created every time a string operation is required.

The `StringBuilder` class addresses the problem of numerous objects being created during the repeated modifications to a string. The `StringBuilder` class allocates space to a string in `Char` units, so that operations may not require additional memory allocations.

Member Name	Member Type	Member Description
Capacity	Property	The number of characters currently allocated for the instance. Not necessarily the same value as the length property.
Chars(Integer index)	Property	Gets or sets the character within the string at the position index.

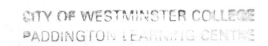

Member Name	Member Type	Member Description
Length	Property	The number of characters in the string. Can be set smaller than the current string value to truncate it.
MaxCapacity	Property	The maximum number of characters that can be allocated for this instance.
Append(<*type*>)	Method	Appends the string representation of the given value. There is an overload for each .NET primitive type. For brevity they are not all listed here.
EnsureCapacity(Integer capacity)	Method	If the current capacity is less than the given capacity, memory is allocated to increase memory to the given capacity.
Insert(Integer position, String strValue, Integer count)	Method	Inserts strValue at the given position, count number of times.
Replace(Char oldChar, Char newChar)	Method	Replaces all occurrences of oldChar with newChar in the instance string.
Replace(String oldString, String newString)	Method	Replaces all occurrences of oldString with newString in the instance string.
Replace(Char oldChar, Char newChar, Integer startPos, Integer count)	Method	Replaces all occurrences of oldChar with newChar in the instance string between positions startPos and count − 1.

Table continued on following page

Member Name	Member Type	Member Description

Replace(String oldString,
 	
    String newString,
 	
    Integer startPos,
 	
    Integer count)
	Method	Replaces all occurrences of oldString with newString in the instance string between positions startPos and count − 1.

ToString()	Method	Returns a reference to a String object whose value is the same as that contained within the StringBuilder instance.

Length and Capacity

The StringBuilder class contains both Length and Capacity properties. Contrary to what might be expected, the Length property is not read-only. If the Length is set to less than the size of the string, the string is truncated. If it is set greater than the current length, then it is padded with spaces at the end. The following code snippet contained within StringBuilderLength.vb demonstrates this behavior.

```
Imports System
Imports System.Text

Module StringBuilderLength
  Sub Main()
    Dim builder As New StringBuilder("Hot dog!")

    Console.WriteLine(builder.ToString()) ' Displays "Hot dog!"

    builder.Length = 3
    Console.WriteLine(builder.ToString()) ' Displays "Hot"

    builder.Length = 10
    Console.Write(builder.ToString()) ' Displays "Hot       "
    Console.WriteLine("(ends)") ' Indicates the string end
  End Sub
End Module
```

Capacity defines the amount of memory available for text manipulation. The default capacity is 16. If you know that the string is going to be greater than 16 characters, you should explicitly set the capacity, which will save at least one memory reallocation. If you provide a string as a parameter to the constructor, the capacity will be set to the nearest exponent of 2. For example, if the string length is 17, the capacity will be 32. The Rotor source code has a CalculateCapacity method in comstringbuffer.cpp. This method is called when a new StringBuilder is created with an initial string. The following C# Rotor code implements the capacity calculation:

```
//Double until we find something bigger than what we need.
while (newCapacity<requestedCapacity && newCapacity>0) {
    newCapacity*=2;
}
```

In the case of a new string the `requestedCapacity` is the length of the string.

The `Capacity` property is independent of `Length`. However, `Capacity` will always be equal to or greater than `Length`.

The following code, contained within `StringBuilderAppend.vb`, demonstrates how the capacity changes as the string grows. The `Append()` method concatenates the given number of specified characters together with the string:

```
Imports System
Imports System.Text

Module StringBuilderAppend
  Sub Main()
    Dim sb As New StringBuilder()

    Console.WriteLine(sb.Capacity & ControlChars.Tab & sb.Length)
    sb.Append("a", 17)
    Console.WriteLine(sb.Capacity & ControlChars.Tab & sb.Length)
    sb.Append("b", 16)
    Console.WriteLine(sb.Capacity & ControlChars.Tab & sb.Length)
    sb.Append("c", 32)
    Console.WriteLine(sb.Capacity & ControlChars.Tab & sb.Length)
    sb.Append("d", 64)
    Console.WriteLine(sb.Capacity & ControlChars.Tab & sb.Length)
  End Sub
End Module
```

The following output is generated on the console:

```
16      0
32      17
64      33
128     65
256     129
```

In this case, there were four memory reallocations. If the initial capacity was set to 256 characters, there would have been no reallocations. Looking at the shared source implementation in the file `stringbuilder.cs`, we can see exactly where the new capacity is calculated.

```
newCapacity = ( currentString.Capacity)*2;

if (newCapacity<requiredLength) {
    newCapacity = requiredLength;
}

if (newCapacity> m_MaxCapacity) {
    newCapacity =  m_MaxCapacity;
}
```

The maximum capacity can be obtained from the property
`StringBuilder.MaxCapacity`. On released implementations of the Microsoft .NET
Framework, this is equal to `Int32.MaxValue`, which is 2,147,483,647 ($2^{31}-1$) That is
quite a few characters and you will run into many other problems, such as lack of
system memory space, before you reach that limit.

The default capacity, maximum capacity, and how the capacity grows, are
implementation specific. For example, the behavior of the shared source
implementation may be different from the released implementation (although the
default capacity is still 16). It is important to take advantage of system behavior to
optimize performance but you need to be aware that if the code is running on another
implementation, you may not get the same benefits.

If you find yourself writing code like the following:

```
If myString.Capacity < myCapacity Then
   myString.Capacity = myCapacity
End If
```

you can replace it with the following equivalent function:

```
myString.EnsureCapacity(myCapacity)
```

If the current capacity is less then the new one, memory will be reallocated. The
current capacity can be reduced as long as it is not less than `Length`. If so, a
`System.ArgumentOutOfRangeException` exception is thrown.

ToString()

We obtain the actual string contained within `StringBuilder` by calling its
`ToString()` method. You can retrieve the whole string, or part of it. The following
code demonstrates both methods.

```
Dim sb As New StringBuilder("This is my string.")
Dim str1 As String = sb.ToString
Dim str2 As String = sb.ToString(5, 5)

Console.WriteLine(str1) ' Displays "This is my string."
Console.WriteLine(str2) ' Displays "is my"
```

The first call to `ToString()` causes a new `String` object to be created, and the
characters are copied to it. This keeps the value semantics of the `String` class.
However, you do get the small performance overhead of allocating the string.

The shared source CLI shows that the second `ToString()` method calls the `Substring()` method of the `String` class. This may not be the case with the final release, as many of the classes may not even be written in C#, but in native code.

```
public String ToString(int startIndex, int length) {
  return m_StringValue.Substring(startIndex, length);
}
```

Many of the other `StringBuilder` methods are duplicated with the `String` methods. In addition, some of the methods in one class call the methods in the other class. We will look at them together in the following section to compare different approaches.

String Operations

All programming languages have support for string operations. Operations on strings fall into the following three categories.

❑   Concatenate strings together

❑   Extract sub-strings from a string

❑   Compare strings

We will look at the operations in detail and then see how they combine for common text operations. The resource cost of the operations will be discussed in terms of performance (time to execute a task) and memory requirements.

While performing these operations, you will often have to choose between the `String` class and the `StringBuilder` class. Some guidelines will be provided here.

> **The relative merits of using `Char` arrays instead of the `String` and `StringBuilder` classes have not been discussed here. Based on some tests, it was found that operations on `Chars` generally ran slower. The shared source CLI provided a clue as to why this might be the case, and it appears as though a `Char` array gets transformed into a `String` before operations are performed on it. Only use `Char` arrays if the operation would make it simpler, and even then it is advisable to test for any performance penalties.**

Concatenation

Let us revisit one of the concatenation examples from Chapter 1 that builds a simple HTML document. The straight translation to Visual Basic .NET would look something like the following:

```
Module HTMLConsole
  Sub Main()
    Dim strHTML As String

    Console.Write("Please enter your name: ")
    Dim userName As String = Console.ReadLine()
    strHTML = "<HTML><HEAD></HEAD><BODY>"
    strHTML = strHTML & "My name is: "
    strHTML = strHTML & userName
    strHTML = strHTML & "</BODY></HTML>"

    Console.WriteLine(strHTML)
  End Sub
End Module
```

Code like this is common because it is written in the way most people think. It is a linear way of programming; start with a string and add each of the pieces until the string is finished. However, this is not the optimal way of doing this. From what we know about the `String` class, the steps taken by the system are the following:

1. The compiler interns the string in the first allocation.

2. In the next line, a concatenation is performed. A new string is allocated, and the interned text and the new text are copied into the string.

3. In the next lines, more concatenations are performed, which again result in new strings being created and characters being copied.

To construct the HTML page, one string is taken from the intern pool and three new ones need to be created. Let us take the same example with our knowledge of how the system stores strings and try to improve performance:

```
Module HTMLConsoleImproved
  Sub Main()
    Const strPrefix As String = "<HTML><HEAD></HEAD><BODY>" _
      & "My name is: "
    Const strSuffix As String = "</BODY></HTML>"

    Console.Write("Please enter your name: ")
    Dim userName As String = Console.ReadLine()
    Dim strHTML As String = strPrefix & userName & strSuffix

    Console.WriteLine(strHTML)
  End Sub
End Module
```

Since some of the text is known beforehand, it is declared as constant. This ensures that it will be placed in the intern pool. At run time, it will not have to be allocated. This approach takes two strings from the intern pool and allocates one string. Memory will be conserved as well, since the constant text is stored once, instead of being allocated many times for each thread running the code.

Based on some performance testing, assigning a new string one million times, this approach was shown to be almost three times as fast as the previous one.

Another approach is to provide a format string. Format strings will be discussed in detail later, but the important point to know for the time being, is that the {0} specifier will be replaced with the replacement parameter:

```
strHTML = String.Format( _
    "<HTML><BODY>My name is: {0} </BODY></HTML>", userName)
```

This approach looks good. There are no explicit string concatenations and the text is easy to read. Unfortunately, it does not perform very well. The Format() method is resource intensive. As a result, it is not a good approach for simple string concatenation. Later in the chapter, we will look at when it is appropriate.

Finally, let's look at using the StringBuilder class to perform concatenation:

```
Dim MHTML As New StringBuilder()

MHTML.Append("<HTML><HEAD></HEAD><BODY>My name is: ")
MHTML.Append(userName)
MHTML.Append("</BODY></HTML>")

Console.WriteLine(MHTML.ToString)
```

In this case, no string is explicitly created. The StringBuilder class looks after all the memory allocation. This approach performs reasonably well but it still seems to take twice as long as the second approach we looked at. However, that is because the creation of a StringBuilder object takes longer than that of a string. If we re-execute all these methods again, just on 10,000 cycles, then we notice something more interesting still. The StringBuilder takes a hundredth of the time even the interned pool concatenation takes. This is partially because interning isn't making much difference here; it still has to create a new string object with every cycle. However, without interning, it would take even longer, depending on how much memory is available, as there would be three times as many string objects being created with each cycle and so garbage collection would need to interrupt the execution repeatedly.

The capacity can also be supplied to the constructor of the StringBuilder. This can improve performance by giving the class a hint as to approximately how much memory will be required. This way it may not have to perform any further allocations. When this was attempted with the same performance tests, the loop took a hundredth less time again. The task was just moving items into memory, and the speed is only dependent on your memory, motherboard, and processor.

There are other ways to perform concatenation but the major ones have been covered here. The optimal is to ensure that the "pieces" of your string that do not change are declared as constants. So, in summary, for just a single concatenation, don't use `StringBuilder`, as the overhead in creating the object will outweigh the performance advantages of the concatenation. For a single concatenation, use constants and other interned strings wherever possible as that can increase performance threefold.

SubStrings

All of the standard Visual Basic sub-string functions are supported in Visual Basic .NET. You can still use `Right()`, `Left()`, and `Mid()`. Please note, however, that `Right()` and `Left()` are just special cases of `Mid()`. Specifically, `Left(theString, numChars)` is the same as `Mid(theString, 1, numChars)`, and `Right(theString, numChars)` is the same as `Mid(theString, Len(theString)-numChars, numChars)`.

The new method call for Visual Basic .NET is `Substring()`. The functionality of `Substring()` and `Mid()` is identical. The one difference is that the `Mid()` function is 1-indexed and `Substring()` is 0-indexed. There is no direct equivalent for `Left()` and `Right()` but `Substring()` can be used to duplicate the functionality just as was demonstrated with `Mid()`.

The following examples show how the functions are equivalent:

```
Dim myString As String = "It's been a long time."
Const numChars As Integer = 4

' The following lines displays true.
Console.WriteLine(Left(myString, numChars) = _
    Mid(myString, 1, numChars))
Console.WriteLine(Right(myString, numChars) = _
    Mid(myString, Len(myString) - numChars + 1))

Console.WriteLine(Left(myString, numChars) = _
    myString.Substring(0, numChars))
Console.WriteLine(Right(myString, numChars) = _
    myString.Substring(myString.Length - numChars))

Console.WriteLine(Mid(myString, 3, numChars) = _
    myString.Substring(2, numChars))
```

The `StringBuilder` class does not have a method to support sub-strings.

Although both `Mid()` and `Substring()` can be used in the same way, it is advisable to always use the `Substring()` method of the `String` object. It is a more object-oriented approach and is part of the .NET Framework class library, so is used the same way across all languages. `Mid()` has been provided for backwards compatibility to get VB6 developers up to speed, but the .NET Framework classes and methods should be used everywhere.

58

Comparing Strings

You might think comparing strings would be straightforward, however, a few choices need to be made here. The String class has four methods for comparing strings, Compare(), CompareTo(), CompareOrdinal(), and Equals().

The Compare() method is a Shared version of the CompareTo() method. The Equals() method is what is called whenever the "=" operator is used, and so is equivalent to it. The CompareOrdinal() method compares two strings without considering the local language or culture; cultures are covered in detail in Chapter 4:

```
Dim str1 As String = "I can't get no"
Dim str2 As String = " satisfaction"

Console.WriteLine(str1.Equals(str2))            ' returns false
Console.WriteLine(str1.CompareTo(str2))         ' returns 1
Console.WriteLine(String.Compare(str2, str1))   ' returns -1
Console.WriteLine(String.CompareOrdinal(str1, str2)) ' returns 41
```

The following shows a simple timing routine for testing the performance of the methods:

```
Module TestOperations
  Sub Main()
    Const NUM_ITER As Integer = 10000000
    Dim result As Integer

    Dim str1 As String = "satisfaction"
    Dim str2 As String = "satisfaction"
    Dim startTime As Integer
    Dim endTime As Integer
    Dim count As Integer

    startTime = Environment.TickCount
    For count = 1 To NUM_ITER
      result = String.Compare(str1, str2)
    Next
    endTime = Environment.TickCount
    Console.WriteLine("Compare: " & CStr(endTime - startTime))

    startTime = Environment.TickCount
    For count = 1 To NUM_ITER
      result = str1.CompareTo(str2)
    Next
    endTime = Environment.TickCount
    Console.WriteLine("CompareTo: " & CStr(endTime - startTime))

    startTime = Environment.TickCount
    For count = 1 To NUM_ITER
      result = CompareOrdinal(str1, str2)
    Next
```

```
        endTime = Environment.TickCount
        Console.WriteLine("CompareOrdinal: " & CStr(endTime-startTime))

        startTime = Environment.TickCount
        For count = 1 To NUM_ITER
          result = str1.Equals(str2)
        Next
        endtime = Environment.TickCount
        Console.WriteLine("Equals (instance): " & CStr(endTime-startTime))

        startTime = Environment.TickCount
        For count = 1 To NUM_ITER
          result = String.Equals(str1, str2)
        Next
        endTime = Environment.TickCount
        Console.WriteLine("Equals (shared): " & CStr(endTime-startTime))
    End Sub
End Module
```

The results of this test should look something like those in the following table. The actual values will be different between environments and even executions, but the relative difference between the functions should be the same. Just make slight alterations to the code to make the strings unequal and non-interned, as the table requires:

Method	Strings Match ?	Number of Strings Interned	Execution Time (ms)
Compare()	Yes	2	2543
CompareTo()	Yes	2	2574
CompareOrdinal()	Yes	2	611
Equals() – Instance	Yes	2	671
Equals() – Shared	Yes	2	80
Equals (=) operator	Yes	2	691
Compare()	No	2	2794
CompareTo()	No	2	2814
CompareOrdinal()	No	2	471
Equals() – Instance	No	2	460
Equals() – Shared	No	2	541
Equals (=) operator	No	2	581
Compare()	Yes	0	2613

Method	Strings Match ?	Number of Strings Interned	Execution Time (ms)
CompareTo()	Yes	0	2644
CompareOrdinal()	Yes	0	601
Equals() – Instance	Yes	0	661
Equals() – Shared	Yes	0	741
Equals (=) operator	Yes	0	691
Compare()	No	1	2153
CompareTo()	No	1	2174
CompareOrdinal()	No	1	400
Equals() – Instance	No	1	351
Equals() – Shared	No	1	420
Equals (=) operator	No	1	501

As you can see, the results vary widely depending on the method used and the strings being compared.

There are some interesting observations about the results. The Compare() method, for instance, was consistently faster than the CompareTo() method, although only marginally. Since the Compare() method is shared, there are fewer overheads in calling it than with an instance method as an instance does not have to be created.

The CompareOrdinal() method is substantially faster than the Compare() and CompareTo() methods. Since the CompareOrdinal() method does not have to worry about culture-specific information, it does not have the overhead of conversions and international support that the other two methods have. This can be used on strings that you know will not be localized, such as various operating system and network variables.

Finally, the Equals() method performance varies widely depending on the strings being compared. Looking at the shared source implementation gives a hint as to why:

```
public static bool Equals(String a, String b) {
  if ((Object)a==(Object)b) {
    return true;
  }

  if ((Object)a==null || (Object)b==null) {
    return false;
  }

  return a.Equals(b);
}
```

Comparing two objects is performed best when comparing their hash codes, which is a very quick operation. If two strings are the same, then they will have the same hash code and, as a result, the equality test is very fast. If they are not the same, the call is forwarded and a character-by-character comparison occurs. There must be some further code in the .NET Framework, as when the two strings were interned and identical, the shared method received an enormous performance boost. This is probably because the references would be identical and so, if it tests for this, the operation would be exceptionally fast.

In general the instance method of Equals() is marginally faster, and the equals operator is slowest of all. The one exception is where both strings are interned and identical, in which case the shared method is much faster. Bear this in mind when choosing what method to use.

Two other useful comparison methods are EndsWith() and StartsWith(). In the shared source snippet, you can see that these methods use the Compare() function; therefore you can expect the performance to be similar. Additionally, if you rewrite the code sample used above to compare these methods, there is a speed difference only if you declare all your variables, like the string lengths, before it starts timing it:

```
public bool EndsWith(String value) {
  if (null==value) {
    throw new ArgumentNullException("value");
  }
  int valueLen = value.Length;
  int thisLen = this.Length;
  if (valueLen>thisLen) {
    return false;
  }
  return (0==Compare(this, thisLen-valueLen, value, 0, valueLen));
}

public bool StartsWith(String value) {
  if (null==value) {
    throw new ArgumentNullException("value");
  }
  if (this.Length<value.Length) {
    return false;
  }
  return (0==Compare(this,0, value,0, value.Length));
}
```

We can assume above that there is therefore no advantage behind using Compare() as opposed to EndsWith() or StartsWith().

Formatting

As discussed in the first chapter, formatting is used to create an end user view of a value from the internal machine representation of the value. Formatting can be described as the conversion of any data type to a string. The advantage of formatting is that the programmer can specify how the conversion happens.

All base data types implement the IConvertible interface. This interface has a ToString() method, which must be implemented by the classes implementing the interface. As you may not know, this method is different from the overload provided through System.Object, but they both return a string representation of the class implementing the interface. Since all base data types implement this interface, you can always retrieve a string representation of the data type. In addition, number, date, and enumeration primitive types also implement the System.IFormattable interface, which contains an additional overload for the ToString() method, and we will be describing it in this section.

This overload is defined as follows:

```
Function ToString(ByVal format As String, _
               ByVal formatProvider As IFormatProvider) _
      As String
```

The first parameter is the format specifier, and the second is the format provider. If the format string is absent, then the System.IConvertible.ToString() method is actually called, which just contains the IFormatProvider argument and uses a default format. We will look at these two arguments in detail in the next section. If neither parameter is provided, then a default format specifier and default format provider will be used by System.Object.ToString(). The richness of formatting in .NET means that you should not even have to perform character-by-character construction of strings.

Formatting is divided into *Numeric* formatting (which includes currency), *Date-Time* formatting, *Enumeration* formatting, and custom formatting. There are many formatting options on all the types. They are not all shown in this chapter. Inspect the .NET Framework SDK's documentation to see all the options available for formatting strings.

Formatting Numbers

For the first example, we will rely on the Pi constant defined within the System.Math class. The formats are listed in the order of default, scientific notation, and fixed-point:

```
Dim val As Double = Math.PI

Console.WriteLine(val.ToString)          ' displays 3.14159265358979
Console.WriteLine(val.ToString("E"))     ' displays 3.141593E+000
Console.WriteLine(val.ToString("F3"))    ' displays 3.142
```

The default format provides information, but isn't too friendly for a user. Scientific notation is an option, but in this case does not help much either. Specifying the number of decimals to display makes the value more presentable. In addition, the value is rounded instead of truncated.

Many developers may also be interested in hexadecimal formatting. It is doubtful that end users would want to see numbers represented in hexadecimal, but certainly if you are logging errors or trace statements then you may want to record them in hex:

```
Dim val As Integer = 65535

Console.WriteLine(val.ToString("x"))     ' displays ffff
Console.WriteLine(val.ToString("X"))     ' displays FFFF
```

It is also possible to format numbers as percentages:

```
Dim val As Single = 0.653

Console.WriteLine(val.ToString("p"))     ' displays 65.30 %
Console.WriteLine(val.ToString("p1"))    ' displays 65.3 %
```

The default formatting puts a space between the number and percent sign. This is customizable by changing the format provider:

```
Dim val As Single = 0.653
Dim myFormat As NumberFormatInfo = _
   NumberFormatInfo.CurrentInfo.Clone()

myFormat.PercentPositivePattern = 1

Console.WriteLine(val.ToString("p", myFormat))    ' displays 65.30%
Console.WriteLine(val.ToString("p1", myFormat))   ' displays 65.3%
```

The first thing to notice is that a new format structure is created by cloning the existing one. Moreover, the NumberFormatInfo class is a member of the System.Globalization namespace, which would have to be imported into your program. The pattern for formatting percentages is changed by setting the PercentPositivePattern property. The new format structure is then passed to the ToString() method. Demonstrations of customizing more of the format will be provided in subsequent examples.

Currency is included as part of number formatting. Results may differ depending on your culture setting. For instance, the currency symbol in the UK is £:

```
Dim val As Double = 12345.89

Console.WriteLine(val.ToString)          ' displays 12345.89
Console.WriteLine(val.ToString("C"))     ' displays $12,345.89 in US
```

There is complete flexibility in the formatting. The following example demonstrates the construction of a nonsense currency:

```
Dim val As Double = 1234567.89
Dim groupSize() As Integer = {2, 1, 3}

Dim myCurrency As NumberFormatInfo = _
    NumberFormatInfo.CurrentInfo.Clone()

myCurrency.CurrencySymbol = "@"
myCurrency.CurrencyDecimalSeparator = "/"
myCurrency.CurrencyGroupSeparator = "-"
myCurrency.CurrencyGroupSizes = groupSize

Console.WriteLine(val.ToString("C", _
    myCurrency))    ' displays @1-234-5-67/89
```

Formatting Dates

The procedure for formatting dates is the same as for formatting numbers; the format strings are just different.

> *The appearance of the output in this section may differ depending on what your machine culture settings are.*

```
Dim dateValue As DateTime = DateTime.Now

' Displays a date like 5/8/2002 10:32:03 AM
Console.WriteLine(dateValue.ToString)

' Displays date like Wednesday, May 8, 2002 10:32 AM
Console.WriteLine(dateValue.ToString("f"))

' Displays May, 2002
Console.WriteLine(dateValue.ToString("y"))

' Displays 18:03:03 PM
Console.WriteLine(dateValue.ToString("T"))
```

Again, you have complete control on how the date string is formatted as the following example illustrates:

```
Dim dateValue As DateTime = DateTime.Now
Dim myDays() As String = _
    {"RelaxDay", "ToughDay", "BlahDay", "LazyDay", "ProductiveDay", _
    "PartyDay", "HomeDay"}

Dim myDateTime As DateTimeFormatInfo = _
    DateTimeFormatInfo.CurrentInfo.Clone()

myDateTime.DayNames = myDays
myDateTime.FullDateTimePattern = "dddd, dd MMMM yyyy HH:mm:ss"

' Displays PartyDay, 19 April 2002 10:32:03
Console.WriteLine(dateValue.ToString("F", myDateTime))
```

This example shows two things. First, how you can override the days of the week and provide your own; second, how you can explicitly provide a format string to control how the date string is put together.

Formatting Enumerations

Finally, we will look at converting enumerations to strings. Consider the following enumeration declaration:

```
Public Enum Music
    Rock = 1
    Blues = 2
    Jazz = 3
    Classical = 4
End Enum
```

You can obtain string information about the enumeration as illustrated in the following code:

```
Dim myMusic As Music = Music.Blues

Console.WriteLine(myMusic.ToString)          ' displays Blues
Console.WriteLine(myMusic.ToString("d"))     ' displays 2
```

You can obtain text from system enumerations the same way:

```
Dim day As DayOfWeek = DayOfWeek.Friday

Console.WriteLine(String.Format("My favorite day is {0:G}", day))
```

This will display the following on the console:

```
My favorite day is Friday
```

The format string "G" displays the enumeration as a string.

Format Choices

Since both StringBuilder and String provide format functionality, you may wonder which to use. Looking at the shared source for the String.Format() method, we see that it creates a StringBuilder object, and calls the AppendFormat() method:

```
public static String Format(IFormatProvider provider, String format,
                            params Object[] args) {
  if (format == null || args == null)
    throw new ArgumentNullException((format==null)?"format":"args");
  StringBuilder sb = new StringBuilder(format.Length +
                                       args.Length * 8);
  sb.AppendFormat(provider,format,args);
  return sb.ToString();
}
```

Since `Format()` is a `Shared` method, there isn't much overhead in calling it. Your choice then comes down to which method makes most sense, and is most readable in the context of the code you are writing.

We will say a little more about formatting in Chapter 4. String formatting can prove very useful when dealing with internationalized strings, but it wouldn't be useful to go into much detail here.

Uses of Strings

We have covered a number of the operations performed with strings. Let us combine some of the operations together to create some practical applications.

Building Strings

We have looked at the issue of building a string that contains HTML. Let us revisit this using the `String` and `StringBuilder` classes. This example illustrates the retrieval of data from a database and displaying it in an HTML table. This is not a demonstration of the best way to do this task; rather it shows how to build up strings. ASP.NET offers superior ways of displaying data, such as with the `DataGrid` control.

With that said, recall that the problem with the method illustrated in Chapter 1, and earlier in this chapter, was too much memory allocation and string copying. The following code addresses the problem using the `String` and `StringBuilder` classes. This has been written as a console application, but it can easily be adapted for ASP.NET, or Windows Forms by just replacing the `Console.ReadLine()` and `Console.WriteLine()` lines:

```
Module HTMLTableConstruction
    Sub Main()
        ' The connection string is specific to your database environment.
        Const CONN_STRING As String = _
            "user id=sa;password=;database=pubs;server=localhost"

        Dim SQLQuery As String
        Dim sb as New System.Text.StringBuilder(256)

        Dim authorName As String = ""
        ' Retrieve author name - Replace with Request(fieldName) for
        ' ASP.NET application
        Console.Write("Please enter author's last name: ")
        authorName = Console.ReadLine()
        ' Remove any spaces that might exist before or after the name.
        authorName = authorName.Trim()

        ' Create the SQL query.
        Dim SQLQuery = String.Format(SELECT * FROM Authors "& _
            "WHERE au_lname LIKE '{0}%'", authorName)
```

```vb
        ' Intern the table tags so as to increase performance
        Const OPENTABLE As String = "<table>"
        Const CLOSETABLE As String = "</table>"
        Const OPENTABLEROW As String = "<tr>"
        Const CLOSETABLEROW As String = "</tr>"
        Const OPENTABLECELL As String = "<td>"
        Const CLOSETABLECELL AS String = "</td>"
        Const OPENTABLEHEADER As String = "<th>"
        Const CLOSETABLEHEADER As String = "</th>"

        Dim conn As New System.Data.SqlClient.SqlConnection(CONN_STRING)
        conn.Open()

        Dim cmd as New System.Data.SqlClient.SqlCommand(SQLQuery, conn)
        Dim dr As System.Data.SqlClient.SqlDataReader = _
            cmd.ExecuteReader()
        Dim numFields As Integer = dr.FieldCount

        sb.Append(OPENTABLE & ControlChars.NewLine)

        ' Create the table headings.
        Dim count as Integer
        For count = 0 to numFields - 1
          sb.Append(OPENTABLEHEADER & dr.GetName(count) & _
                    CLOSETABLEHEADER)
        Next

        ' Iterate through the rows and add the data to the HTML table.
        While (dr.Read())
          sb.Append(ControlChars.NewLine & OPENTABLEROW)
          For count = 0 To numFields-1
            sb.Append(OPENTABLECELL & dr(count).ToString() & _
                      CLOSETABLECELL)
          Next
          sb.Append(CLOSETABLEROW)
        End While

        conn.Close()
        sb.Append(ControlChars.NewLine & CLOSETABLE & _
                  ControlChars.NewLine)
        Console.WriteLine(sb.ToString())
    End Sub
End Module
```

The first interesting piece of code is the SQL statement for the query:

```vb
        authorName = authorName.Trim()
        ...
        Dim SQLQuery = String.Format(SELECT * FROM Authors "& _
          "WHERE au_lname LIKE '{0}%'", authorName)
```

The Trim() method is used to remove any leading or trailing whitespace from the entry; this would be essential in a WebForms application. There is a small performance hit here, because a new string is created for the trimmed string. Next, the Format() method is used to create the SQL statement. Concatenation using interned strings could have been used here instead of the Format() method. A specific situation where you would use the Format() method over concatenation is if you needed to format the text you were inserting into the SQL Statement. We then define a number of constants, to ensure that the system interns them (although it would happen anyway), before passing the SQL statement to a command object, where the command is executed on the connection:

```
Dim cmd as new System.Data.SqlClient.SqlCommand(SQLQuery, conn)
Dim dr As System.Data.SqlClient.SqlDataReader = _
    cmd.ExecuteReader()
Dim numFields As Integer = dr.FieldCount

sb.Append(OPENTABLE & ControlChars.NewLine)

Dim count As Integer
For count = 0 to numFields - 1
    sb.Append(OPENTABLEHEADER & dr.GetName(count) & _
            CLOSETABLEHEADER)
Next
```

The HTML is built inside one StringBuilder object. Notice that when it was declared it was given a default capacity of 256 characters. Remember that if a capacity is not provided, then the default is 16. The total characters are going to be more than that so we can minimize the amount of memory reallocation by providing a value closer to the size of the result.

The HTML is made part of the StringBuilder object using the Append() method. The first Append() method contains a fixed string and character. The compiler will recognize this and reduce it to a single string. The strings in the second Append() call cannot be evaluated until run time, so we get a performance hit here. Once the header information is in place, we can iterate through the rows:

```
While (dr.Read())
    sb.Append(ControlChars.NewLine & OPENTABLEROW)
    For count = 0 To numFields - 1
        sb.Append(OPENTABLECELL & dr(count).ToString() & _
                CLOSETABLECELL)
    Next
    sb.Append("CLOSETABLEROW")
End While
```

This loop is where most of the work is, as there is another nested loop inside. In most cases, the StringBuilder object copies the characters into the memory it has allocated for the string. When it hits the capacity, it needs to reallocate and copy. Considering that it doubles the capacity each time, this should not be an issue.

The `AppendFormat()` method could be used instead of string concatenation as illustrated below:

```
While (dr.Read())
  sb.Append(ControlChars.NewLine & OPENTABLEROW)
  For count = 0 To numFields - 1
    sb.AppendFormat("<td>{0}</td> ", dr(count).ToString())
  Next
  sb.Append(CLOSETABLEROW)
End While
```

This is an effective approach if you want to specify the format of the fields to display. It is also somewhat more readable. However, formatted strings are slower to manipulate than concatenation:

```
conn.Close ()
sb.Append(ControlChars.NewLine & CLOSETABLE & _
  ControlChars.NewLine)
Console.WriteLine(sb.ToString())
```

Finally, the HTML is completed and in an ASP.NET application the string would be sent to the client. In this application, it just outputs to the console:

Tokenizing

Tokenizing is the process of extracting specific content from text. Compilers use tokenizing extensively since they need to separate the language keywords from the delimiters. Tokenizing is also used in natural language processing to remove words from sentences. Consider the following sentence:

"I just want the words, not the punctuation, and not the spaces, from this sentence."

One approach is to process the sentence character by character. This is tedious and error-prone. Although Java has a `StringTokenizer` class to make this process easy, the .NET Framework does not supply a class like this, so you have to write more code. The following snippet extracts the words from the sentence and outputs them to the console.

```
Dim myString As String = _
  "I just want the words, not the punctuation, and not the spaces," _
  & " from this sentence."
Dim separators() As Char = {" ", ",", ".", ":", ";", "?", "!"}
Dim startPos As Integer = 0
Dim endPos As Integer = 0

Do
  endPos = myString.IndexOfAny(separators, startPos)

  If endPos = -1 Then
    endPos = myString.Length
  End If
```

```
   If endPos <> startPos Then
     Console.WriteLine( _
       myString.Substring(startPos, (endPos - startPos)))
   End If
   startPos = (endPos + 1)
Loop Until startPos >= myString.Length
```

You will see the following output on the console:

```
I
just
want
the
words
not
the
punctuation
and
not
the
spaces
from
this
sentence
```

First, the variables are declared. The characters identified as the token separators are stored in an array. Variables for the start and end position of each token are declared:

```
Dim myString As String = _
   "I just want the words, not the punctuation, and not the spaces," _
   & " from this sentence."
Dim separators() As Char = {" ", ",", "."}
Dim startPos As Integer = 0
Dim endPos As Integer = 0
```

The IndexOfAny() method is the key part of this tokenizing routine. Given a list of separators and a starting position it finds the next character location that contains one of the separators. The method returns –1 if no separators are found. In this case, the end position is set to the end of the string:

```
Do
   endPos = myString.IndexOfAny(separators, startPos)

   If endPos = -1 Then
     endPos = myString.Length
   End If
```

The token is extracted from the string using Substring() and written to the console. The start position is updated to one character past the end position before the next token is searched for:

```
If endPos <> startPos Then
  Console.WriteLine( _
     myString.Substring(startPos, (endPos - startPos)))
End If
startPos = (endPos + 1)
Loop Until startPos >= myString.Length
```

Most of the routine is efficient since it is a linear walkthrough of the characters in the string. The expensive part is the Substring() operation, since that creates a new string. In the code download for this chapter, a StringTokenizer class has been created that works mostly in the same way as the Java class of the same name.

Reversing a String

You may need to reverse a string. Some languages offer this as built-in functionality, but not the .NET Framework. The following example demonstrates a good approach to reversing a string:

```
Dim myString As String = "If there's a bustle in your hedgerow"
Dim myChars As Char() = myString

Array.Reverse(myChars)

Console.WriteLine(myString)
Console.WriteLine(myChars)
```

Any class derived from Array can use the Reverse() method to reorder the elements in the array. To reverse the string we create a character array from the string and call the reverse method. The resulting array has the characters in reverse order.

The code displays the following on the console:

```
If there's a bustle in your hedgerow
woregdeh ruoy ni eltsub a s'ereht fI
```

However, as you'll discover in Chapter 4, one character can be made up of a pair of Chars. Reversing this pair would make such a character invalid. In the code download we provide a method that allows you to reverse characters, preserving these "surrogate pairs" if a Boolean argument is passed to the method.

Insert, Remove, and Replace

A category of operations on strings is to insert, remove, or replace portions of a string. Both the String and StringBuilder classes support these operations. Most of these operations can also be performed using regular expressions. We look at regular expressions in Chapters 5-7.

For these examples, we will use the following sample file (albums.txt) as a source of strings. You will notice that the following code reads the file as Unicode. Be sure that the text file is saved in the same format as it is read. Notepad for instance allows you to Save As Unicode:

```
Led Zeppelin, Led Zeppelin [I], 1969
Frank Zappa, We're Only in It for the Money, 1968
Beatles, Sgt. Pepper's Lonely Hearts Club Band, 1967
Jimi Hendrix, Are You Experienced?, 1967
```

The following code will be the test harness for loading the data and processing it. The results are sent to the console:

```
Const NAME As String = "album.txt"
Dim ReadLine As Stream
Dim WriteLine As TextWriter
Dim sb As StringBuilder

ReadLine = File.OpenRead(NAME)
WriteLine = Console.Out

Dim ReadLineSReader As StreamReader = New StreamReader(ReadLine, _
    System.Text.Encoding.Unicode)

ReadLineSReader.BaseStream.Seek(0, SeekOrigin.Begin)

While (ReadLineSReader.Peek() > -1)
    sb = New StringBuilder(ReadLineSReader.ReadLine())
    ' insert string operation here
    WriteLine.WriteLine(sb.ToString)
End While
```

If we use the following code to add a column on the end:

```
sb.Append(", Rock")
```

this displays the following on the console:

```
Led Zeppelin, Led Zeppelin [I], 1969, Rock
Frank Zappa, We're Only in It for the Money, 1968, Rock
Beatles, Sgt. Pepper's Lonely Hearts Club Band, 1967, Rock
Jimi Hendrix, Are You Experienced?, 1967, Rock
```

The first column could be removed using the following code:

```
sb.Remove(0, sb.ToString().IndexOf(",") + 1)
```

This results in the following output:

```
Led Zeppelin [I], 1969
We're Only in It for the Money, 1968
Sgt. Pepper's Lonely Hearts Club Band, 1967
Are You Experienced?, 1967
```

The delimiter could be replaced with the following code:

```
sb.Replace(",", " |")
```

This gives the following output:

```
Led Zeppelin | Led Zeppelin [I] | 1969
Frank Zappa | We're Only in It for the Money | 1968
Beatles | Sgt. Pepper's Lonely Hearts Club Band | 1967
Jimi Hendrix | Are You Experienced? | 1967
```

In this case, there is a performance hit. To make the output look better, a space and a pipe replace the comma. This means the system cannot do a simple character-for-character replacement. Other characters have to be moved and potentially more memory allocated.

Finally, we can prefix each line with line numbers using this code. This assumes m_lineNumber is declared and initialized to zero somewhere previously:

```
sb.Insert(0, m_lineNumber.ToString("000 "))
m_lineNumber = m_lineNumber + 1
```

This results in the following output:

```
000 Led Zeppelin, Led Zeppelin [I], 1969
001 Frank Zappa, We're Only in It for the Money, 1968
002 Beatles, Sgt. Pepper's Lonely Hearts Club Band, 1967
003 Jimi Hendrix, Are You Experienced?, 1967
```

Choosing Between String and StringBuilder

For insert, remove and replace operations you have a choice between the String and StringBuilder classes. The following table shows some performance results of these operations when the code was executed on a 1.3GHz Intel Celeron processor, with 256MB of memory:

Class	Method	String Interned	Execution Time (ms)
String	Insert()/Remove()	Yes	691
String	Insert()/Remove()	No	851
StringBuilder	Insert()/Remove()	N/A	441
String	Replace()	Yes	981
String	Replace()	No	982
StringBuilder	Replace()	N/A	761

By running these tests, you can see that StringBuilder is consistently faster than String for Replace(), Remove(), and Insert() operations. If we're using the String class, operations on an interned string are faster than a non-interned string for Insert() and Replace() operations, but not by enough to make a significant difference.

The main reason StringBuilder performs much better than the String class is because String has to allocate a new string and copy the characters. StringBuilder can perform the operations in the same memory space. StringBuilder suffers in performance only if it reaches its capacity and needs to allocate more memory. However, it suffers no more than String does and it reallocates memory far less often than String, if at all. As with the performance tests for concatenation, all you have to be aware of is that creating a StringBuilder can take longer. Using a similar test to the one shown below, on the same machine, using the same number of iterations, it was found that on a 114 character string, the creation of a StringBuilder took just 790ms longer. The gap increases depending on the size of the string.

The following code was used to obtain the results for the previous table:

```
Imports System.Text

Module PerfTest
   Const NUM_ITER As Integer = 1000000

   Public Sub Main()
     Dim str1 As String = "It's been a long time " & _
       "since I rock and rolled."
     Dim str2 As String
     Dim str3 As String
     Dim test As Boolean
     Dim sb As New StringBuilder(str1)

     ' Make sure we have a string that's not interned.
     str2 = str1.Replace("."c, "!"c)
```

```vb
Dim startTime As Integer
Dim endTime As Integer
Dim count As Integer
' INSERT/REMOVE - String, interned.
startTime = Environment.TickCount
For count = 1 To NUM_ITER
  str3 = str1.Insert(12, "really ")
  str1 = str3.Remove(12, 7)
Next
endTime = Environment.TickCount
Console.WriteLine("INSERT/REMOVE - interned String: " & _
  CStr(endTime - startTime))

' INSERT - String, not interned.
startTime = Environment.TickCount
For count = 1 To NUM_ITER
  str3 = str2.Insert(12, "really ")
  str1 = str3.Remove(12, 7)
Next
endTime = Environment.TickCount
Console.WriteLine("INSERT/REMOVE - non interned String: " & _
  CStr(endTime - startTime))

' INSERT - StringBuilder
startTime = Environment.TickCount
For count = 1 To NUM_ITER
  sb.Insert(12, "really ", 1)
  sb.Remove(12, 7)
Next
endTime = Environment.TickCount
Console.WriteLine("INSERT/REMOVE - String Builder: " & _
  CStr(endTime - startTime))

' REPLACE - String, interned.
startTime = Environment.TickCount
For count = 1 To NUM_ITER
  str3 = str1.Replace("rock and rolled", "had the blues")
Next
endTime = Environment.TickCount
Console.WriteLine("REPLACE - interned String: " & _
  CStr(endTime - startTime))

' REPLACE - String, not interned.
startTime = Environment.TickCount
For count = 1 To NUM_ITER
  str3 = str2.Replace("rock and rolled", "had the blues")
Next
endTime = Environment.TickCount
Console.WriteLine("REPLACE - non interned String: " & _
  CStr(endTime - startTime))
```

```
' REPLACE - StringBuilder
startTime = Environment.TickCount
For count = 1 To NUM_ITER
  sb.Replace("rock and rolled", "had the blues")
Next
endTime = Environment.TickCount
Console.WriteLine("REPLACE - String Builder: " & _
  CStr(endTime - startTime))
End Sub
End Module
```

Summary

Text manipulation using the String and StringBuilder classes has been extensively covered in this chapter. When faced with performing operations on text, you often have a number of approaches to choose from. This chapter gave you background on how the String and StringBuilder classes operate, to try to guide you in making the best decisions.

The following tips are recommended to optimize performance of string operations.

❑ Store strings as constants whenever possible to ensure the intern pool is used and so to minimize the number of machine instructions required.

❑ If the String class will do the job effectively, use it instead of StringBuilder. For example, if the operation is a single string assignment.

❑ If you are looping to build up a large block of character data, use StringBuilder.

❑ Only use Compare() if you require international strings. Otherwise, use CompareOrdinal.

❑ Use Equals() rather than CompareOrdinal() if you only need to know if the strings are the same.

❑ Always use the Equals() method, rather than the "=" operator.

This chapter did not properly address Internationalization, which also has an impact on how you structure your string manipulation solutions. Another approach to solving some of the problems listed in this chapter is through using regular expressions. Internationalization within Visual Basic .NET is covered in detail in Chapter 4, whereas Regular Expressions are explained in Chapters 5-7. In the next chapter we look at the issues involved when moving strings between data types and storing them in arrays and collections.

VB.NET

Text Manipulation

Handbook

3

String Conversion

When writing code, there are many cases where information needs to be converted from one type to another. For instance, you may need to convert user input of a date from a string to an actual date representation on which calculations can be done, or you may need to transform a number to a string so that it can be displayed using a format that shows two decimal places and a currency symbol. The .NET Framework provides you with easy ways to achieve these goals.

The ToString() Method

Every object, because it inherits from the System.Object base class, has a ToString() method that provides a string that represents the object This includes the system base types, such as Integer or Double, which also implement the ToString() method, as they are also objects. The default implementation for the ToString() method returns the fully qualified name of the type of the instance of the object-derived class. For instance, if you use the following code, it will return a string that contains "System.Object".

```
Dim obj As Object = New Object()
MessageBox.Show(obj.ToString())
```

However, this method can and should be overridden, whenever it makes sense to do so, so that this method returns a human-readable, culture-sensitive string that represents the current object. For instance, the Integer class implements the ToString() method in this way. The following code provides a useful string representation of the integer value.

```
Dim i As Integer = 123456
MessageBox.Show(i.ToString())
```

Also, please note that derived classes that require more control over the formatting of the returned string should implement the IFormattable interface, which uses the thread's current culture for its ToString() method. You'll read much more about cultures in the next chapter, but if you remember, this specifies what region-specific information is to be used. For instance, an instance of the Double class, whose value is zero, might return 0.00 or 0,00 after its ToString() method call, depending on the current culture.

Now that we know that objects can be converted to strings by using the ToString() method, let's see how to convert numeric values to strings.

Representing Numeric Values as Strings

Let's review the numeric formats that are supported by the .NET Framework and how numeric data, including percentage and money amounts, can be formatted and represented as strings. Before we explore the NumberFormatInfo class, let's look at some of the more interesting numeric features enabled by the .NET Framework. The simplest way of representing a number of a string can be seen below:

```
12345.ToString()
```

This will output 12345 as a string. While this is useful, the formatting, or rather lack thereof in this case, isn't very impressive. This is because we did not specify a proper format for the string, and by default, the ToString() method will use the standard formatting for numbers, with no specification of decimal separator and no grouping.

Now, we can go one step further and specify some formatting information here as well, such as:

```
12345.ToString("n")
```

In this case, we provided formatting information (the "n" value) to indicate that we want 12345 to be formatted as a number when being represented as a string. The formatting will now take into account the currently selected CurrentCulture (see next chapter for more details on cultures) at the thread level in order to provide us with a string that represents this number.

If the current culture were "en-US", you would get the following result:

```
12,345.00
```

If the current culture were "fr-FR", the result would be:

```
12 345,00
```

You can format numeric results by using the String.Format() method, or for Console applications, you can use the Console.Write method, which in turn calls the String.Format() method. The format is specified using format strings.

The following code sample uses the currency format (selected by the "C" specifier when using the ToString() method) to display the actual value of the integer. Since the author is located in the United States and the machine is configured as a regular en-US machine, the value is displayed using the symbol for US dollars.

```
Module ToStringCulture
    Sub Main()
        Dim MyInt As Integer = 100
        Dim MyString As String = MyInt.ToString("C")
        MessageBox(MyString)
    End Sub
End Module
```

If you type this code and run it on your machine, in the UK, with English settings properly configured, then the output will be in Pounds Sterling:

This happens because the application uses the current culture set at the current thread level if no culture information is passed to the ToString() method.

The following code example uses the CultureInfo class to specify the culture that the ToString() method and format string will use. This code creates a new instance of the CultureInfo class called MyCulture and initializes it to the French culture using the string "fr-FR". This object is then passed to the ToString() method as an additional parameter along with the C string format specifier that we used in the previous example to produce a French monetary value.

```
Imports System
Imports System.Globalization
Imports System.Windows.Forms

Module ToStringCulture
    Sub Main()
        Dim MyInt As Integer = 100
        Dim MyCulture As New CultureInfo("fr-FR")
        Dim MyString As String = MyInt.ToString("C", MyCulture)
        MessageBox.Show(MyString)
    End Sub
End Module
```

This should result in the following:

This is interesting as the culture is being taken into account. The current CultureInfo object implements the IFormatProvider interface and has a NumberFormatInfo member that is actually responsible for providing the information, such as the grouping symbol, the actual size of the groups, the decimal separator symbol, and more. Actually, the NumberFormatInfo class also implements the IFormatProvider to supply formatting information to applications.

NumberFormatInfo

The `NumberFormatInfo` class defines how numeric values are formatted and displayed, depending on the culture. This class contains information, such as currency, decimal separators, and other numeric symbols.

To create a `NumberFormatInfo` for a specific culture, create a `CultureInfo` object for that culture and retrieve the `CultureInfo.NumberFormat` property. If you want to create a `NumberFormatInfo` for the culture of the current thread, use the `CurrentCultureInfo` property.

To create a `NumberFormatInfo` for the invariant culture, use the `InvariantInfo` property for a read-only version, or use the `NumberFormatInfo` constructor for a writable version. Note that it is impossible to create a `NumberFormatInfo` for a neutral culture (a culture that only deals with a language and has no region/country information), because there is no indication of formatting associated with a neutral culture.

Numeric values are formatted using standard or custom patterns stored in the properties of a `NumberFormatInfo`. To modify how a value is displayed, the `NumberFormatInfo` must be writable, so that custom patterns can be saved in its properties. Since the default `NumberFormatInfo` object associated with a `CultureInfo` as a member of this class is not writable, we will need to clone this object, using the `Clone()` method to create another instance that we can modify.

The format string takes the form Ann, where A is the format specifier, and nn is the precision specifier. The format specifier controls the type of formatting applied to the numerical value, and the precision specifier controls the number of significant digits or decimal places.

If the format string is not specified, or set to `Nothing` or an empty string, the general format specifier ("G") is implicitly used.

The table below provides a list of all the standard format specifiers and examples of their use:

Format Character	Format Description	Example	Output
C or c	Currency	1000.ToString("C") (-1000).ToString("C")	$1,000.00 ($1,000.00)
D or d	Decimal	1000.ToString("D")	1000
E or e	Scientific (exponential)	100000.ToString("E")	1.000000E+005

Table continued on following page

Format Character	Format Description	Example	Output
F or f	Fixed-point	`1000.ToString("F4")` `1000.ToString("F0")`	1000.0000 1000
G or g	General	`1000.ToString("G")`	1000
N or n	Number	`1000.ToString("N")`	1,000.00
X or x	Hexadecimal	`1000.ToString("X")` `1000.ToString("x")` `&h1000.ToString("x")`	3E8 3e8 1000
P or p	Percentage	`1.ToString("P")`	100.00 %
r or R	Roundtrip. This is used to ensure that the string representation can be converted back to a number. It is not available for the `Integer` type but works for `Double`	`Dim d as Double = _` `    1000.0` `d.ToString("R")`	1000

Note that the format character is not case sensitive, except in the case of "x" and "X", where the case of the format characters determines the casing used for hexadecimal numbers. The formatting information displayed in the table above only applies to the "en-US" culture. If another culture were used, output could be different.

The `NumberFormatInfo` class implements the `ICloneable` interface, so that `NumbeFormatInfo` objects can be duplicated using the `Clone()` method. This is very useful when you intend to customize an instance of the `NumberFormatInfo` class associated with a `CultureInfo` in order to provide custom formatting. The example below shows exactly this. This short program retrieves the current culture and customizes it so that the new currency symbol is "*" and the new group separator is "|". Then it outputs a value of `123456` using this format.

The `CurrencyPositivePattern` requires some explanation. The .NET Framework uses a set of patterns, referenced by numbers (it is actually an enumeration), which indicate where the currency symbol is located (in front of the string or at the end of it) and whether a space is to be inserted before the currency symbol or not.

```
Imports System
Imports System.Globalization
Imports System.Threading

Module ChangeCultureFormat
    Sub Main()
        ' Retrieve current culture information by cloning it so that we
        ' can manipulate its NumberFormat member
        Dim ci As CultureInfo = _
            CType(Thread.CurrentThread.CurrentCulture.Clone(), _
                CultureInfo)
        Dim nfi As NumberFormatInfo = ci.NumberFormat

        ' Set our format to "123|456*"
        nfi.CurrencyPositivePattern = 1
        nfi.CurrencyGroupSeparator = "|"
        nfi.CurrencySymbol = "*"
        nfi.CurrencyDecimalDigits = 0
        ci.NumberFormat = nfi

        ' Set the thread culture to our modified CultureInfo object
        Thread.CurrentThread.CurrentCulture = ci

        ' Display the actual value using the proper formatting
        Console.WriteLine(123456.ToString("C"))
        Console.ReadLine()
    End Sub
End Module
```

The output when executing this should be:

```
123|456*
```

Representing Date and Time as a String

The DateTime value type represents dates and times with values ranging from 12:00:00 midnight, January 1, year 1 A.D. (or C.E. – Common Era, which is the new cross-culture name for "AD") to 11:59:59 P.M., December 31, 9999 C.E.

The DateTime type implements the IFormattable interface, allowing it to be formatted as a string with one of the overloads of DateTime.ToString(). The standard format provider class used for formatting DateTime objects in the .NET Framework is DateTimeFormatInfo.

The DateTimeFormatInfo Class

This class defines how `DateTime` values are formatted and displayed, depending on the culture. It contains information, such as date patterns, time patterns, and AM/PM designators. To create a `DateTimeFormatInfo` for a specific culture, create a `CultureInfo` for that culture and retrieve the `CultureInfo.DateTimeFormat` property. To create a `DateTimeFormatInfo` for the invariant culture, use the `InvariantInfo` property for a read-only version, or use the `DateTimeFormatInfo` constructor for a writable version. Like the `NumberFormatInfo` class, it is impossible to create a `DateTimeFormatInfo` for a neutral culture.

Format strings are interpreted as standard format specifiers if they contain only one of the single format specifiers listed in the table below. If the specified format character is a single character and is not found in the following table, an exception is thrown. If the format string is longer than a single character in length (even if the extra characters are whitespaces), the format string is interpreted as a custom format string. The patterns produced by these format specifiers are influenced by the settings in the Regional Options of the Windows Control Panel as these affect the current culture, unless the user preferences are overridden.

The `DateSeparator` and `TimeSeparator` characters associated with the `DateTimeFormat` property of the current culture define the date and time separators displayed by format strings.

However, in cases where the `InvariantCulture` is used (when referenced by the "r", "s", and "u" specifiers), the characters associated with the `DateSeparator` and `TimeSeparator` characters do not change depending on the current culture, but remain attached to the invariant culture.

The .NET Framework provides a long list of formats that are supported for date and time (the full list is available on MSDN). Here are the most common ones, which are also mapped to member functions of the `DateTimeFormatInfo` class (with some sample data for the en-US culture):

- ❏ "d": the short date pattern (5/20/2002, for example), also available directly through the `DateTimeFormatInfo.ShortDatePattern` property

- ❏ "D": the long date pattern (Monday, May 20, 2002, for example), also available directly through the `DateTimeFormatInfo.LongDatePattern` property

- ❏ "t": the short time pattern (3:51 PM, for example), also available directly through the `DateTimeFormatInfo.ShortTimePattern` property

- ❏ "T": the long time pattern (3:51:04 PM, for example), also available directly through the `DateTimeFormatInfo.LongTimePattern` property

Of course, besides standard formats, custom ones are also supported. The following code example illustrates how to use a custom format string with `DateTime` objects:

```
Imports System.Threading
Imports System.Globalization

Module CustomDateTimeFormat
  Sub Main()
    Dim dt As DateTime = DateTime.Now
    Dim dfi As New DateTimeFormatInfo()
    Dim ci As New CultureInfo("nl-BE")

    ' Use the DateTimeFormat from the culture associated with
    ' the current thread.
    Console.WriteLine(dt.ToString("d"))
    Console.WriteLine(dt.ToString("m"))

    ' Use the DateTimeFormat from the specific culture passed.
    Console.WriteLine(dt.ToString("F", ci))

    ' Make up a new custom DateTime pattern, and use it
    dfi.MonthDayPattern = "MM-MMMM, ddd-dddd"
    Console.WriteLine(dt.ToString("m", dfi))

    ' Reset the current thread to a different culture.
    Thread.CurrentThread.CurrentCulture = New CultureInfo("fr-BE")
    Console.WriteLine(dt.ToString("d"))
  End Sub
End Module
```

The results would be similar to the following, depending on the current date, time, and culture:

```
5/29/2002
May 29
woensdag 29 mei 2002 15:01:13
05-May, Wed-Wednesday
29/05/2002
```

Representing Other Objects as Strings

So far, we have dealt with numbers and date and time but what if we were creating a class and wanted to make sure that our class can be represented as a String properly? Well, this is only slightly more complicated: our class will inherit from the Object class and so we just need to provide overload(s) for the ToString method in the class.

Here we will create a Coordinate class that contains two values, X and Y:

```
Class Coordinate
  Inherits Object

  Private mx As Integer
  Private my As Integer

  Public Sub New(ByVal X As Integer, ByVal Y As Integer)
    mx = X
    my = Y
  End Sub

  Public Overrides Function ToString() As String
    Return "(" & _x.ToString() & ", " & _y.ToString() & ")"
  End Function

  Public Shared Sub Main()
    Dim c As Coordinate = New Coordinate(10, 20)
    Console.WriteLine(c.ToString())
  End Sub
End Class
```

This is the really simple and naive approach. A more elaborate approach would be to enable formatting parameters. It would be interesting to support the different formatting options available for the numeric format so that we could, for instance, display the coordinate as hexadecimal numbers.

In order to do so, we simply need to implement an overload for the ToString() method that implements the IFormattable interface, and change the current ToString() overload so that it uses the one that implements the formatting support. This is done here with the code below:

```
Imports System.Globalization
Imports System.Threading

Class Coordinate
  Inherits Object

  Implements IFormattable

  Private mx As Integer
  Private my As Integer

  Public Sub New(ByVal X As Integer, ByVal Y As Integer)
    mx = X
    my = Y
  End Sub

  Public Overloads Overrides Function ToString() As String
    Return ToString("g", CultureInfo.CurrentCulture)
  End Function
```

```
Public Overloads Function ToString(ByVal format As String, _
                         ByVal fp As IFormatProvider) As String _
                         Implements IFormattable.ToString
    Return String.Format("({0}, {1})", mx.ToString(format, fp), _
                         my.ToString(format, fp))
End Function

Public Shared Sub Main()
    Dim c As Coordinate = New Coordinate(1000, 2000)
    Console.WriteLine(c.ToString())
    Console.WriteLine(c.ToString("X", Nothing))
    Console.WriteLine(c.ToString("N", New CultureInfo("en-GB")))
End Sub
End Class
```

The default ToString() method uses the current culture and the "g" format, which is the general number format.

The output of this sample application is:

```
(1000, 2000)
(3E8, 7D0)
(1,000.00, 2,000.00)
```

Representing Strings with Strings

There are many cases where we need to transform strings into strings. While this may sound strange, let's just see why we may want to do this.

Let's assume that we have the following code:

```
Imports System

Module StringConcatenation
    Sub Main()
        Dim list As String() = {"car", "pen"}
        Dim item As String
        Dim message As String

        For Each item In list
            message = "This is my new " + item
            Console.WriteLine(message)
        Next
        Console.ReadLine()
    End Sub
End Module
```

The output of this code is:

```
This is my new car
This is my new pen
```

This looks perfectly fine. However, in many cases, this code is wrong when dealing with international strings. It is wrong because it makes an assumption, which is that all languages work like English. Many languages work in different ways.

Japanese, for instance, uses a different word order, where the verb is at the end of the sentence for sentences like the ones above. In addition, in other languages such as French and Italian, nouns have gender (masculine or feminine) and adjectives change depending on the gender and the number of the nouns they refer to.

It is now easy to see why the code above would not always work appropriately. The simple concatenation used above is not good enough and we need a better mechanism. This is exactly what the `String.Format()` method provides, as shown in the next chapter.

From String to Other Types

So far, we have seen how to format data from a numeric value or a date time object to as string. However, there are cases where we need to do the opposite transform, which is transforming a string into a `DateTime` or a number. This is exactly what the `Parse()` and `ParseExact()` methods are for.

Converting Strings to Numbers

All numeric types (such as `Integer` and `Double`) provide a `Parse()` method that enables you to convert strings to numbers very easily, while taking into account the formatting that may have been applied to the string representations. The `Parse()` method accepts a format provider, which allows you to specify and parse culture-specific strings. This means that you can also apply the same customization that can be applied for formatting.

If no format provider is specified, then the provider associated with the current thread is used. If you want to specify a format, you need to make sure that the `NumberStyles` enumeration flags that you pass to the `Parse()` method will actually match the format you want to use, otherwise a `FormatException` will be thrown. For instance, in the en-US culture, a string that contains a comma cannot be converted to an integer value using the `Parse()` method if the `NumberStyles.AllowThousands` enumeration is not passed.

The following code example is invalid and it will raise an exception. It shows an improper way to parse a string containing nonnumeric characters:

```
Imports System.Globalization

Module BadParsing
   Sub Main()
      Dim myCultureInfo As CultureInfo = new CultureInfo("en-US")
      Dim myString As String = "1,000"
      Try
         Dim myInt As Integer = Integer.Parse(myString, myCultureInfo)
         Console.WriteLine(myInt)
         ' Raises Exception
      Catch ex As System.FormatException
         Console.WriteLine("Commas cannot be included in string " & _
                           "to convert")
         Console.WriteLine("Exception was: {0}", ex.ToString())
      End Try
   End Sub
End Module
```

We only need to modify this code slightly to make it work properly by specifying the NumberStyles.AllowThousand flag when parsing the string:

```
Imports System.Globalization

Module GoodParsing
   Sub Main()
      Dim myCultureInfo As CultureInfo = new CultureInfo("en-US")
      Dim myString As String = "1,000"
      Dim myInt As Integer = Integer.Parse(myString, _
         NumberStyles.AllowThousands, myCultureInfo)
      Console.WriteLine(myInt)
   End Sub
End Module
```

We can also use a custom format to do some parsing. In order to show this, let's extend the sample we used when demonstrating how to format numbers using a custom format and just add parsing capabilities to this sample.

This short program retrieves the current culture and customizes it so the currency symbol is "#" and the group separator is ":". It will then output an integer (2364) based on a string with these characters inserted. This can be extremely valuable when dealing perhaps with an HTML form that could receive input from users in another locale.

```
Imports System.Globalization
Imports System.Threading

Module CustomizeCulture
   Sub Main()
      ' Retrieve current culture information by cloning it
      ' so that we can manipulate its NumberFormat member
      Dim ci As CultureInfo = _
         CType(Thread.CurrentThread.CurrentCulture.Clone(), CultureInfo)
```

```
        Dim nfi As NumberFormatInfo = ci.NumberFormat

        ' Set our format to "2:364#"
        nfi.CurrencyPositivePattern = 1
        nfi.CurrencyGroupSeparator = ":"
        nfi.CurrencySymbol = "#"
        nfi.CurrencyDecimalDigits = 0
        ci.NumberFormat = nfi

        ' Set the thread's culture to our modified CultureInfo object
        Thread.CurrentThread.CurrentCulture = ci

        ' Display the actual value using the proper formatting
        Console.WriteLine(2364.ToString("C"))

        ' Now parse a string using our custom format
        Dim myInt As Integer = Integer.Parse("2:364#", _
            NumberStyles.AllowCurrencySymbol & _
            NumberStyles.Currency & NumberStyles.AllowThousands)
        Console.WriteLine("{0:N}", myInt)
    End Sub
End Module
```

The `Parse()` method is called with a combination of the `Currency`, `AllowCurrencySymbol`, and `AllowThousands` `NumberStyles` flags in order to match the format that is currently specified using the current thread's culture.

This sample output is now:

```
2:364#
2,364.00
```

Converting String to Date and Time

In this section we cover the subtleties in converting a string to date and time, because dates are formatted differently in different locales.

Parsing Date and Time

The `DateTime` object has both a `Parse()` and a `ParseExact()` method that can be used to convert a string representation of a date or time into a `DateTime` object. The difference between the `Parse()` method and the `ParseExact()` method is that the `Parse()` method converts any valid string representation, whereas the `ParseExact()` method only converts strings that match the format that you specify. If you are using standard `DateTime` patterns (as defined earlier by the `DateTime` format table) then both methods can be used.

Parse()

The code below shows how to use the `Parse()` method to parse a string that contains a date:

```
Imports System.Globalization

Module Parse
  Sub Main()
    Dim myString As String = "05/28/2002"
    Dim myDateTime As DateTime = DateTime.Parse(myString)
    Console.WriteLine("{0:F}", myDateTime)
  End Sub
End Module
```

Provided the current culture is set to English (United States), the output is:

```
Thursday, May 28, 2002 12:00:00 AM
```

It should also be noted that a `CultureInfo` could be passed so that the date/time information is parsed according to the specified culture. If we modify the code slightly to pass an English (United Kingdom) culture, as indicated below, we get different results:

```
Imports System.Globalization

Module ParseUK
    Sub Main()
      Dim myCultureInfo As CultureInfo = New CultureInfo("en-GB")
      Dim myString As String = "28/05/2002"
      Dim myDateTime As DateTime = DateTime.Parse(myString, _
        myCultureInfo)
      Console.WriteLine("{0:F}", myDateTime)
    End Sub
End Module
```

The output for this would be:

```
Tuesday 28 May 2002 00:00:00 AM
```

It is important to note that because date format depends on the culture being used, it is not always possible to figure out what date is meant if the culture information is not provided. For instance, 02/01/2002 may be either January 2, 2002 or February 1, 2002, depending on the culture that is used. Since this can easily lead to incorrect dates being stored, it is a good practice to always set the culture info explicitly in any date handling code, and to ensure that the date is stored in a culture independent format – which is exactly what the invariant culture provides in the .NET Framework (see next chapter for more details on this).

Another interesting feature of the `Parse()` method is that, by default, any information about the date or time that is not contained in the passed string is filled with the current date and time value for this information.

ParseExact()

The `ParseExact()` method only converts the specified string pattern to a `DateTime` object and if the string that is passed does not match the pattern, then a `FormatException` is thrown. In the following code example, the `ParseExact()` method is passed a string object that matches the en-US short date pattern.

```
Imports System.Globalization

Module ParseExact
    Sub Main()
        Dim myCultureInfo As CultureInfo = New CultureInfo("en-US")
        Dim myString As String = "05/28/2002"
        Dim myDateTime As DateTime

        myDateTime = DateTime.ParseExact(myString, "d", _
            myCultureInfo)
        Console.WriteLine("{0:d}", myDateTime)
    End Sub
End Module
```

The output of this code varies depending on the current culture settings. On a US locale, for instance, the output will be: 5/28/2002. On a UK locale, the output will be: 28/05/2002.

Moving Strings Between Collections and Arrays

This is a small section on members of the `System.Collections` namespace, and objects of type `System.Array`. Because collections and arrays store their members differently, some mention is worthwhile here. Before we do though, we need to briefly describe what the `CType()` method does.

All objects have a `ToString()` method, so it may seem pointless to use `CType()` to move an object to a string. However, the difference is in the implementation. The `ToString()` method can contain many instructions and it is not always obvious to the Visual Studio IDE that it is of type `System.String`. `CType()` is very fast, as all it does is see if the .NET Framework allows casting to occur in this manner. An object can always be cast to an object it inherits from, and it can be cast to its own data type. This is useful if you want to perform a string operation on an item contained in an array or collection. No cultural information is ever considered when using the `CType()` method, and you may have to apply `String.Format()` to its results.

CType() with strings is often a useful language construct to make it explicit that the data type you are dealing with is a string. With this mentioned, we can now move on to discussing arrays.

Arrays

A System.Array object can be defined of fixed or variable size, and the object itself does not contain the contents of any other objects. If you define an array of value types, then it will contain the values, but as System.String is a reference type, then an array of strings will only contain references to the location of the strings. In addition, an array can only contain items of the same type. This is because the .NET Framework prefers to know the exact size of the array. Value types are of fixed size, so an array that contains ten integers, for instance, will consume 40 bytes of memory. This means that the heap can exactly allocate the space needed for the array. An array of ten strings would consume the same amount of memory as an array of ten integers, as references are also 32-bit. As all references are the same, then you can define an array of type System.Object and it will consume the same amount of memory for strings and all other objects.

We can see this in practice in the following code. Remember that in arrays, unlike collections, GetValue(index) is used to return the contents at the specified index, and SetValue(item, index) is used to change or add a new element at the specified index. Arrays are normally resized using ReDim, and you cannot insert more elements than the array allows.

```
Module ArrayExample
    Sub Main()
        Dim count As Integer
        Dim firstArray() As String = {"what", "did", "you", "do"}
        For count = 0 To firstArray.Length - 1
            Console.WriteLine(firstArray.GetValue(count) & _
                " - Type: {0}", firstArray.GetValue(count).GetType())
        Next
        Console.WriteLine("Type of firstArray is {0}", _
            firstArray.GetType())
    End Sub
End Module
```

There are some interesting things to point out about this code. Firstly, when the array is first defined, it happens in a few stages. Four areas of the heap are allocated to contain the strings "what", "did", "you", and "do". Then, the array object is constructed, and is limited to 4 elements. The references to the four strings are then inserted in each of the elements of the array. If you change any of the elements in this array, it will create a new string object and insert a reference to it.

Now, look at the first `Console.WriteLine()`. There is no need to cast this to type string as the compiler can see that it is a string at compile time. In the next part of the line, we use a formatting string to output the results of `GetType()`. Because `GetType()` returns a `System.Type`, it would have to be cast to a string, and the formatting instruction does this explicitly. This `For` loop returns `System.String` four times. The second `Console.WriteLine()` uses a formatting string again to return the type of the array. Here, rather than returning `System.Array`, or `System.Object`, it returns `System.String[]`. This is because although Visual Basic uses parentheses `()` to define an array, IL uses the square brackets instead. So, this is saying that it is an array object that contains elements of type `System.String`. Arrays are simple to deal with, as the `GetValue()` method always returns the expected type.

Now, if we were to `ReDim` this array, what would happen is that a new `Array` object would be created of the specified size, and the contents of the first would be copied into the first elements of the second. This is quite inefficient, and so the .NET Framework has provided collections so that we can store different objects of different types, and like the `StringBuilder` object discussed in the last chapter, attempt to reduce the amount of memory copying that occurs.

ArrayLists

An `ArrayList` is the `StringBuilder` of the array world. Like the `StringBuilder`, on initialization it permits 16 elements when the default constructor is used, and it also allows a value to be passed to its constructor so you can specify that it be resized to contain a different number of elements. `ArrayLists` store any object of type `System.Object` – which is everything. This is a boon as it means that any object can be contained, but it is also a burden as it means that objects returned would often need to be cast to its original type for the compiler not to complain about operations you wish to perform. This is generally a good idea anyway, as you may not know for certain what the type is of the object contained at a specific position within the `ArrayList`. An `ArrayList`, like an array, stores its elements in specific indices, but it can contain different types, and fewer memory allocations occur if more items need to be added. Unlike an array, an `ArrayList` uses the `Add()` method to append a new item, the `Item()` method to retrieve an item at a specific index, and numerous other methods, like `Insert()`, `Remove()`, `RemoveAt()`, `Sort()`, and `IndexOf()` to perform more powerful operations. `Insert()` and `RemoveAt()` will move the contents of the `ArrayList` up or down one, depending on the method, and so they can be quite expensive. Let's look at an `ArrayList` in action:

```
Imports System.Collections

Module ArrayListExample
  Sub Main()
    Dim myList As New ArrayList()
    myList.Add("Humpty Dumpty sat on the wall")
    myList.Add("Humpty Dumpty had a great fall")
    myList.Add("All the king's horses and all the king's men")
```

```
        myList.Add("Couldn't put humpty together again")
        myList.Add(6)
        myList.Add(6.3)
        myList.Add(True)
        Dim count As Integer
        For count = 0 To myList.count - 1
            Console.WriteLine("{0}" & ControlChars.Tab & "Type: {1}", _
                myList.Item(count), myList.Item(count).GetType)
        Next
    End Sub
End Module
```

This outputs:

```
Humpty Dumpty sat on the wall    Type: System.String
Humpty Dumpty had a great fall   Type: System.String
All the king's horses and all the king's men    Type: System.String
Couldn't put humpty together again         Type: System.String
6        Type: System.Int32
6.3      Type: System.Double
True     Type: System.Boolean
```

As you can see, the items returned are the expected types, and the `String.Format()` method happily converts the other types into strings.

IDictionary Objects

These include `HashTable` and all other key-value pair collections. Thankfully, these work in exactly the same way as the other collections. The key can be any object. `String.Format()` will work on any of the string items contained in any collection. It is advisable to use `CType()` with `IDictionary` objects, as well as with `ArrayLists` so that the compiler, and a third-party reader of the code, will know that the developer intends this item to be of the `String` type, but that is not essential.

Summary

In this chapter you have learned the best methods for converting between strings and other data types, taking into account that different data types may be entered differently, or output differently in different locales. We have covered the details of converting from numbers and dates, which may need formatting in a completely different way depending on the locale. We have also covered the reverse of this, sending a formatted string to a specific data type.

The last section showed how collections contain strings – as references to objects. It showed some of the issues involved when referencing the members of `Arrays`, `ArrayLists`, and `IDictionary` collections. In short, there was very little to learn about these objects. The collections only contain references to separate `String` objects.

The next chapter covers the culture-specific issues touched on this chapter in more detail, and describes how to make use of Unicode in the .NET Framework.

97

VB.NET

Text Manipulation

Handbook

4

4

Internationalization

Dealing with text well is one of the major challenges of building a truly international application and involves many aspects, from ensuring that the localizability requirements are met, to performing capitalization and lowercasing, sorting strings, displaying strings and characters, dealing with Unicode intricacies such as surrogate pairs, combining characters, and more. Fortunately, the .NET Framework provides a set of classes that actually help you handle text correctly for the diverse cultures supported by the .NET Framework. In brief, this chapter covers:

❑   Unicode – what it is and how it is encoded in .NET

❑   What cultures are

❑   The different kinds of cultures and how they are dealt with

❑   Sorting and the various issues involved with sorting for different cultures

❑   Dealing with Unicode characters, including surrogate pairs, and combining characters

By the end of this chapter, you will understand exactly how strings are dealt with in .NET, and how to make use of the new Unicode default set to ensure your applications are internationalized. You will also become aware of the issues of dealing with Unicode, such as the different ways different languages sort their alphabets. Before we explore all these features and the classes .NET provides to assist you, let's investigate the standard the .NET Framework uses for dealing with characters and strings., Unicode.

Unicode

While applications and users deal with text, computers as you probably know only operate with numbers – so computers treat letters, digits, and other characters by assigning a value for each one. Traditionally, characters have been stored as binary numbers ranging from decimal 0 to 127, complying with the ASCII standard.

Later, additional encodings (such as the MS-DOS or Windows code pages) were created that stored characters as 8-bits, opening up the range from 128 to 255 so that additional characters could be accommodated from languages with different or wider alphabets, such as Russian, Greek, Spanish, and French. However, not all additional characters could be provided at the same time, so support for different languages was divided between different encodings. In Microsoft Windows, one encoding (code page 1252) provided support for all Western European languages and other encodings were necessary for Central and Eastern European languages, such as Russian and Greek.

In addition, other encodings (such as Shift-JIS used in Japan) were devised for East Asian languages, which use many more characters. These encodings mix characters encoded on one byte and those encoded on two bytes, making most string operations, such as the ones to find the next character, far more difficult. While all these encodings provided a way to deal with one, and sometimes several languages at a time, provided they were written using the same set of characters, none of them provided a way to deal with all languages at once. This was because none of these encodings provided enough characters for that purpose, and this limitation has had drastic consequences. The European Union, for instance, had to use several encodings to support its languages. Also adding to the complexity was the fact that a value would represent a different character in a different encoding, as well as a character maybe having different values in different encodings, creating many problems when exchanging data between different machines.

The Unicode standard changes that. It provides the capacity to encode all the characters used for all the written languages in the world. Each character is assigned a name and a value that is unique. This unique value is called a **code point** and is usually expressed as a hexadecimal number following the prefix "U" and the "+" symbol. For example, the code point U+0042 represents the character "B" in the Unicode standard, and is given the character name of "LATIN CAPITAL LETTER B".

The original goal of Unicode was to use a single 16-bit encoding, providing code points for more than 65,000 characters. However, these 65,000 characters are not enough to encode all the characters used by all of the languages of the world. Therefore, the Unicode standard supports additional mechanisms that allow for over a million characters, which should provide enough space for all the written languages of the world, present or past. This makes the Unicode standard somewhat more complicated and will be detailed in the section *Dealing with Characters*, later.

Finally, characters are grouped logically in the Unicode standard, by ranges that correspond to the different writing scripts used by the different languages in the world. The coding starts at U+0000 with the standard ASCII characters, and then from U+0080 onwards, represents ranges defined for Greek, Cyrillic, Hebrew, Arabic, and most other scripts – ultimately it should support every script.

Encoding Formats

The Unicode Standard (http://www.unicode.org) defines three encoding formats that can be used to encode the same data in byte (8 bits), word (16 bits), or double word (32 bits) orientation. All three formats encode the same data and the data can be converted easily and without any loss between these three encoding formats.

UTF-8 is a popular encoding for HTML and XML. With UTF-8, Unicode characters are converted into bytes. Its main advantage is that Unicode characters that correspond to the familiar ASCII character set are also encoded on a single byte, which has the same value as its ASCII counterpart. For instance, the Unicode string "ABC" is encoded as a series of bytes 0x41, 0x42, 0x43, just as it would be if the string were an ASCII string. Unicode characters that are outside the normal 256-character range of UTF-8 (that is, characters whose code points are higher than U+00FF) are encoded on two or three bytes. The .NET Framework provides support for the UTF-8 encoding through an encoding class.

UTF-16 is the most common Unicode encoding and this is the one people refer to implicitly when speaking about Unicode. It represents most characters as single 16-bit code units, and some as a pair of 16-bit units. This topic will be explored further in the *Dealing with Characters* section. Strings within the .NET Framework use UTF-16, but for the most part, this is transparent to the developer.

UTF-32 is useful when the developer needs to use fixed-width characters, as it provides a way to encode all Unicode characters simply by using 32 bits. However, it is an expensive format because each character is encoded on four bytes, and it is therefore not as common as the other two encodings. The .NET Framework does not provide built-in support for UTF-32.

Finally, another encoding format, UTF-7, is mentioned here for completeness. This encoding format provides a representation of the Unicode character repertoire, with each character encoded as a series of 7-bit entities. This format uses shift characters to encode characters that are not represented as characters in the ASCII range. These shift sequences are pairs of ASCII characters that are rarely seen, and indicate that the next 2 or 3 characters are to be interpreted as a character outside the ASCII range. This format should really only be used in the context of 7-bit transports such as mail and news transports. The .NET Framework provides an encoding class that lets you convert Unicode characters used internally by the .NET Framework to UTF-7 sequences.

.NET Framework Encoding Classes

Having seen the basics of Unicode, we will now look at the encoding classes provided by the .NET Framework. The System.Text namespace provides a series of encoding classes that allow you to convert strings between Unicode (UTF-16) and other encodings.

The Encoding Class

The Encoding class is the base class from which the other encoding classes are derived. It provides methods to convert arrays and strings of Unicode characters, to and from arrays of bytes that are encoded using a Windows code page.

The following code example shows how to use the encoding class to convert strings between Unicode and code pages 1252 (Windows Latin 1) and 932 (Shift-JIS, Japanese). You will notice that converting Japanese characters using the ConvertToEncoding() method yields different results if the code page specified is 1252 or 932. When code page 1252 is specified, these characters are not recognized and are converted to question marks, whereas when the 932 code page is specified, then the proper Japanese characters are being generated.

```vbnet
Imports System.Windows.Forms
Imports System.Text

Module ConvertEncoding
  Sub Main()
    ConvertToEncoding("Hello, world", 1252)
    ConvertToEncoding("Hello, world", 932)

    Dim japaneseString As String
    japaneseString = ChrW(&H307B) & ChrW(&H308B) & ChrW(&H305A) & _
      ChrW(&H3042) & ChrW(&H306D)

    ConvertToEncoding(japaneseString, 1252)
    ConvertToEncoding(japaneseString, 932)

    Dim bytes As Byte() = {65, 66, 67, 233, 230}
    ConvertFromEncoding(bytes, 1252)
  End Sub

  Public Sub ConvertToEncoding(ByVal text As String, _
                               ByVal codePage As Integer)
    Dim targetEncoding As Encoding
    ' Get the encoding for the specified code page and
    ' get the byte representation of the specified string
    targetEncoding = Encoding.GetEncoding(codePage)

    Dim targetBytes As Byte()
    targetBytes = targetEncoding.GetBytes(text)
```

```
    ' Display the bytes and their values
    Dim message As String = String.Format( _
      "String ""{0}"" has been converted to: ", text)

    Dim count As Integer
    For count = 0 To targetBytes.Length - 1
      message += String.Format("{0} ", targetBytes(count))
    Next

    MsgBox(message)
  End Sub

  Public Sub ConvertFromEncoding(ByVal bytes As Byte(), _
                                 ByVal codePage As Integer)
    Dim targetEncoding As Encoding
    ' Get the encoding for the specified code page and
    ' convert the byte array to a Unicode string
    targetEncoding = Encoding.GetEncoding(codePage)

    Dim targetString As String
    targetString = targetEncoding.GetString(bytes)

    ' Display the bytes and the string
    Dim count As Integer
    Dim byteString As String = String.Empty

    For count = 0 To bytes.Length - 1
      byteString += bytes(count).ToString() & " "
    Next

    Dim message As String
    message = String.Format( _
      "Bytes ""{0}"" have been converted to string: ", byteString)
    message += " " + targetString
    MsgBox(message)
  End Sub
End Module
```

The output of this code sample, assuming you have international fonts installed (which can consume 230MB of space on a Windows XP system) should be as follows:

As you can see from the two screenshots, the string "Hello, world" is converted in an identical manner on both 1252 (Western Europe) and 932 (Japan) code pages. This is because the ASCII characters are present in all code pages.

The screenshot above shows that in code page 1252, the string has been converted to a set of characters of value 63, (a question mark). This is because these characters are not present in this code page and are therefore not understood when the conversion from Unicode to code page 1252 occurs.

In the screenshot below, the Unicode Japanese characters have been correctly converted to their equivalent representations in code page 932, as these characters are present in this code page, which was designed to support Japanese.

Finally, the conversion can also be performed the other way round, and characters from code page 1252 can be converted successfully into Unicode characters:

The code uses the Encoding.GetEncoding() method, passing a code page as its argument to obtain the actual encoding that is used to format the byte array. Then it uses the Encoding.GetBytes() method to convert arrays of Unicode characters into array of bytes. A reversing method, called GetChars(), can be used to convert arrays of bytes to arrays of Unicode characters.

A number of Encoding-derived classes are also provided in the System.Text namespace, including:

❑ The ASCIIEncoding class, which encodes Unicode characters as single 7-bit ASCII characters and only supports characters whose values are in the [U+0000-U+007F] range. If you are trying to convert a Unicode character that is not is not in this range, you will get an exception and the character will not be encoded.

❑ The UnicodeEncoding class, which encodes each Unicode character as two consecutive bytes. Different operating systems use different byte orders when storing data internally; some use the big endian order where the most significant byte is stored first and some use the little endian order where the most significant byte is stored last. The UnicodeEncoding class provides support for both little endian and big endian byte ordering, which makes this class especially useful when converting from the .NET Framework (which is little endian) to exchange data with a computer such as some mainframes and Unix systems (which are big endian).

❑ The UTF7Encoding class, which encodes Unicode characters using the UCS Transformation Format 7-bit form (UTF-7), which supports all Unicode character values and converts them to a 7-bit variable length format.

❑ The UTF8Encoding class, which encodes Unicode characters using the UTF-8 encoding, which also supports all Unicode characters.

You can use the Encoding class, as used in the example, to convert data back and from Unicode for all code pages that are actually supported on your machine. For instance, this is how you can support the new GB-18030 encoding used in the People's Republic of China. Provided you have installed the proper support files for this encoding on your machine (which you can download from Microsoft China's web site), you will then be able to use this encoding in your .NET Framework-based applications through the Encoding class.

If we were dealing with a larger amount of data, or data that comes from a stream and is only available in sequential blocks, we would probably need to use the Decoder and Encoder classes to perform the conversion. These classes, unlike the GetBytes() and GetChars() methods, maintain state information that is required to support data conversion of data spanning several blocks.

Dealing with Strings

Considering the complexity usually associated with strings in an international context, the best way to deal with strings is probably by not dealing with the strings at all. Of course, this is really extreme and not readily achieveable in a real-world application, so the idea here is really to limit the string handling to what is absolutely necessary, as each operation may introduce significant complexity and performance issues. Fortunately, the .NET Framework provides a great deal of help in dealing with this complexity, and enables us as developers to create applications that support international strings in a straightforward manner. However, there are some general truths about operations on international strings, such as that operations done properly on international strings are generally more costly than similar operations that do not care about culture-correctness. Another interesting aspect is that it is always easier to deal with whole strings and not with characters one by one, as international strings may contain combinations of characters that cannot be separated at random without corrupting data.

Before we look into standard string operations, such as capitalization, lowercasing, and sorting, we need to look at cultures and how they can affect string operations.

The CultureInfo Class

The `CultureInfo` class is the most important class in the `System.Globalization` namespace. It provides culture-specific information, such as the culture name, its associated language, country/region, calendar, and cultural conventions. This class also provides access to culture-specific instances of other classes that provide additional culture-specific information, such as `DateTimeFormatInfo`, `NumberFormatInfo`, `CompareInfo`, and `TextInfo`. These objects contain the information required for culture-specific operations, such as casing, formatting dates and numbers, and comparing strings. Therefore, by specifying a culture, it is possible to use a set of common preferences for information on strings, and date and number formats that correspond to users' cultural conventions.

Culture Names

The culture names are derived from the RFC 1766 standard. This standard uses the format `language[-country/region]`", where `language` is a lowercase two-letter (sometimes three-letter) code, derived from the ISO-639-1 standard, and `country/region` is an uppercase two-letter code derived from the ISO 3166 standard. Here are a few examples:

❑ "en" represents the English language

❑ "en-US" represents English (United States)

❑ "kok-IN" represents Konkani (India)

A culture name may or may not contain the `country/region` information in its name, and it is possible to have cultures whose names are only specified by the language information. For instance, Japanese (as a language) is specified as `ja` and Japanese as spoken in Japan is specified as `ja-JP`.

In addition, some culture names have suffixes that specify the script; for example, `-Cyrl` specifies the Cyrillic script, `-Latn` specifies the Latin script. For instance, `sr-SP-Cyrl` indicates Serbian (Cyrillic) (Serbia) and `sr-SP-Latn` indicates Serbian (Latin) (Serbia). This is different from the MSDN documentation at the time of writing.

The Different Types of Culture

While the .NET Framework implements over 200 cultures, these cultures can be divided into three groups:

❑ The **invariant culture**, which is unique

❑ The **neutral** cultures

❑ The **specific** cultures

Figure 1 shows a subset of the overall culture tree, where only the invariant culture, the neutral English (en) and French (fr) cultures, and the specific French-related cultures are displayed.

Figure 1

The Invariant Culture

The invariant culture is a unique culture that is at the root of the culture tree implemented by the .NET Framework. It is associated with the English language, but not with a country or region, and is a culture that does not exist in the real world. It is a completely culture-insensitive culture.

This may seem quite strange, but there is some logic to it; there are many processes requiring culture-independent results, such as system services. Typical applications of the invariant culture are when dealing with date and time storage for a web service, and capitalization of file names that are to be passed to the operating system. Storing data in a culture-independent format guarantees a known format that does not change (at least within the same version of the .NET Framework,). When users from different cultures need to access data that is stored using the invariant culture format, this data can be formatted appropriately for the user by converting it to a culture that is appropriate for the specific user.

In other cases, such as when used directly for user interface elements, the invariant culture produces results that might be linguistically incorrect, or culturally inappropriate. You are therefore recommended to avoid using the invariant culture for any user interface item.

Neutral Cultures

A neutral culture is a culture that is associated with a language but not with a country or region. As such, a neutral culture is very useful for language-only related operations, but cannot be used for retrieving information, such as date and time formatting, as these are very much country- and region-dependent, and may vary within the same language. For instance, date and time formats differ between the United States and the United Kingdom, although the language can be considered English in both cases.

Names for neutral cultures are specified using the *languageCode2* format indicated above. For instance, Arabic is specified with `ar`. Neutral cultures cannot be used to perform string operations, such as capitalization and lowercasing or sorting. To perform these, you need to create a specific culture.

Specific Culture

A specific culture is a culture that provides information for both the language and the country or region. For example, `de` is the neutral German culture and `de-DE` is a specific culture that represents German (Germany). The major difference between a neutral culture and a specific one is that a specific culture provides additional information about the date, time, currency, and number formatting options associated with the specific region or country.

The Two Roles of CultureInfo

An international-aware application needs to handle international data (date, time, currencies, characters that are part of the application data, etc.). In addition, it wants to be localized so that international users can use the application in the easiest, most productive fashion. However, the latter point (localization) is not a strict requirement for an international-aware application.

In both cases, the `CultureInfo` class plays an important role as a provider of cultural preferences. Since these two roles are distinct, even though there are many cases where the same culture is used for both, the .NET Framework implements a mechanism for both roles, which are referred to as the `CurrentCulture` and the `CurrentUICulture`.

The `CurrentCulture` and the `CurrentUICulture` are set at the thread level for an application, which enables a multi-threaded application to use different cultures on different threads. If you do not specify these values, they are inherited from the operating system so that you always have a valid `CurrentCulture` and `CurrentUICulture` defined.

CurrentUICulture

The `CurrentUICulture` value determines how the resources are loaded for a form, and is used for culture-specific lookup of resource data. The only purpose of the `CurrentUICulture` value is to indicate the language the resource manager should use to load the resources associated with the form if this one is localizable. You can use either a neutral or a specific culture to set the `CurrentUICulture`.

CurrentCulture

The CurrentCulture value determines everything else – date formatting, number formatting, string casing and comparison, and so on. The CurrentCulture value can only be set to specific cultures such as en-US or en-GB. This prevents the problem of identifying the correct currency symbol to use for en.

The two culture settings do not need to have the same value. In the design of your application, it may be important to set them separately. For instance, if you are building an application for the United States but you want the user interface to display menus in Spanish, you can set the CurrentCulture to en-US so that the number formatting will be correct, and the CurrentUICulture to es so that the localized resources are actually displayed in Spanish. Another interesting aspect is when running a US application that is not localized for Japan. In this case, the CurrentCulture will be set to ja-JP so that the date, time, currency and number formats will be all Japanese, whereas the user interface will remain in English with the CurrentUICulture set to en.

Setting the CurrentCulture and the CurrentUICulture

First, it should be noted that there are cases where you don't want or need to set these cultures explicitly. For instance, if you are developing a Windows Form application, you usually should avoid setting these values (at least the CurrentCulture one) explicitly, as the operating system provides you with implicit default values that match the current user choice (for CurrentCulture) and settings (for CurrentCulture).

Implicit Values

If the CurrentCulture property is not set explicitly, then a default value is provided by the system, picked up from the GetUserDefaultLCID API in Windows. This default value is affected by changes to Regional Options | Set Locale in Control Panel.

If the CurrentUICulture property is not set explicitly in an application's code, it is set by default when the application starts with the language used for the Windows resources. This default cannot be changed by the user unless they use an MUI (Multilingual User Interface) version of Windows, in which case, an additional option is available in the control panel that lets you change this default value.

Explicit Values

While the default values work in some cases, there are cases where you will need to set the CurrentUICulture or CurrentCulture explicitly. For instance, if you are developing a server application (such as when using ASP.NET), the default local values are picked up on your server and they are very likely to be different from what your users may expect on their client machines. In that case, setting the values explicitly for the current culture and the current UI culture is necessary.

This is done by setting the culture properties of the current thread to instances of the CultureInfo class you want:

```
Imports System.Globalization
Imports System.Threading
...
    Thread.CurrentThread.CurrentUICulture = New CultureInfo("en")
    Thread.CurrentThread.CurrentCulture = New CultureInfo("ja-JP")
```

In both samples, the current UI culture will be set to English, whereas the current culture will be set to Japanese.

You now have a better understanding of the cultures and the `CultureInfo` class, so we can now dig into the actual string handling specifics.

Uppercasing and Lowercasing

It is important to note that operations such as uppercasing, lowercasing, and string comparison are culture-sensitive, and that this impacts on both linguistic correctness and performance. In particular, performance is impacted as potentially more complicated lookup and calculations need to occur behind the scenes so that the correct operation happens for a given culture.

Uppercasing

The `String` class provides the `ToUpper()` method, which capitalizes a string. The easiest way to call this method is without any parameters:

```
myString = "This is a string"
myCapStr = myString.ToUpper()
```

This call will actually use the culture that is specified at the current thread level, and use it to perform the capitalization. If the selected culture happens to be en-US, these sample strings would contain:

this is a string
THIS IS A STRING

If the current thread's current culture is set to `tr-TR` (Turkish, Turkey), then the output will be different, as Turkish uses a different capitalization rule for the "I" character. There are four "I" characters in Turkish and they are matched according to the table below:

Lowercase	Uppercase
i (U+0069)	İ (U+0130)
ı (U+0131)	I (U+0049)

Since the conversion to uppercase for the "i" character is different in Turkish, our sample will have a different string as an output:

this is a string
THİS İS A STRİNG

Another way to call the String.ToUpper() method, is to pass a CultureInfo parameter to this method. In this case, the passed CultureInfo parameter is used instead of the current thread's culture to perform the capitalization operation.

So, for instance, the following code:

```
myString = "this is a string"
myCapStr1 = myString.ToUpper(New CultureInfo("en-US")
myCapStr2 = myString.ToUpper(New CultureInfo("tr-TR")
```

produces the following results:

this is a string
THIS IS A STRING
THİS İS A STRİNG

Lowercasing

The String class also provides the String.ToLower() method that performs the reverse operation, lowercasing. Just like the ToUpper() method, the ToLower() method either takes a CultureInfo parameter or no parameter, in which case the current thread's culture is used to perform the lowercasing operation.

When Culture-Sensitive Operations are Not Desired

Since both uppercasing and lowercasing operations are culture-sensitive, there are no guarantees that an operation performed using one culture will provide the same results when using another culture, as we have seen in the previous section.

While using culture-sensitive operations is desirable when dealing with user interface strings, so that strings can be displayed properly to the users based on the correct capitalization and lowercasing rules for their cultures, there are cases, such as when dealing with system objects, where this may be a problem. For instance, imagine that you are trying to validate a path; this path name contains some "I" characters and you have two strings, one in uppercase and another in lowercase that are set to the path name. It would be very difficult to actually figure out that these two strings refer to the same file if the two strings do not match, because the current culture has different capitalization rules from the culture that was originally used to produce the path name. In this case, it is important that the conversion rules are always the same, and this is where the invariant culture is useful.

Sorting

There are two ways a string can be sorted: either in a culture-insensitive manner, which only considers the actual code point values of the characters being sorted, or in a culture-sensitive manner that ensures the sorting is performed according to the sorting rules available for the selected culture.

Let's illustrate this with an example. There are two strings: "ciao" and "character", and we'll first sort these strings using an ordinal sort (which only checks the values of the code points):

"ciao"	"character"
U+0063	U+0063
U+0069	U+0068
U+0061	U+0061
U+006F	U+0072
	U+0061
	U+0063
	U+0074
	U+0065
	U+0072

We see that the second character in the ciao string (i) has a code point value that is higher than the second character of the character string (h). Therefore, the ordinal comparison returns that "ciao" > "character", as you might expect.

Now, let's assume that we want to use a culture-sensitive sort. If we select the en-US (English, United States) culture, the alphabetical rules for this culture indicate that "h" should be sorted before "i", and so the comparison also returns "ciao" > "character". However, if we change the culture to use the cs-CZ (Czech, Czech Republic) culture, then the rules of the Czech language specify that "ch" is to be treated for comparison and sorting purposes as a single entity that appears after "c". In this case, the comparison between our two strings results in "ciao" < "character".

As you can see, using a culture-specific sorting method provides us with the sorting order that closely matches the user's language experience and expectations. As a rule, user interface items, such as list boxes, combo boxes, and other tabular data lists should use a culture-specific sorting method, so that they match the user's expectations.

So far, we have seen the theory, but you should now want to see how to apply this to .NET.

String.CompareOrdinal()

The String class provides the CompareOrdinal() method that can be used to compare two strings without considering the current culture. For instance, the following code snippet compares two strings using the CompareOrdinal() method and writes the results to the command line:

```
Module CompareOrdinalMethod
  Sub Main()
    Dim firstString As String = New String("ciao")
    Dim secondString As String = New String("character")

    Select Case String.CompareOrdinal(firstString, secondString)
    Case Is < 0
      Console.WriteLine("""{0}"" < ""{1}""", firstString, _
        secondString)
    Case 0
      Console.WriteLine("""{0}"" = ""{1}""", firstString, _
        secondString)
    Case Is > 0
      Console.WriteLine("""{0}"" > ""{1}""", firstString, _
        secondString)
    End Select
  End Sub
End Module
```

Running this application should result in the following output:

```
"ciao" > "character"
```

In real-world applications, you may want to use the String.CompareOrdinal() method to compare strings when you are dealing with system objects (for instance file names) and you don't want the order of the sort to change depending on the culture, such as when you are creating an index or hash table.

String.Compare()

The Compare() method implements a culture-sensitive string comparison. There are several overloads for this method that specify whether the comparison should be case-sensitive or not; or in other words, provide a CultureInfo object to use instead of the current thread's culture. You can also specify indices and lengths in the strings to be compared so that you effectively compare sub-strings.

Let's look at what the example above might be if we were using the Compare() method:

```
Imports System.Globalization

Module CompareMethod
  Sub Main()
    Dim firstString As String = New String("ciao")
    Dim secondString As String = New String("character")
```

```
      Select Case String.Compare(firstString, secondString, True, _
        New CultureInfo("cs-CZ"))
      Case Is < 0
        Console.WriteLine("""{0}"" < ""{1}""", _
          firstString, secondString)
      Case 0
        Console.WriteLine("""{0}"" = ""{1}""", _
          firstString, secondString)
      Case Is > 0
        Console.WriteLine("""{0}"" > ""{1}""", _
          firstString, secondString)
      End Select
    End Sub
  End Module
```

In this case, the comparison would yield "ciao" < "character", as we specified
the Czech (Czech Republic) culture to perform the comparison. Note that we passed
the Czech (Czech Republic) culture as a parameter to the String.Compare() method,
as shown in the section on capitalization and lowercasing above. We also indicated
that the comparison should be case-insensitive by specifying the value True for the
third parameter passed to the String.Compare() method, which is the IgnoreCase
flag for this overload of the Compare() method.

String.CompareTo()

This method is similar to the Compare() method but it cannot be used as a shared
method and does not provide any way to specify if the comparison should be case-
sensitive or not (it is case-sensitive). The code snippet below implements our
comparison using the CompareTo() method:

```
Imports System.Globalization
Imports System.Threading

Module CompareToMethod
  Sub Main()
    Dim firstString As String = New String("ciao")
    Dim secondString As String = New String("character")

    Thread.CurrentThread.CurrentCulture = New CultureInfo("cs-CZ")

    Select Case firstString.CompareTo(secondString)
      Case Is < 0
        Console.WriteLine("""{0}"" < ""{1}""", firstString, _
          secondString)
      Case 0
        Console.WriteLine("""{0}"" = ""{1}""", firstString, _
          secondString)
      Case Is > 0
        Console.WriteLine("""{0}"" > ""{1}""", firstString, _
          secondString)
      End Select
    End Sub
  End Module
```

Using the CompareInfo Class

There are cases, for specific cultures, where the culture-sensitive sorting provided by the Compare() method is not enough for some more advanced ordering.

For instance, Japanese uses two syllabaries named Hiragana and Katakana, and each contain characters that are pronounced in identical manners, but are written differently. There are cases, when dealing with Japanese text, where you may want characters that are pronounced the same way to be treated as equal, and cases where they should be treated differently. If you wish to support this functionality in your code, you will need to use another class provided by the .NET Framework – the CompareInfo class.

The CompareInfo Class

The CompareInfo class implements a set of methods for culture-sensitive string comparisons. Unlike most other classes in the .NET Framework, an instance of this class cannot be created by using a constructor, but needs to be created using the GetCompareInfo() method. This method accepts several overloads that let you specify an integer that is a Windows LCID identifier, or a string that is a culture identifier (CultureInfo). A list containing Windows LCIDs, which provide alternative sort orders, is available in the MSDN documentation (http://support.microsoft.com/directory/article.asp?ID=KB;EN-US;Q224804&).

In order to create a CompareInfo object for the en-US culture, you can use:

```
Dim ci As CompareInfo = CompareInfo.GetCompareInfo(1033)
```

or:

```
Dim ci As CompareInfo = CompareInfo.GetCompareInfo("en-US")
```

Another way to retrieve a CompareInfo object is to get the CompareInfo member that is contained in a CultureInfo class (in particular, the one in the current culture) with the following syntax:

```
Dim ci As CompareInfo = CultureInfo.CurrentCulture.CompareInfo
```

The most interesting method of this class is Compare(), which also provides several overloads. The most interesting ones are those that provide a CompareOptions parameter, which can be used to fine-tune the comparison, as with the following overload, for instance, which takes strings as its first two parameters, and a CompareOptions as its third:

```
Compare(string1 As String, string2 as String, _
        options as CompareOptions)
```

115

The CompareOptions enumeration contains the following members that can be combined to customize the comparison options used for the CompareInfo.Compare() function:

Member Name	Description
IgnoreCase	Indicates that the string comparison must ignore case. In the case of the en-US culture, if this value is set, then abc and ABC compare equally, whereas they don't otherwise.
IgnoreKanaType	Indicates that the string comparison must ignore the Kana type.
	The Japanese language uses two syllabaries, **hiragana** and **katakana**, which represent phonetic sounds in the Japanese language. Hiragana is used for native Japanese expressions and words, while katakana is used for words borrowed from other languages, such as "computer". The same phonetic sound can be expressed in both hiragana and katakana. If the IgnoreKanaType flag is specified, then the hiragana character for one sound is considered equal to the katakana character for the same sound. In this case, "バナナ" (banana written properly in katakana) is equal to "ばなな" (banana, written using hiragana).
IgnoreNonSpace	Indicates that the string comparison must ignore non-spacing combining characters, such as diacritics. If this value is set, "é" will be equal to "e".
IgnoreSymbols	Indicates that the string comparison must ignore symbols, such as whitespace characters, punctuation, currency symbols, the percent symbol, mathematical symbols, the ampersand, etc, for example, the Kashida used in Arabic is in this category and will be ignored for comparison purposes if this value is set.
IgnoreWidth	Indicates that the string comparison must ignore the character width. For example, Japanese katakana characters can be written as full-width or half-width and, if this value is selected, the katakana characters written as full-width are considered equal to the same characters written in half-width.
	In this case, "バ゙ナナ" equals "バナナ"
None	Indicates the default option settings for string comparisons, which is a comparison that provides the same results as a case-sensitive sort operated with String.Compare()

116

Member Name	Description
Ordinal	Indicates that the string comparison must be ordinal. This is equivalent to turning the string comparison into an ordinal string comparison as described at the beginning of the *Sorting* section.
StringSort	Indicates that the string comparison must use the string sort algorithm, where the hyphen and the apostrophe, as well as other non-alphanumeric characters, come before alphanumeric symbols.

Dealing with Characters

Directly dealing with characters, when manipulating international strings, is not a very good idea. There is a lot of complexity that one needs to deal with when doing so. While at first Unicode seems to be an easier model than the code pages systems it has replaced, there is still significant complexity linked to two classes of Unicode characters: **surrogate pairs** and **combining characters**.

The best advice that can be given here is to avoid dealing with single characters altogether and to only deal with strings. However, if you really need to deal with single characters, then the information below should help you. Before we see how to deal with this complexity, it should be noted that Unicode provides information about each character that is defined within the standard. This allows us to know which characters are potentially problematic. The .NET Framework exposes information about Unicode characters through the Char class.

Necessary Information about Characters

The Char class provides several methods that are useful in determining the role of a character and its properties. The base method is Char.GetUnicodeCategory(), which indicates the category to which the character belongs.

The following code snippet shows how to retrieve the Unicode category for the character "a":

```
Dim uc As UnicodeCategory = Char.GetUnicodeCategory("a"c)
```

The Char class also provides a series of Is methods that actually loosely match the different Unicode categories. MSDN contains a table that lists all the categories that are available (http://msdn.microsoft.com/library/default.asp?url=/library/en-us/cpref/html/frlrfSystemGlobalizationUnicodeCategoryClassTopic.asp).

Surrogate Pairs

So far, what we have seen from Unicode is not very different in terms of handling characters from existing code pages. Let's now look at the complexity associated with surrogate pairs and combining characters.

Unicode is often thought of as a simple mechanism with all characters defined in 16-bit quantities. However, this is not true. That definition would provide for 65,536 characters, which is not enough to represent all the characters that are available in all the different scripts worldwide. In particular, there are over 85,000 Chinese characters. This means that characters need to be defined on more than 16-bits in order to provide a greater range. In order be able to support these supplemental characters, Unicode defines a mechanism that permits an additional 917,476 characters without having to use 32-bit characters, and while preserving compatibility with the existing set of characters. This mechanism is known as the surrogate pair mechanism.

The Unicode standard defines a surrogate pair as a coded character representation for a single abstract character that consists of a sequence of two code units, where the first unit of the pair is a **high surrogate** and the second is a **low surrogate**. In simple terms, this means that to represent a character value which is higher than can be encoded on 16 bits, we can substitute a pair of 16-bit characters (the high surrogate and the low surrogate) that represent the same value.

How This Works

There is a reserved area of 1,024 characters at the high end of the Unicode code space, from U+D800 through to U+DBFF for high surrogates. There is also a reserved area of 1,024 characters following this, from U+DC00 through to U+DFFF for low surrogates. Combining one high-range value with one low-range value makes a unique surrogate pair. We use two 16-bit Unicode values together and their unique pairing maps at display time to a real-world character. No other characters or symbols are ever assigned inside these two reserved areas. Also, since surrogates have no interpretation except when they occur as part of a surrogate pair; standing alone, a surrogate is meaningless. Therefore, whenever an application encounters a Unicode value from either one of these reserved areas, it can only be one half of a surrogate pair.

The transformation between a Unicode value of N (which is a value between 0 and 10FFFF (hexadecimal)) and a pair of surrogate characters is defined in the following manner. First the high surrogate:

```
(N - 0x10000) / 0x400 + 0xD800
```

Whereas the low surrogate can be calculated by:

```
(N - &h10000) mod &h400 + 0xDC00
```

Let's see an example. If a character has a scalar value of 2002F, the matching surrogate pair is as follows, with the high surrogate being 0xD840 ((0x2002F-0x10000)/0x400 + D800), and the low surrogate being 0xDC2F ((0x2002F-0x10000) mod 0x400 + 0xDC00).

Why Support Surrogates

Version 3.1 of the Unicode standard introduced the characters that are represented by surrogates. Here is a list of the ranges that are so defined by the Unicode Standard version 3.2:

Range Name	Range Start	Range End
Old Italic	U+10300	U+1032F
Gothic	U+10330	U+1034F
Deseret	U+10400	U+1044F
Byzantine Musical Symbols	U+1D000	U+1D0FF
Musical Symbols	U+1D100	U+1D1FF
Mathematical Alphanumeric Symbols	U+1D400	U+1D7FF
CJK Unified Ideographs Extension B	U+20000	U+2A6DF
CJK Compatibility Ideographs Supplement	U+2F800	U+2FA1F
Tags	U+E0000	U+E007F
Supplementary Private Use Area-A	U+F0000	U+FFFFF
Supplementary Private Use Area-B	U+100000	U+10FFFF

While some of the characters defined here are not very often used, the CJK (China, Japan, Korea) characters available in the CJK Unified Ideographs Extension B and the CJK Compatibility Ideographs Supplement ranges are essential for the East Asian markets. The Han ideographs used in China, Japan, and Korea are numerous and the original Unicode implementation only captured the most commonly used ideographs; it did not capture all of them. Over time, there have been requests for Unicode support for more of these ideographs and more have been added: first as CJK Extension A, which is within the main Unicode range, and then as CJK Extension B, which is a range that is accessible through surrogate pairs.

Creating such characters with Unicode surrogate pairs ensures that the world remains on the same Unicode code page, removing the need to move to an even larger one later. There are potentially over a million (1,048,576) surrogate pairs that could be assigned via this method. It is not expected that the need for characters will outgrow the surrogate range.

Handling Surrogates

To a large extent, the Microsoft .NET Framework provides uniform support for Unicode strings, whether they contain surrogates or not. This means that there are actually only a few cases where you need to worry about surrogates.

Surrogate pairs are predictable in their form. They are always composed of one high-range value in the first pair member, and one low-range value in the second pair member. Surrogate pairs are also easy to reference. Each pair will always be composed of two 16-bit values. Since pairs always combine in high and low combinations, that provides an easy way to backtrack to the start of a sequence of surrogate pairs. The following sections list cases that typically arise when developing an application and provide information about the level of support that needs to be implemented by developers who are dealing with surrogates.

Displaying Surrogates

Both Windows Forms and Web Forms display surrogates correctly, provided they are using a font that contains glyphs for the characters to be displayed, such as "Arial Unicode". Console-based applications do not display surrogates, as the console does not provide any non-proportional font that can display them correctly.

To display surrogates correctly for a Windows Form control, a font must be selected in the form designer, or the font property for a control needs to be changed at run time through code. In the example below, a FontDialog control is used in order to select a font and then assigns the newly selected font to a label that displays the actual surrogate pair. If this font supports surrogates, the control will then display them correctly.

The screenshot below shows a Windows Form based application developed with the Microsoft .NET Framework that displays a set of surrogate characters. No special handling is necessary for display, apart from finding a font that can display characters represented by surrogate pairs.

The complete source code for this example can be found in the code download, but the relevant methods are shown below. First the method that deals with the Select Font... button:

```
Private Sub ButtonFont_Click(ByVal sender As System.Object, _
                             ByVal e As System.EventArgs) _
              Handles ButtonFont.Click
  FontDlg.Font = CharDisplay.Font
  If System.Windows.Forms.DialogResult.OK = FontDlg.ShowDialog() Then
    CharDisplay.Font = FontDlg.Font
  End If
End Sub
```

There is nothing complicated in the above class. It just pops up the font dialog and changes the Font property of the CharDisplay item (the box that displays the character) to the selected font. The interesting code is contained in the Display() method below:

```
Private Sub Display(ByVal codepoint As Integer)
  If codepoint < &H10000 Then
    CharDisplay.Text = "" & Convert.ToChar(codepoint)
  Else
    CharDisplay.Text = "" & _
      Convert.ToChar(GetHighSurrogate(codepoint)) & _
      Convert.ToChar(GetLowSurrogate(codepoint))
  End If
End Sub
```

Here you pass the full code point of the character and if it is not a surrogate pair (code value less than H10000) then it just displays it, after converting it to a System.Char and appending it to the end of an empty string to perform implicit conversion to a string. If it is a surrogate, then it calls two methods, GetHighSurrogate() and GetLowSurrogate() and returns the Char of each, appending them to the textbox, where the Windows OS and the supplied font converts them into the required character. The two methods are shown below:

```
Private Function GetHighSurrogate(ByVal codepoint As Integer) _
                  As Integer
  Return (codepoint - &H10000) / &H400 + &HD800
End Function

Private Function GetLowSurrogate(ByVal codepoint As Integer) _
                  As Integer
  Return (codepoint - &H10000) Mod &H400 + &HDC00
End Function
```

As you can see, these just implement the equations shown previously and return the requested high and low surrogates. The reverse of these methods is:

```
Private Function MakeCodePoint(ByVal high As Integer, _
                              ByVal low As Integer) As Integer
  Return (high - &HD800) * &H400 + (low - &HDC00) + &H10000
End Function
```

The code above just uses the same equations shown previously to retrieve the code value
for the high and low surrogates. The event code for the two Show buttons is shown below:

```
Private Sub ButtonCV_Click(ByVal sender As System.Object, _
                           ByVal e As System.EventArgs) _
            Handles ButtonCV.Click
  ' Retrieve information from the code value text box
  Dim str As String = ValueInput.Text
  Dim ncp As Integer = Convert.ToInt32(str, 16)
  If ncp < &H10000 Then
    HighInput.Text = "n/a"
    LowInput.Text = "n/a"
  Else
    HighInput.Text = Convert.ToString(GetHighSurrogate(ncp), 16)
    LowInput.Text = Convert.ToString(GetLowSurrogate(ncp), 16)
  End If
  Display(ncp)
End Sub

Private Sub ButtonSP_Click(ByVal sender As System.Object, _
                           ByVal e As System.EventArgs) _
            Handles ButtonSP.Click
  Dim high As Integer = Convert.ToInt32(HighInput.Text, 16)
  Dim low As Integer = Convert.ToInt32(LowInput.Text, 16)

  ' Check that both high and low surrogates are in correct ranges
  If ((high < &HD800) Or (high > &HDBFF) Or (low < &HDC00) _
                      Or (low > &HDFFF)) Then
    ValueInput.Text = "n/a"
  Else
    Dim ncp As Integer = MakeCodePoint(high, low)
    ValueInput.Text = Convert.ToString(ncp, 16)
    Display(ncp)
  End If
End Sub
```

The first method handles the clicking of the first Show button, and the second handles
the second. ButtonCV_Click() first checks to see if the value entered in the textbox
is outside the surrogate pair range. If so, then it enters "n/a" into the relevant textboxes.
If not, then it uses the GetHighSurrogate() and GetLowSurrogate() methods
shown earlier to input the correct values into the textboxes. It then shows this
character in CharDisplay using the Display() method.

The second method is simpler and combines the two values in the textboxes together
using MakeCodePoint() and passes this value to Display() before entering it into
the previous textbox.

As mentioned earlier, the full code can be found in the code download.

Surrogates Input

Now that we have seen what surrogate pairs are and how to display them, let's see how they can be entered.

Programmatic Input

Programmatically, surrogates are very simple to input as they are defined just like any other Unicode characters and can be input using the same syntax. For instance, the following lines of VB code create a string that contains a character that is represented by a pair of surrogates:

```
Dim mySurrogatePairString As String
mySurrogatePairString = ChrW(&HD840) & ChrW(&HDC0B)
```

The ChrW() function used here is a very useful function that lets you specify a character by its associated numeric value and converts this value to a character, and it can be found in the Microsoft.VisualBasic namespace. In this case, as we are adding a surrogate pair to the string, we need to first specify the high surrogate value and then the low surrogate value.

User Input

User input depends on an Input Method Editor (**IME**) that allows a user to input characters directly. An IME is a mechanism provided by Windows for East Asian languages that allows you to enter characters by typing a phonetic value, by drawing the character, or by direct keyboard input. There are different IMEs for Chinese, Japanese, and Korean. If users have installed an appropriate IME, then the surrogate character will be input correctly.

Sorting

No special provision needs to be made for surrogates while sorting, as no linguistically significant sort order is defined for these characters. So, basically, the sort order for surrogate characters is defined as ordinal order, and surrogate pairs will just sort according to the value of the character that they represent.

Combining Characters

Many languages that use either Latin script or other scripts have characters that present diacritic marks. For instance "é" is an "e" with an acute accent. There are two ways to think about such a character. The first one is to consider that this is a character that is always pre-composed (the "é" is a character by itself, with its own code point). The other way to think about it is to consider "é" to be an "e" (which we will call a base letter) followed by a non-spacing acute accent. In this case, the, "é" is a **composite character** created by rendering "e" and "´" together. A composed character sequence is typically made up of a base letter, which occupies a single space, and one or more non-spacing marks, which are rendered in the same space as the base letter. In this case, we can have letters that are actually represented as a series of several characters, which provides yet another added complexity when dealing with strings.

The Unicode Standard provides both combining characters and pre-composed characters to retain compatibility with established standards such as Latin 1, which includes many pre-composed characters such as "ü" and "ñ". In the case where such a character is a composite character, the base character comes first, followed by one or more non-spacing marks. If a text element is encoded with more than one non-spacing mark, the order in which the non-spacing marks are stored isn't important if the marks don't interact typographically. If they do, order is important. The Unicode Standard specifies how successive non-spacing characters are applied to a base character.

Dealing with Surrogate Pairs and Combining Characters

While there is no special requirement for handling surrogates and combining characters as far as displaying and sorting is concerned, approaching a string in a naive way by considering that each element represents a character will lead to problems when inserting or deleting characters, or even just traversing the string in order to count the number of actual displayable items.

In well-formed text, a low surrogate can only be preceded by a high surrogate and a high surrogate can only be followed by a low surrogate. The case with combining characters is a little different as it is easy to err by deleting the base character and getting the non-spacing marks applied wrongly to the preceding character.

If we are dealing with surrogate pairs, the following string, for instance:

"AB∂C"

is represented in the following manner internally:

0041	0042	D801	DC00	0043
A	B		∂	C

If we are using the following code to retrieve the first three text elements from the string described above, we will not get the appropriate result as we will retrieve the first two characters (AB) and the high surrogate (but not the low surrogate that needs to be associated to the high surrogate to have meaning).

```
Dim str As String
str = "AB" & ChrW(&HD801) & ChrW(&HDC00) & "C"
Dim strFirstThree = str.Substring(0, 3)
```

In order to perform the operation correctly, we need to retrieve additional information on the characters (whether they are surrogates or not). Thus, if we are writing a program that needs to deal with individual characters within a string, we need to make sure that when we delete a character or take a sub-string, we are not breaking a surrogate pair by separating a high surrogate from a low surrogate. The good news is that it is not hard to detect surrogates, as performing range checking will indicate if a character is a surrogate or not. We could definitely do this manually by walking the string directly and performing tests along the way, but the .NET Framework provides two methods that do all the tedious work.

More importantly, these methods also do the work for combining characters that would need to be taken care of as well if we were to implement code to handle strings manually.

StringInfo.ParseCombiningCharacters()

The `StringInfo` class provides a method named `ParseCombiningCharacters()` that can parse a string into text elements. The .NET Framework defines a text element as a unit of text that is displayed as a single character; a **grapheme**. A text element can be a base character, a surrogate pair, or a combining character sequence.

StringInfo.GetTextEnumerator()

The `StringInfo` class provides another method, `GetTextEnumerator()`, which enables you to achieve the same results as are obtained by using the `ParseCombiningCharacters()` method: parsing the text into text elements. The `StringInfo` class provides access to the `TextEnumerator` class via the `StringInfo.GetTextEnumerator()` method.

The `StringWalk` code example in the code download shows how to use either the `ParseCombiningCharacters()` method or the `GetTextElementEnumerator()` method to "walk" a string and retrieve all the text elements contained in the string, including surrogate pairs and combining characters.

Formatting Unicode Strings

The `String.Format()` method lets you format a string by providing format specification in a format string and additional objects. These will be formatted according to the format specifiers. This is often essential for correct formatting of a string with international characters. For instance, we can rewrite:

```
message = "This is my new" + item
```

as:

```
message = String.Format("this is my new {0}", item)
```

While this has an impact in terms of performance, as the `String.Format()` method is more costly than the string concatenation that we used previously, it is good practice as it makes the code much easier to localize into another language. For instance, if we were to port the modified code to Japanese, the only thing we would have to do would be to change the formatting string to: "これは私の新しい {0} です" and the code would handle Japanese correctly.

Another interesting aspect of the `String.Format()` method is that it can also be used to format numeric values, dates, and times as well as strings. For instance, the following code:

```
Module FormatDate
  Sub Main()
    Dim message As String
    message = String.Format("Date is {0}, value is {1}, " & _
                            "word is {2}", DateTime.Now, 1234, "car")
    Console.WriteLine(message)
  End Sub
End Module
```

Produces this output:

```
Date is 18/05/2002 14:24:05, value is 1234, word is car
```

Of course, the format specifiers that we have seen earlier for the numeric and the date and time values can be used as well, so if we replace the line:

```
message = String.Format("Date is {0}, value is {1}, " & _
                        "word is {2}", DateTime.Now, 1234, "car")
```

by:

```
message = String.Format("Date is {0:d}, value is {1:C}, " & _
                        "word is {2}", DateTime.Now, 1234, "car")
```

the output is now (if the current culture is set to English (United States)):

```
Date is 5/18/2002, value is $1,234.00, word is car
```

Additionally, a `CultureInfo` (or any other class that implements the `IFormatProvider` interface) can be passed as a parameter for one of the overrides of the `String.Format()` method.

If we modified the code to pass the Swedish (Sweden) culture as below:

```
message = String.Format(New CultureInfo("sv-SE"), _
                        "Date is {0:d}, value is {1:C}, " & _
                        "word is {2}", DateTime.Now, 1234, "car")
```

We would get the following results:

```
Date is 2002-05-18, value is 1.234,00 kr, word is car
```

Finally, if you are building Console applications, the sequence:

```
message = String.Format("This is a {0}", "car")
Console.WriteLine(message)
```

can be replaced by the following code, which uses the `String.Format()` method internally:

```
Console.WriteLine("This is a {0}", "car")
```

Summary

We've seen in this chapter that dealing with international strings and characters is not always easy. The .NET Framework does a great job of providing a lot of support for dealing with this complexity but some caution still needs to be applied.

If you only need a couple of points to take away, know when you need to deal with cultures and culture-sensitive information – essentially when performing user-interface related operations, such as sorting strings that are to be displayed in a listbox – and avoid dealing with individual characters as much as possible as this introduces a much higher level of complexity.

VB.NET

Text Manipulation

Handbook

5

5

Introducing Regular Expressions

Regular expressions, often referred to by their shorthand of **regexes**, are a very powerful way of manipulating and examining string data. A regular expression is a series of characters, special and otherwise, that are transformed into an algorithm against which to match text. Although new to Visual Basic, they have been used extensively in Unix systems and even web scripting languages like JavaScript. You may be familiar with wildcard characters such as "%" and "?" in SQL expressions, or "*" in MS DOS. These allow us to do searches without specifying all the possible characters, for example "del *.txt" would delete all files with the .txt extension. Regular expressions allow for similar expressions but are much more powerful. In fact, regular expressions have a simple language of their own that allows us to specify precisely what we are looking to match. In one line we can match patterns of text that would take many lines without regular expressions. However, the downside is that regular expressions can be tricky to create, and are quite cryptic. In this, though, they are not unlike many successful programming languages, such as Perl. Once you get used to them regular expressions are certainly easy enough to use.

The most common sort of problem we can use regular expressions for is data validation. Web Form controls that come with Visual Studio .NET, such as the Regular Expression Validator control, use regular expressions to validate data entered by the user. The control comes with a small number of standard regular expressions to check items such as zip codes, e-mail addresses, and Internet URLs. We'll be seeing in the following chapters how we can validate our own data using our own customized regular expressions, especially since the stock regular expressions provided with the Validator don't quite cover every possible eventuality. Regexes allows us to match against patterns of characters, such as three letters, followed by two numbers, followed by either a letter, or another two numbers. This would take a lot of code without regexes, but is very straightforward to implement with them.

However, it's not just validating data that regular expressions are useful for; we can use them for any situation where we have text-based data we need to manipulate. Let's say we have a string containing HTML tags and we want to extract each tag, then extract the value of attributes for each tag. Regular expressions make this task easier and take only a few lines of code.

This chapter will gently introduce the .NET aspects of regular expressions, and the regular expression syntax supported. We'll be leaving most of the more advanced features until the next chapter.

System.Text.RegularExpressions

That's enough of theory, we'll now move on to practice. The key to regular expression implementation in .NET is the System.Text.RegularExpressions namespace, which contains the eight classes listed below:

❑ Regex – contains the regular expression and has various methods to make use of that regular expression

❑ MatchCollection – contains all the matches found by a regular expression

❑ Match – contains all the text matched by a single match

❑ GroupCollection – contains all the groups in a single match

❑ Group – contains the details of a single group in a group collection

❑ CaptureCollection – contains all the Capture objects for a single group

❑ Capture – returns the string matched by a single capture within a group

❑ RegexCompilationInfo – provides details needed to compile Regex into a standalone assembly

Of these, the most important one is the Regex class; the other classes provide useful specialized functions, but they are not as commonly used. We'll be looking at the Regex, Match, and MatchCollection classes in this chapter. All this functionality is provided within the System.dll assembly.

The Regex Class

The Regex class not only allows us to create regular expressions, but it also provides a number of useful methods for manipulating string data using regular expressions. We would create a Regex object if we had a regular expression that we wanted to use repeatedly on different strings. However, many of the class's methods are shared methods; this means that if we are just using the regular expression once, then it's more efficient not to create a Regex object, but to simply use the methods required. So if we want to use the shared Replace() method, we can just write:

```
Regex.Replace(inputstring, regularexpression, replacementString)
```

We'll see that a number of options are supported by the Regex class, and these alter the way the regular expression syntax works. The more commonly used ones are shown below; we'll be discussing the rest throughout the next two chapters:

RegexOptions

Flag	Description
IgnoreCase	Makes the pattern matching case insensitive. The default is that matches are case sensitive.
RightToLeft	Searches input string from right to left. The default is from left to right which suits languages like English that read from left to right but not languages like Arabic or Hebrew where its from right to left.
None	Sets no flags. This is the default.
MultiLine	Specifies that ^ and $ can match the beginning and the end of lines as well as the beginning and end of the string. This means that you can get different matches for each line, separated with a newline character. However, the "." character, which you will read about later in *Matching Different Classes of Characters*, will still not match newline characters.
SingleLine	Specifies that the "." special character matches any character, not any character except a newline. Default is that the "." special character does not match a newline. This is often used with the MultiLine option.

Some of the above only make sense when we have looked at the appropriate regular expression syntax. The default is that none of the flags are set. This means searches are, by default, case sensitive and inspected from left to right.

We can use the RegexOptions enumeration to set the flags, for example:

```
RegexOptions.IgnoreCase
```

We either pass this to the regular expression constructor, or as in the case of the shared methods, pass it to the method as a parameter:

```
Regex.IsMatch(MyString, "ABC", RegexOptions.IgnoreCase Or
    RegexOptions.RightToLeft)
```

To set more than one flag we just OR each flag together, so in the above example the flag options set are IgnoreCase and RightToLeft. Note it's a logical Or not a Boolean Or. It is performing a bit-wise operation to return a different value that the method can interpret correctly. To remove all the flags in code, we can use None.

Class Constructor

Here we show various ways of creating a `Regex` object and the parameters it takes, especially the `RegexOptions` parameter and how that allows us to specify things like whether the search should be left to right, if it should be case sensitive, and more.

The two main constructors are:

```
Regex(regular_expression_pattern_string)
Regex(regular_expression_pattern_string, options_enumeration)
```

The first parameter is the regular expression for the match. Taking a very simple example, let's consider matching `ABC`:

```
Dim myRegEx As New Regex("ABC")
MessageBox.Show(myRegEx.IsMatch("The first three letters of " _
    & "the alphabet are ABC"))
```

If you wanted to match `ABC` or `abc` or any combination of upper or lower case, you could do this by setting the case-insensitive option flag and passing this to the constructor:

```
Dim myRegEx As New Regex("ABC", RegexOptions.IgnoreCase)
MessageBox.Show(myRegEx.IsMatch("Hello abc there"))
```

A further point to note is that by default, the `Regex` object matches against ASCII text. You can specify Unicode characters using a format described later, but the engine will turn a Unicode string into ASCII whenever it can. There is an option to change this, shown in the next chapter, but this halves the performance so, against the advice provided so far, treat a string as ASCII, unless you have a good reason not to. As regexes match against specific patterns, this is less of an issue, as a string in a different language/character set would not match anyway.

IsMatch() Method

The `IsMatch()` method tests a string to see if there is a match on the regular expression pattern. If a match is found, then the method returns `True`, otherwise, `False` is returned. The `IsMatch()` method has a shared overload, so we can use it without explicitly creating a `Regex` object.

The method takes three parameters:

```
Public Shared Regex.IsMatch(input_string, regular_expression_string, _
                            regex_options_enumeration) As Boolean
Public Shared Regex.IsMatch(input_string, regular_expression_string) _
                    As Boolean
Public Regex.IsMatch(input_string) As Boolean
Public Regex.IsMatch(input_string, start_position_int32) As Boolean
```

The first two overloads, as you can see, are the shared methods, whereas the latter two operate on a Regex object. The parameters for the first two overloads are all strings, except for the regex_options_enumeration, which we saw earlier in the *Class Constructor* section. The start_position_int32 parameter allows you to specify what position in the string to begin matching. Therefore, to test if a string contains the words "Wrox Press" we could use IsMatch() like this:

```
Dim inputString As String = "Welcome to the publishers, " _
    & "Wrox Press Ltd"
If Regex.IsMatch(inputString, "wrox press", RegexOptions.IgnoreCase) _
    Then
    MessageBox.Show("Match Found")
Else
    MessageBox.Show("No Match Found")
End If
```

The above will show a match found if the input string contains "wrox press". As we have set the IgnoreCase option, it'll be case insensitive so "Wrox press" will also be matched. We've used the shared method because we are only using the regular expression once, and so there is no need to instantiate a new Regex object. Creating a Regex object is useful where we want to save state: the details of the regular expression, its options, and details of its matches.

Replace() Method

This method, again with a shared overload, replaces a matched pattern with the string specified. This method has many variations; we'll just look at the basic ones here, and investigate the more advanced options in the next chapter.

As a shared method, we have the following overloaded methods:

```
Shared Regex.Replace(input_string, _
                     regular_expression_string, _
                     replacement_string)

Shared Regex.Replace(input_string, _
                     regular_expression_string, _
                     replacement_string, _
                     Regex_options_enumeration)
```

So, using the shared method, if we wanted to replace all instances of "Wrox press" with "Wrox Press" we'd write:

```
Dim inputString As String = "Welcome to the publishers Wrox press ltd"
inputString = Regex.Replace(inputString, "wrox press", "Wrox Press")
```

Without using the shared method, we have the choice of specifying a maximum number or replacements, and a start index.

```
RegexObject.Replace(input_string, _
                    replacement_string, _)

RegexObject.Replace(input_string, _
                    replacement_string, _
                    max_number_of_replacements)

RegexObject.Replace(input_string, _
                    replacement_string, _
                    max_number_of_replacements,_
                    start_at_character_index)
```

If we want to replace all the matches made while using one of these overloads, then we can pass -1 as the max_number_of_replacements argument.

So let's say we have the string "123,456,123, 123,789,123,888" and we want to replace the 123s from 456 onwards with xxx but only want to replace a maximum of two of them, the code would look like this:

```
Dim inputString As String = "123,456,123, 123,789,123,888"
Dim regExp = New Regex("123")
inputString = regExp.Replace(inputString, "xxx", 2, 4)

MessageBox.Show(inputString)
```

The first 123 won't be replaced because we passed 4 as the final argument, which means the search for patterns only starts at character index 4; the fifth character, which in this case is the 4 of the 456. The two 123s between the 456 and the 789 will be replaced with xxx. However, the final 123 won't be replaced because we specified in the third argument that only a maximum of two replacements should be made.

Split()

This splits a string at each point where the matching pattern is found. It returns the results as an array of strings. Again, there are shared overloads, as well as ones for Regex instances. The two shared methods are:

```
Regex.Split(input_string, regular_expression_pattern)

Regex.Split(input_string, _
            regular_expression_pattern, _
            Regex_options_enumeration)
```

Let's say we have a comma-delimited string; to split it we could write:

```
Dim inputString As String = "123,ABC,456,DEF,789"
Dim splitResults() As String
Dim stringElement As String
Dim resultsString As String
splitResults = Regex.Split(inputString, ",")
```

```
For Each stringElement In splitResults
    resultsString += stringElement & ControlChars.CrLf
Next
MessageBox.Show(resultsString)
```

This code will result in the message box shown below:

The string was split where each comma was found, the comma is not included, and each split string is placed in an array element.

The public non-shared methods are similar to those we saw for the Replace() method in that they allow us to specify a maximum number of splits, and where the pattern matching should start from:

```
RegexObject.Split(input_string, _
                  separator_string)

RegexObject.Split(input_string, _
                  separator_string, _
                  max_number_of_splits)

RegexObject.Split(input_string, _
                  separator_string, _
                  max_number_of_splits, _
                  start_at_character_index)
```

If we pass "0" as the argument for the maximum number of splits, then all the matching splits will be made; the same as for the normal default behavior.

The Match and MatchCollection Classes

The Match and MatchCollection classes allow us to obtain the details of each match made via a regular expression. The Match class represents a single match made, whereas the MatchCollection class is a collection of Match objects, one for each successful match made. We need to use the Regex object's Match() or Matches() methods to retrieve the matches.

135

Let's look first at the `Regex.Match()` method, which has the following overloaded methods:

```
Match(inputString)
Match(inputString, startAt)
Match(inputString, startAt, number_of_characters_to_search)
Shared Match(inputString, regular_expression_pattern, RegexOptions)
Shared Match(inputString, regular_expression_pattern)
```

The first three are instance methods; the last two are shared. All of them return a `Match` object as their result, which will contain details of the match made. Note that it's just the first match made, not all matches.

Let's look at a simple example of the second overload listed above:

```
Dim userInputString As String = "A sailor went to sea to sea"
userInputString += ", to see what he could see could see."
Dim matchMade As Match
Dim myRegex As New Regex("se.")
matchMade = myRegex.Match(userInputString, 20)
Do While matchMade.Success
  MessageBox.Show(matchMade.Value)
  matchMade = matchMade.NextMatch()
Loop
```

The input string is a line from a folk song but the repetition of words helps to emphasize the point. The regular expression is `"se."` The `"."` character, as you will learn later, matches any character. Normally, this regular expression would match every occurrence of see or sea in this string. However, when we use the `Regex` class's `Match()` method:

```
matchMade = myRegex.Match(userInputString, 20)
```

we specify that the match should start from the twenty-first character (remember that character indices begin at 0). Moreover, it will only find the first match, which in this case is the second "sea". However, although we can see in the example that a match will be successful, we often won't know this in practice, and so this is where the `Success` property of the `Match` class proves useful. We use the `Success` property in a `Do-While` loop, so that while a match success is true, then we keep looping:

```
Do While matchMade.Success
  MessageBox.Show(matchMade.Value)
  matchMade = matchMade.NextMatch()
Loop
```

To get the next match, we use the `Match.NextMatch()` method. This will search from the point immediately after the last successful match of the `Match` object. Some of the more useful methods and properties of the `Match` class are detailed in the following tables:

Method	Description
NextMatch()	Returns a new `Match` with the results for the next match, starting at the position at which the last match ended (at the character beyond the last matched character).
Result()	Returns the expansion of the passed replacement pattern. This is used with groups as shown in the next chapter. It will group the results of all the different regular expression replacement patterns together and return them as a whole.
Synchronized()	Returns a `Match` instance equivalent to the one supplied that is safe to share between multiple threads in a multithreaded application.

Property	Description
Captures	Returns a collection of capture objects, one for each capture matched by the capturing group. Groups and captures are covered in the next chapter.
Groups	Returns a collection of group objects, one for each `Regex` group matched by the regular expression.
Index	The position in the input string where the first character of the match was found.
Length	The length of the match
Success	Returns `True` or `False` depending on whether the match was successful or not.
Value	Gets the matched substring from the input string.

Finally, let's look at the `MatchCollection` class. Using the `Regex.Matches()` method, we can obtain a reference to a `MatchCollection` object; this collection class will contain a `Match` object for each match made by the regular expression. It's especially useful where we are dealing with multiple matches and is a useful alternative to using the `Match.NextMatch()` method. The `MatchCollection` class has two main properties that we will find useful, `Count` and `Item`. `Count` returns the number of items matched, and `Item` allows us to access each particular `Match` object in the collection by its index, or we can use the `For Each` loop.

To obtain a `MatchCollection` we need to use the `Regex.Matches()` method, which has the following overloads, which all return a `MatchCollection` object:

```
Matches(inputString As String)
Matches(inputString As String, startAt As Integer)
Shared Matches(inputString As String, _
               regular_expression_pattern As String)
```

```
Shared Matches(inputString As String, _
               regular_expression_pattern As String, _
               regexOptions As RegexOptions)
```

In the example below we use the Shared `Matches()` method to access the third match made, 3C:

```
Dim userInputString As String = "A sailor went to sea to sea"
userInputString += ", to see what he could sea could sea"
Dim matchesMade As MatchCollection
matchesMade = Regex.Matches(userInputString, "se.")
If matchesMade.Count >= 3 Then
  MessageBox.Show(matchesMade(2).Value)
End If
```

We define `matchesMade` as a `MatchCollection` object, then set it to the `MatchCollection` object returned by the `Regex` method `Matches()`. Here we have used the shared `Matches()` method, rather than explicitly create a `Regex` object.

We then check that there are three or more matches made by using the `Count` property, then display the details of the third match, which is item index 2 in the collection.

Regex Tester Example

In the previous section, we have touched on what some of the methods of the `Regex` object do. In this section, we'll be creating an application that will make the creation and testing of regular expressions very easy. Even though it's a simple example, you should find it very useful, and it can be used to test the regular expressions in the later chapters as well. The appearance of the application is shown opposite:

It allows you to enter regular expressions, set all the options, and then test using the IsMatch(), Replace(), Split(), and Matches() methods described above.

For example if you enter "\d\d\d[a-z]" into the regular expression textbox, select the IgnoreCase option, and enter the text "456A 321B 789 78AA 444E" into the Text to Match On box and click the Matches() button, you'll see the following:

We'll learn about the \d and [a-z] regular expression syntax shortly but you can deduce from the Regular Expression Tester that \d matches a single number character and [a-z] matches any single letter that is in the range a to z. Setting the IgnoreCase flag means lower and upper case characters are matched. We have only covered and will only be covering the MultiLine, IgnoreCase, and SingleLine options. We'll cover the options in the next chapter.

We need to create a new Windows Application (call it RegexTester) and change the initial class definition to the following:

```
Imports System.IO
Imports System.Text
Imports System.Text.RegularExpressions

Public Class frmRegexTester
```

Here are the controls that need to be added to the form:

Name	Control Type	Text
cmdTestRegex	Button	IsMatch()
cmdReplace	Button	Replace()
cmdSplit	Button	Split()
cmdMatches	Button	Matches()
cmdOpenRegex	Button	Open Regex
cmdSaveRegex	Button	Save Regex
grpOptions	GroupBox	Regex Options
chkSingleLine	CheckBox	SingleLine
chkRightToLeft	CheckBox	RightToLeft
chkMultiLine	CheckBox	MultiLine
chkIgnorePatternWhiteSpace	CheckBox	IgnorePatternWhiteSpace
chkIgnoreCase	CheckBox	IgnoreCase
chkExplicitCapture	CheckBox	ExplicitCapture
chkECMAScript	CheckBox	ECMAScript
OpenFileDialog1	OpenFileDialog	
SaveFileDialog1	SaveFileDialog	

For the following controls, additionally set the MultiLine property to True, and the Scrollbars property to Vertical:

Name	Control Type
txtRegex	TextBox
txtInputText	TextBox
txtResults	TextBox
txtReplacementText	TextBox

You can see in the previous screenshot where to add these and the label controls, and what text should be bold. The Open and Save buttons are there for convenience; it's useful to be able to save the more complex regular expressions. We'll start by adding the code to save the regular expression. Double-click on the Save Regex button and change its Click event:

```
  Private Sub cmdSaveRegex_Click(ByVal sender As System.Object, _
                                 ByVal e As System.EventArgs) _
         Handles cmdOpenRegex.Click
    SaveFileDialog1.ShowDialog()
  End Sub
```

This shows the Save File dialog, allowing the user to select the drive, directory, and file name for the text file that will hold the regular expression. If the user then clicks OK to save the file, the FileOk event fires and it's here that we add the code to save the file:

```
  Private Sub SaveFileDialog1_FileOk( _
            ByVal sender As System.Object, _
            ByVal e As System.ComponentModel.CancelEventArgs) _
            Handles SaveFileDialog1.FileOk
    Dim filePath As String = SaveFileDialog1.FileName
    Dim streamWriterRegex As StreamWriter = File.CreateText(filePath)
    streamWriterRegex.Write(Me.txtRegex.Text)
    streamWriterRegex.Close()
  End Sub
```

We obtain the file path from the SaveFileDialog.FileName property just selected by the user, and then use the StreamWriter class to create a new text file. We use its Write() method to save the regular expression to the file.

Opening a regular expression involves a similar method to SaveFileDialog1_FileOK. First, we need to add code to show the open dialog upon pressing the cmdOpenRegex button:

```
  Private Sub cmdOpenRegex_Click(ByVal sender As System.Object, _
                                 ByVal e As System.EventArgs) _
         Handles cmdOpenRegex.Click
    OpenFileDialog1.ShowDialog()
  End Sub
```

If the user then clicks the OK button, then the FileOk event of OpenFileDialog1 will fire. We now insert the code to read in the regular expression from the file:

```
  Private Sub OpenFileDialog1_FileOk( _
            ByVal sender As System.Object, _
            ByVal e As System.ComponentModel.CancelEventArgs) _
            Handles OpenFileDialog1.FileOk
    Dim filePath As String = OpenFileDialog1.FileName
    Dim streamReaderRegex As StreamReader = File.OpenText(filePath)
    Me.txtRegex.Text = streamReaderRegex.ReadToEnd()
    streamReaderRegex.Close()
  End Sub
```

This is similar to the method that saves the regular expression, except this time we use the `StreamReader` object to read in the text, and set the `txtRegex.Text` property to its value.

That's the opening and saving of the regular expression dealt with, so now let's see how we can determine which `Regex` options need to be set, based on which checkboxes have been checked by the user. As this is something all of our `Regex` testing buttons will need to do, we create a `Private` function called `GetSelectedRegexOptions()` that will be called by each of the other buttons' `Click` events:

```
Private Function GetSelectedRegexOptions() As RegexOptions
    Dim selectedRegexOptions As RegexOptions
    If Me.chkIgnoreCase.CheckState Then
        selectedRegexOptions = RegexOptions.IgnoreCase _
                        Or selectedRegexOptions
    End If

    If Me.chkECMAScript.CheckState Then
        selectedRegexOptions = RegexOptions.ECMAScript _
                        Or selectedRegexOptions
    End If

    If Me.chkExplicitCapture.CheckState Then
        selectedRegexOptions = RegexOptions.ExplicitCapture _
                        Or selectedRegexOptions
    End If

    If Me.chkIgnorePatternWhiteSpace.CheckState Then
        selectedRegexOptions = RegexOptions.IgnorePatternWhitespace _
                        Or selectedRegexOptions
    End If

    If Me.chkMultiLine.CheckState Then
        selectedRegexOptions = RegexOptions.Multiline _
                        Or selectedRegexOptions
    End If

    If Me.chkRightToLeft.CheckState Then
        selectedRegexOptions = RegexOptions.RightToLeft _
                        Or selectedRegexOptions
    End If

    If Me.chkSingleLine.CheckState Then
        selectedRegexOptions = RegexOptions.Singleline _
                        Or selectedRegexOptions
    End If

    Return selectedRegexOptions
End Function
```

Although containing a lot of code, this function is just a long list of if statements that check each checkbox. If one is checked then it Ors the RegexOption together.

Taking the top of the code:

```
Dim selectedRegexOptions As RegexOptions
If Me.chkIgnoreCase.CheckState Then
    selectedRegexOptions = RegexOptions.IgnoreCase _
                            Or selectedRegexOptions
End If
```

We define the selectedRegexOptions variable as type RegexOptions, and this will hold the final tally of options set.

In the If statement, we check to see if the checkbox chkIgnoreCase has been checked by the user; if it has we then set to IgnoreCase by using a logical Or statement to set RegexOptions to include that option. Note that it's a logical Or, not a Boolean Or – it adds to whatever existing options are set – it does not remove them.

The remainder of the function continues in the same manner until all the checkboxes and Regex options have been set as requested by the user. We then return the results held in selectedRegexOptions.

Each of the buttons has the name of the method used with the regular expression entered in the top box. Let's start with the easiest one, the IsMatch() button. The following code needs to be added to its Click event:

```
Private Sub cmdTestRegex_Click(ByVal sender As System.Object, _
                                ByVal e As System.EventArgs) _
                Handles cmdTestRegex.Click
    Try
        Dim selectedRegexOptions As RegexOptions = _
            GetSelectedRegexOptions()
        Dim testRegex As New Regex(Me.txtRegex.Text, selectedRegexOptions)
        If testRegex.IsMatch(Me.txtInputText.Text) Then
            Me.txtResults.Text = "MATCH FOUND"
            Me.txtResults.ForeColor = Drawing.Color.Red
        Else
            Me.txtResults.Text = "NO MATCH FOUND"
            Me.txtResults.ForeColor = Drawing.Color.Black
        End If
    Catch ex As ArgumentException
        Me.txtResults.ForeColor = Drawing.Color.Red
        Me.txtResults.Text = _
            "There was an error in your regular expression when " _
            & ControlChars.CrLf & ex.Message
    End Try
End Sub
```

The code is placed inside a `Try...Catch` statement; this is particularly useful in this case because if we make a mistake in our regular expression syntax, the `Catch` clause will grab the exception, and will then write it out to `txtResults`. The error message usually gives enough detail to hint at where the regular expression syntax is wrong.

At the start of the `Try` clause, we create a new variable to hold the `RegexOptions` enumeration and initialize it to the user-selected options with our `GetSelectedRegexOptions()` method created above.

Then we use the `IsMatch()` method to check to see if any match is made using the regular expression on the text in the `txtInputText` textbox. If a match has been found, then `True` is returned, and we set the `txtResults` textbox to "MATCH FOUND" in red letters. If no match is found, then "NO MATCH FOUND" is output in black letters.

Let's now turn to the **Replace()** button and the code for its `Click` event:

```
Private Sub cmdReplace_Click(ByVal sender As System.Object, _
                             ByVal e As System.EventArgs) _
              Handles cmdReplace.Click
    Try
        Dim selectedRegexOptions As RegexOptions = _
          GetSelectedRegexOptions()
        Dim replaceRexex As New Regex(Me.txtRegex.Text, _
                              selectedRegexOptions)
        Me.txtResults.ForeColor = Drawing.Color.Black
        Me.txtResults.Text = replaceRexex.Replace( _
          Me.txtInputText.Text, Me.txtReplacementText.Text)
    Catch ex As ArgumentException
        Me.txtResults.ForeColor = Drawing.Color.Red
        Me.txtResults.Text = "There was an error in your " _
                      & "regular expression when " _
                      & ControlChars.CrLf & ex.Message
    End Try
End Sub
```

Again, we have a `Try...Catch` clause that will capture any errors in our regular expression syntax and write them to `txtResults`. Inside the `Try` clause, we obtain the `RegexOptions` and then create a new `Regex` object using the regular expression in the `txtRegex` textbox. However, we then use the `Replace()` method, which replaces the matches made by the regular expression on the text in `txtInputText` with text inside the `txtReplacementText` textbox and displays the results in the `txtResults` textbox.

The next button to describe is the **Split()** button, and its `Click` event code is as follows:

```
Private Sub cmdSplit_Click(ByVal sender As System.Object, _
                           ByVal e As System.EventArgs) _
              Handles cmdSplit.Click
    Try
```

```
      Dim selectedRegexOptions As RegexOptions = _
        GetSelectedRegexOptions()
      Dim splitRegex As New Regex(Me.txtRegex.Text, _
                              selectedRegexOptions)
      Dim splitResults() As String
      Me.txtResults.ForeColor = Drawing.Color.Black
      splitResults = splitRegex.Split(Me.txtInputText.Text)
      Dim stringElement As String
      Dim resultsString As New _
        StringBuilder(Me.txtInputText.Text.Length)
      For Each stringElement In splitResults
        resultsString.Append(stringElement & ControlChars.CrLf)
      Next
      Me.txtResults.Text = resultsString.ToString()
    Catch ex As ArgumentException
      Me.txtResults.ForeColor = Drawing.Color.Red
      Me.txtResults.Text = "There was an error in your " _
                      & "regular expression when " _
                      & ControlChars.CrLf & ex.Message
    End Try
  End Sub
```

Our `Try...Catch` clause is as with the previous methods – it captures any errors in the regular expression. We then get the selected `RegexOptions` and use them with the regular expression string to create a new `Regex` object.

We declare an array, `splitResults`, that will hold the results, if any, returned by the `Split()` method; remember it returns each split data item as a string in a string array. We then execute the `Split()` method on the `Regex` object, and store the results in the `splitResults` variable.

Having got the results in the array, we now need to loop through each array element using a `For Each` loop, and append the results to the `resultsString` `StringBuilder` object: This was initialized to the size of the string being split, to increase performance.

```
    For Each stringElement In splitResults
      resultsString.Append(stringElement & ControlChars.CrLf)
    Next
```

Finally, we write out the results to the textbox, `txtResults.Text`:

```
    Me.txtResults.Text = resultsString.ToString()
```

The final button we need to cover here is the Matches() button, and its event code is as follows:

```
Private Sub cmdMatches_Click(ByVal sender As System.Object, _
                        ByVal e As System.EventArgs) _
            Handles cmdMatches.Click
  Try
    Dim selectedRegexOptions As RegexOptions = _
      GetSelectedRegexOptions()
    Dim matchesRegex As New Regex(Me.txtRegex.Text, _
      selectedRegexOptions)
    Dim matchesFound As MatchCollection
    Dim matchMade As Match
    Dim resultsString As New StringBuilder()
    matchesFound = matchesRegex.Matches(Me.txtInputText.Text)

    Dim nextMatch As String = "------- NEXT MATCH -------" & _
      ControlChars.CrLf
    For Each matchMade In matchesFound
      resultsString.Append(matchMade.Value & ControlChars.CrLf)
      resultsString.Append(nextMatch)
    Next
    Me.txtResults.ForeColor = Drawing.Color.Black
    Me.txtResults.Text = resultsString
  Catch ex As ArgumentException
    Me.txtResults.ForeColor = Drawing.Color.Red
    Me.txtResults.Text = "There was an error in your " _
                    & "regular expression when " _
                    & ControlChars.CrLf & ex.Message
  End Try
End Sub
```

We start, as with the previous click events, with a Try...Catch clause to capture any regular expression exceptions while creating a new Regex object. However, we now want to obtain the text of each match made by the regular expression. To do this we need to use the MatchCollection and Match objects, to hold the text of each of these matches. Variable matchesFound is set to the MatchCollection object returned by the Matches() method. This collection object contains Match objects, one for each match made. We loop through this collection using a For Each loop, where each Match.Value property is appended to the resultsString StringBuilder object, along with a string to indicate the match boundaries.

Finally, the code writes the results to the txtResults textbox.

Fundamental Regular Expression Syntax

So far, with only two short exceptions, we have only used the Regex methods with plain character matches for our regular expression, for example matching the actual characters "ABC". However, this is nothing more than we can do with the String class and its similar methods. If we just want to match actual characters then it's much more efficient to use the String class's methods; the Regex methods are more powerful but also consume greater processing power.

However, where regular expressions show their power is when matching not specific characters, but patterns of types of character instead. For example in the next section, we see how to match any character that is a whitespace character (spaces, tabs, and so on).

Matching Different Classes of Characters

Shown below are the special character classes in regular expression syntax. These groups replace one single character. Therefore, a \d will match any digit.

Character Class	Characters it Matches	Example
\d	Any digit from 0 to 9	\d\d matches 72, but not aa or 7a
\D	Any character that is not a numerical digit	\D\D\D matches abc, but not 123
\w	Any word character, as in A-Z, a-z, 0-9, and the underscore character _	\w\w\w\w matches Ab_2, but not £$%* or Ab_@
\W	Any non-word character	\W matches @, but not the letter a
\s	Any whitespace character; includes tab, newline, carriage return, form feed, and vertical tab	Matches all traditional whitespace characters, as defined in HTML, XML, and other standards
\S	Any non-whitespace character	Every character bar whitespace: A%&g3:, etc.
.	Any character	"." matches any single character, except a newline character
[...]	Any one of the characters between the brackets	[abc] will match a single character a, or b, or c, but nothing else. [a-z] will match any character in the range a to z.
[^...]	Any character, but not one of those inside the brackets	[^abc] will match any character except a or b or c, but A or B or C could be matched by this pattern [^a-z] will match any character which is not in the range a to z, but all uppercase letters could be matched by this pattern

So to match a telephone number in the format 1-800-888-5474, the regular expression could be:

```
\d-\d\d\d-\d\d\d-\d\d\d\d
```

Any \d will match any character in the digit class and the "-" matches a dash. To test it works in code:

```
MessageBox.Show(Regex.IsMatch("1-800-888-5474", _
    "\d-\d\d\d-\d\d\d-\d\d\d\d"))
```

Try this and you'll see a message box with True displayed to show that it's valid. If you change the string to be tested:

```
MessageBox.Show(Regex.IsMatch("X-800-888-5474", _
    "\d-\d\d\d-\d\d\d-\d\d\d\d"))
```

False will be displayed. To match a date, presented as "Jul 31 2001", our regular expression would be:

```
[a-zA-Z][a-zA-Z][a-zA-Z] \d\d \d\d\d\d
```

[a-zA-Z] will match any character from lowercase a to lowercase z, and uppercase A to uppercase Z. Therefore, what we are saying is match any pattern consisting of exactly three letters which are in the range a-z or A-Z, followed one space, followed by exactly two digits, followed by another space, and finally with exactly four digits.

A good idea in this situation is to use the IgnoreCase option to say the match is case insensitive and just have [a-z] or [A-Z].

If we wanted to allow dashes between date digits as well as spaces, such as "Jul 31 2001", we'd change our regular expression to:

```
[a-z][a-z][a-z][ -]\d\d[ -]\d\d\d\d
```

Something you're probably starting to notice is there is a lot of repetition of characters. In the regular expression above, we have three instances of [a-z], two of \d in the middle, and at the end, four \d special characters. To help us in this situation, regular expression syntax has special repetition characters and these are the topic of a later section, *Specifying Repetition*.

Specifying Match Position

Now we will look at the regular expression language aspects that allow us to specify where the match should start, end, or occur between. For example using ^ to specify the match must start at the beginning of the string or if it should be between words. The regular expressions seen so far would allow any characters before and after the matched characters.

149

The position characters allow us to specify where in a string the pattern should be found. This is called "anchoring" the pattern. By anchor, we mean that (at least) one end of the regex is fixed to a point in the string to be matched. Therefore, anchors stop the normal behavior of searching all the string for any match.

There are eight special position characters and these are shown in the table below:

Position Character	Description
^	The following pattern must be at the start of the string, or if it's a multi-line string, at the beginning of a line. For multi-line text, (a string that contains carriage returns) we need to set the multi-line flag.
$	The preceding pattern must be at the end of the string, or if it's a multi-line string then at the end of a line.
\A	The proceeding pattern must be at the start of the string; the multi-line flag is ignored.
\z	The preceding pattern must be at the end of the string; the multi-line flag is ignored.
\Z	The proceeding pattern must be at the end of the string or before a new line at the end of the string.
\b	This matches a word boundary, essentially the point between a word character and a non-word character. Remember a word character is any of [a-zA-Z0-9_]. The start of a word.
\B	Match a position that is not a word boundary; not the start of a word.

If we are using regular expressions to do validation of user input, then we'll often want to make sure that only the data we want is there and there is nothing before or after the data. For example "1234 4567 1234 1232" is a valid credit card number. However, if "XXXX1234 4567 1234 1232" is entered then the input is invalid. To solve the problem we can use a "^" (caret) character at the start of the regular expression to ensure the card number is the first thing in the string and the $ character to ensure that the pattern is also the end of the string. By implementing this method, we ensure sure that the card number pattern is the first, last, and only thing in the string. So, our regular expression for a credit card becomes:

```
^\d\d\d\d \d\d\d\d \d\d\d\d \d\d\d\d$
```

It's with the "^" and "$" special characters that the setting of the MultiLine option becomes important. If the MultiLine option is set, then "^" matches the position following a \n or \r (Cr/Lf) character as well as the position at the very beginning of the string, and "$" matches the position preceding \n or \r, as well as the position at the very end of the string.

150

If the MultiLine option is not set then "^" only matches the position at the beginning of a string, and $ only matches the position at the end of a string, up to the first \n or \r. Repetition characters were mentioned earlier with regards to the telephone matching example in the last section; now we will describe them.

Specifying Repetition

Repetition characters not only make our regular expressions more compact, they also allow us to specify how often a character or, as we'll see shortly, group of characters occur. Let's start by looking at the basic repetition characters available.

Repetition Character	Meaning	Example
{n}	Match n of the previous item	x{2} matches xx, but not x or xxx
{n,}	Match n or more of the previous item	x{2,} matches two or more xs, that is xx, xxx, xxxx, xxxxx, ...
{n,m}	Match at least n and at most m of the preceding item, if n is 0, that makes the character optional	x{2,4} matches xx, xxx, and xxxx, but not x or xxxxx
?	Match the previous item zero or one times, essentially making it optional	x? matches x or nothing.
+	Match the previous item one or more times	x+ matches x, or xx, or any number of x greater than zero
*	Match the previous item zero or more times	x* matches nothing x, x, xx, or any number of xs

After learning from this table, and the earlier section on anchoring regular expressions, let's change the telephone and date regular expressions we saw earlier. First, the telephone regular expression can be changed from:

```
\d-\d\d\d-\d\d\d-\d\d\d\d
```

to:

```
^\d-\d{3}-\d{3}-\d{4}$
```

The updated regular expression will match exactly the same pattern, reading 1 digit, followed by a dash, followed by 3 digits, followed by a dash, followed by 3 digits, followed by a dash, and finally followed by 4 digits. It will also anchor it so that there can be no other characters either side of this pattern.

Let's also update our short date matching expression from:

```
[a-zA-Z][a-zA-Z][a-zA-Z][ -]\d\d[ -]\d\d\d\d
```

to:

```
^[a-zA-Z]{3}[ -]\d\d[ -]\d{4}$
```

We haven't changed the \d\d in the middle to \d{2} as it would add an extra character and so lengthen the expression rather than shortening it, which would be pointless.

Even more useful than the shorthand of {n} are the "?", "+", and "*" special repetition characters. Let's say we wanted to match a 16-digit credit card number. When users enter credit card numbers, they sometimes enter the whole number with no spaces, and sometimes they split it up into groups of four digits with spaces between the groups as it's printed on the card itself. This could present a problem as it would mean either stripping out spaces using a Replace() before performing the regular expression pattern match, or having two regular expressions to match each situation – as follows:

```
\d{16}
```

and

```
\d{4} \d{4} \d{4} \d{4}
```

Using the "?" repetition character, which matches the previous character zero or one times, we can combine the two regular expressions like this:

```
^\d{4} ?\d{4} ?\d{4} ?\d{4}$
```

Now the "?" following the space after the digits means the space must appear zero or one times. Additionally, we only match if the pattern fills the entire string by anchoring at both ends.

Greedy and Lazy Expressions

The quantifiers we have looked at so far have all been what is termed **greedy**; in other words the regular expression engine will do its very best to match as many characters as it can, as long as the rest of the expression is possible. Think of it like this: When the regex engine comes across one of these repetition characters, it will move from the left to the right as far as that particular component of the regular expression will allow it to. \d*3, for instance, would match numbers until there were no more numbers grouped together to match against. Once it has grabbed as much as possible, the engine will attempt to match the 3. If it cannot, and it will not be able to immediately as it has already matched all the numbers, then it will remove one character from the previous match and try again, and it will repeatedly do this until a match can be made, where it will continue. This means that where there is a quantitative decision to be made, the engine will take as much as it can first, and grudgingly release one character at a time if a later character cannot be matched. You can see how this works in Figure 1, below. It uses the \d*3 regex, and attempts to match against the string "123456789fgfd".

Figure 1

Each of the points where a decision can be made is placed on a stack. This means that on failure, the engine returns to the last decision point and makes the next decision available to it. In Figure 1, this was to attempt to match one less digit. If all options have been considered, it is popped off the stack and the previous decision is returned to. If there are no more decisions on the stack, then it knows that there is no match and the IsMatch() method returns False.

The best way to demonstrate this is with an example. Let's use a different example, one to match ISBNs. Different ISBN forms are often used by different publishers and individuals. What is the same is that there are always ten digits and the last digit can be an "X" (the last digit is a check digit, with eleven possibilities). To allow for the different forms, we will permit any number of "-" or whitespace characters to separate the number at any point in the sequence. So for a particular book we could use "1-861007-13-2" or "1-86100-713-2", for instance. One regular expression that could be used is the following:

```
^(\d[- ]*){9}[\dxX]$
```

This is quite straightforward if you break it up. This says that at the start there must be one digit. It then says there can be a hyphen, or zero or more of any whitespace characters. It then repeats this sequence a further eight times (as {9} is a shorthand for repeating the sequence a further eight times), and the brackets represent a group; groups are covered in the next chapter. At the last character, it states there can be one of a digit, an "x", or an "X". We will use the following ISBN to match against:

```
1-861-0007 132
```

If you look closely at the sequence, you can see that there are too many digits there; an extra zero has been added. There is only one greedy quantifier used in this example, but let's look at how the regular expression matches this. This is best illustrated in a bulleted list:

1. 1 is matched.

2. "-" is matched, but there is also another choice of matching whitespace that could have been made here, so this position is placed on the stack.

3. 8 is matched.

4. "-" was not found. The engine moves to the next decision and no whitespace is found, which as the "*" character is used, is deemed valid and so matches. There are no further decisions to be made, and so nothing extra is left on the stack.

5. 6 is matched.

6. "-" was not found. The engine moves to the next decision and no whitespace is found, which as the "*" character is used, is deemed valid and so matches. There are no further decisions to be made, and so nothing extra is left on the stack.

7. 1 is matched.

8. "-" is matched, but there is also another choice of matching the whitespace that could have been made here, so this position is placed on the stack.

9. 0 is matched.

10. "-" was not found. The engine moves to the next decision and no whitespace is found, which as the "*" character is used, is deemed valid and so matches. There are no further decisions to be made, and so nothing extra is left on the stack.

11. 0 is matched.

12. "-" was not found. The engine moves to the next decision and no whitespace is found, which as the "*" character is used, is deemed valid and so matches. There are no further decisions to be made, and so nothing extra is left on the stack.

13. 0 is matched.

14. "-" was not found. The engine moves to the next decision and no whitespace is found, which as the "*" character is used, is deemed valid and so matches. There are no further decisions to be made, and so nothing extra is left on the stack.

15. 7 is matched.

16. This case is different from the previous case. "-" was not found, so it moves on to the next choice, zero or more whitespace characters. It tries to grab as much as possible, which in this case is two space characters. It then passes control to the next instruction and sticks on the stack the decision to match 2 whitespace characters.

17. 1 is matched.

18. "-" was not found. The engine moves to the next decision and no whitespace is found, which as the "*" character is used, is deemed valid and so matches. There are no further decisions to be made, and so nothing extra is left on the stack.

19. 3 is matched, but there was also a choice of x or X, so this decision point is placed on the stack.

Now, it finds that it should be at the end of the string, but there is still another character, so it has to walk back through its decisions, selecting a different one for each to see if it can match. In this case, there are four decision points to return to and try again: those at positions 2, 8, 16, and 19 in the above list. It returns to the last decision point at point 19 and tries to see if either "x", or "X" can be matched instead. As the number is 3, they cannot and so this decision point is removed from the stack.

It now moves to position 16, where it tries to match one less whitespace character – one space. It succeeds and so starts moving forwards again. There are still more decisions possible, though, as there could be no whitespace characters so this point is left on the stack. However, the engine wants to match a digit and cannot, so it fails and returns to the last point (16). It attempts the match with no whitespace characters and it will remove this decision from the stack, as there are no more decisions that could be made. It fails again as there is a space character at the next position, when the regex engine still wants a digit.

155

It now returns to the next decision point in the stack, which is at point 8. "-" was matched here, but the other decision wasn't attempted so it tries that. However, there are no whitespace characters there, it is still a "-", and so this match fails. It removes this point from the stack, and moves to the last decision point at point 2. It attempts to do the same with this character, but fails again. There are no more decisions to return to in the stack, so the match fails.

This is a very long and convoluted way of determining failure. However, because the engine has to make decisions at various points in the expression, it is actually essential for this kind of regex engine. However, there are ways of improving the regular expression to reduce the number of decision points to which it has to return. This has to be considered because the regex engine starts again from the last decision point, and in some choices of string and regex, it can work its way to the end again before discovering failure and having to work back once more. Alternatively, it can still succeed without matching everything expected. Thankfully, there are ways of stopping wildcards from being greedy.

To perform a non-greedy, or **lazy**, match with the wildcard characters, we simply use the quantifiers we have seen so far but add "?" after them. The difference is that with the non-greedy repetition the regex engine will always favor as few matches as possible. Another example will help make this clearer.

Let's imagine we want to match a single line of a text file. In this file we have the lines:

```
This is the first line.
This the second line.
The final line.
```

We want each match to capture just one whole line. Therefore, we are looking for one or more whitespace or non-whitespace characters. We want it to start at the beginning of a line and end at the end of a line. Our first attempt at a regular expression might be this:

```
^[\w\W]+$
```

Let's try this with our Regular Expression Tester, with the MultiLine option checked:

The Matches() button will show what sub-strings actually matched. When we click the Matches() button, we see that there is just one match, the whole string. We wanted the match to start at the beginning of a line and end at the end of a line, but it only matched once.

The problem is the Regex engine is greedy. Moreover, the match it first made is valid; it starts at the beginning of a line, has one or more \w or \W characters in it, and ends at the end of the string. The problem is just it matched too much; it matched all the lines in between as well. In this case, the MultiLine option is irrelevant. The problem is with our greedy repetition character "+". The solution is to use a non-greedy repetition instruction, in this case "+?". If we change our regular expression to:

```
^[\w\W]+?$
```

and hit the Matches() button again, we'll see this time that each line is contained within one match:

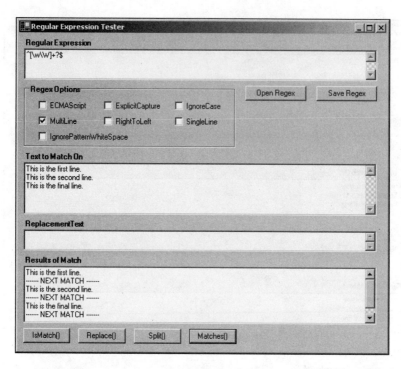

Now the Regex engine only matches as many characters as it needs to for a successful match. So this means it starts at the first line, matches all the characters until it hits the end of the line and then stops matching. The \W character could match against a newline character, because the MultiLine option states that it can. So as the "$" character follows, it stops.

There are no hard and fast rules governing when you should use lazy matching, but it is often quite clear from what your characters are asking for. By looking at what your instruction will and won't match, you can decide if you want it to be greedy. If you are using the "." character with a wildcard, you will often want to use the non-greedy version as it would otherwise match all of the rest of the string before it moves on to the next regex instruction. A greedy instruction will discover how many it can match and then count down if a failure occurs later, whereas a lazy match will try with as few as possible until a later instruction fails, where it tries again with one more occurrence. If the Regex engine reaches a character it cannot match while using a lazy wildcard, or it reaches the end of the string while it was attempting to increase the number of characters to match against, then it will fail and so step back through the decision stack.

Greediness and laziness will need to be applied at different times; you will want to take into account how far through the string the lazy character would match, how large the string is likely to be in total, and how many repeated characters you are likely to have. Let's show another example, the ISBN example used earlier. We'll change the regex to:

```
^(\d[-\s]*?){9}[\dxX]$
```

We'll use the same string as before:

```
1-861-0007  132
```

Here it will attempt to match 0 or more whitespace characters and will first start from 0. The difference in the matching routine here is that when it gets to the point where there are 2 whitespace characters, it will attempt to match against 1 character first, but this will fail because the next character wants to match a digit. This means that when it does match 2 spaces, then it leaves nothing on the stack as there are no more than 2 whitespace characters there and so there are no more decisions that can be made there. In terms of performance, the greedy search will often be faster matching a string, but its eagerness to succeed can mean that you don't match what you expect to. You should be able to make a more informed decision now, however, by considering how these operators work when you build up your expression.

Specifying Alternatives

You've seen how we can use [] to specify some alternatives. However, it only matches against single characters. The alternation character allows you to provide fuller choices.

Let's say we wanted to match "Paul" or "John" with a regular expression. Without the alternation character we'd need two regular expressions and therefore two different comparisons, but with this character, we can write just one:

```
Paul|John
```

The alternation character becomes even more useful when coupled with grouping, which we see in the next chapter. With all alternation decisions, the engine will attempt to match the first choice first, and step through each from left to right.

Special Characters

In the previous sections, we have seen many regular expression characters. We've seen that if we want to match any word character we write \w, or if we want to match the previous character one or more times then we use "+". However you may want to match an actual + sign rather than indicating zero or more characters. Alternatively, you may want to match characters that cannot be typed in; for example non-standard characters and characters such as the tab or line feed. Thankfully, there are escape sequences that can be used to specify these characters. "\" is the character indicating that what follows is an escape sequence of characters. What follows indicates what character each escape sequence represents, so \t represents a tab. A list of these are shown in the following table :

Escape Sequence	Description
\\	Matches actual "\"
\.	Matches "." character
*	Matches "*" character
\+	Matches "+" character
\?	Matches "?" character
|	Matches "|" character
\(	Matches "(" character
\)	Matches ")" character
\{	Matches "{" character
\}	Matches "}" character
\^	Matches "^" character
\$	Matches "$" character
\n	Matches newline
\r	Matches carriage return
\t	Matches tab
\v	Matches vertical tab
\f	Matches form feed
\nnn	Matches ASCII character specified by octal number nnn; so \103 matches an uppercase C
\xnn	Matches ASCII character specified by hexadecimal number nn; so \x43 matches C
\unnnn	Matches the Unicode character specified by the four hexadecimal digits represented by nnnn
\cV	Matches a control character; for example \cV matches *Ctrl-V*

Let's say we have the string, "The price is $1.95 and it is available now", and want to match the "$" and replace it with a "£". The dollar must be escaped; otherwise, it is interpreted as meaning the pattern must be at the end of the string.

```
Dim myString As String = "The price is $1.95 and it is available now"
MessageBox.Show(Regex.Replace(myString, "\$", "£"))
```

Another example is a string that only contains a URL, which you want to split into its separate parts, for example `www.subdomain.domain.com` into:

```
www
subdomain
domain
com
```

We need to split the input string at each point there is a "." character. However the "." is part of the regular expression syntax and therefore we need to tell the Regex parser we mean a literal ".", and not the regular expression syntax version. We escape it by simply adding a "\" in front of it, this means our regular expression will be: "\.".

Summary

In this chapter, we have covered the basics of regular expression syntax and how regular expressions are implemented in the .NET Framework.

In this chapter we covered:

- ❑ In .NET, regular expression functionality is provided via the `System.Text.RegularExpressions` namespace, and is contained within `System.dll`.

- ❑ The most important class is the `Regex` class. This allows to us create and use regular expressions to test for patterns of characters, search, replace, and split strings. The class has a number of shared methods that remove the need to create a `Regex` object if we just want to use a regular expression once.

- ❑ Regular expression syntax allows us to specify not just to match actual characters, but also to specify matches for a type of character, for example digits, letters, and whitespace.

- ❑ The number of times a character should be matched can be specified with the repetition characters.

- ❑ The alternative character "|" is a logical OR statement in that it allows one or other of the patterns to be matched.

- ❑ When we want to specify characters that can't be typed in using the keyboard, or when we want to match a character that is normally part of regular expression syntax we can use one of the special characters.

In the next chapter, we look at the more advanced aspects of regular expression syntax. We also look at the trickier aspects of the .NET regular expression support and cover the other classes in the `System.Text.RegularExpressions` namespace.

VB.NET

Text Manipulation

Handbook

6

Advanced Regex Concepts

In this chapter, we'll be covering the more advanced regular expression syntax we left out of the previous chapter. We'll also be looking at other .NET Framework classes that deal with regular expressions, like the Group and GroupCollection classes. We'll give examples of the more tricky aspects of regular expressions: groups, using groups in substitutions, and backreferences.

Groups, Substitutions, and Backreferences

In this section, we'll look at the .NET Group and GroupCollection classes, substitutions, and backreferences. It's no coincidence that we're discussing these all in the same section, as they are all related. Groups allow us to specify that a pattern of characters should be considered as a distinct item. One example of where we might do this is when matching someone's whole name, where although the whole match should be of the whole name, we want to split the match up into first name and last name. Using the Group and GroupCollection classes we can then access the first and surname parts of the match separately.

Substitutions and backreferences allow us to use the characters matched by a group. Substitutions allow the group to be used in replacement operations as part of the text that replaces the pattern. Let's say we wanted to replace all instances where someone had typed in a word twice accidentally, for example, "and and", with just one word. We can place one of the matched words in a group, and then replace the whole match with just the group ("and and" becomes "and"). We'll see how this works shortly when we look at substitutions.

Backreferences allow us to reuse the pattern matched by a group later in the regular expression, that is, reference a previously matched group. For example, if we want to match the open and close tag of an HTML element we obviously want to match the open tag first, for example, "<p>", and then match the same close tag, ("</p>"). However, we don't know in advance what the start tag will be, so we can't specify the close tag's contents unless we use backreferences. So, in our example, let's say for our input string we had the following HTML string:

```
<P>some text</P><H2>some heading</H2>
```

In our simple example an HTML start tag consists of a letter followed optionally by a number (obviously real HTML has more complex tags but this will do for out simple example). To match the start tag we could use the regular expression:

```
<[a-zA-Z]\d?>
```

This will produce two matches in our input string: <P> and <H2>.

So, for the first match the closing tag must be </P> and for the second it must be </H2>. The important bits are the P and the H2, as it's these that must be matched in the closing tag, so we need to group them in the start tag matching pattern:

```
<([a-zA-Z]\d?)>
```

The brackets specify the grouping of the pattern. So, for each match there is now one group, and in the example the group will contain P and H2.

So in our closing tag we just need to match </ and > with whatever the contents of the first group were inside, which will be: </P> and </H2>.

So the full regular expression would be:

```
<([a-zA-Z]\d?)>[^<]*</\1>
```

This matches the start tag, making sure the tag type is captured within a regex group. Then any characters are matched so long as they are not a "<" character, that is we've not hit a new start or close tag. We tell the close tag to match <\, then the contents of group1 (the \1 specifies group1), and finally ">".

Simple Groups

In the sections below, we explain the grouping characters that can be used in regular expressions.

Capturing: ( )

This groups together the characters matched by the pattern inside the brackets. It's a capturing group; this means the characters matched by the pattern become part of the final match, unless the ExplicitCapture option is set, which would mean that, by default, the characters are not part of the match.

As an example, let's look at the following input string: ABC1 DEF2 XY. A regular expression that matches three characters A to Z and then one digit would look like:

```
([A-Z]{3})\d
```

This will produce the following two matches:

```
1st Match = ABC1
2nd Match = DEF2
```

Each match will have one group:

```
1st match's 1st group = ABC
2nd match's 1st group = DEF
```

With back referencing we can access the group via its number within the regular expression and also via .NET using the Group and GroupCollection classes. If the ExplicitCapture option is set then the contents captured by the groups will not be available.

Non-Capturing: (?:)

This groups together the characters matched by the pattern inside the brackets. It's a non-capturing group; this means the characters matched by the pattern will not be captured as a group, though it will form part of the final match results. It's basically exactly the same as the group type above but with the ExplicitCapture option set.

As an example, let's look at the following input string: 1A BB SA 1 C. The regular expression that matches a digit **or** a letter from A - Z, followed by any word character looks like:

```
(?:\d|[A-Z])\w
```

This regular expression will produce three matches:

```
1st Match = 1A
2nd Match = BB
3rd Match = SA
```

However, there will be no groups captured.

Capturing-By-Name: (?<name>)

This groups together the characters matched by the pattern inside the brackets and gives the group the name specified between the angle brackets. Within the regular expression we can use the name for backreferencing, instead of having to use a number. It's a capturing group, even if the ExplicitCapture option is set; this means the characters matched within the group are available for backreferencing or accessible from the Group class, as we'll see shortly.

Consider the following input string:

Characters in Seinfeld included Jerry Seinfeld, Elaine Benes, Cosmo Kramer and George Costanza

The regular expression to match their first and last names and capture the last name in a group called lastName is:

```
\b[A-Z][a-z]+ (?<lastName>[A-Z][a-z]+)\b
```

This produces four matches:

```
1st match = Jerry Seinfeld
2nd match = Elaine Benes
3rd match = Cosmo Kramer
4th match = George Costanza
```

There is one group in each match, the lastName group:

```
1st match lastName group = Seinfeld
2nd match lastName group = Benes
3rd match lastName group = Kramer
4th match lastName group = Costanza
```

The groups will be captured regardless of whether the ExplicitCapture option is set or not.

Comparing Simple Groups

The easiest group to use from those explained above is the capturing group. By simply placing part of our regular expression inside brackets, we can tell the regex engine to treat the pattern as a distinct entity. This can be especially useful when used with the alternation character "|". For example, if we wanted to match an individual's title, for example, Mr, Mrs, Miss, Ms, Dr, and then their last name, we could use the following expression:

```
(Mr|Mrs|Miss|Ms|Dr) [A-Z][a-z]*
```

Within the brackets we have five possible matches that can be made, either Mr or Mrs or Miss or Ms or Dr. The pattern inside the brackets requires only that we match one of these. Following the group is a space, then a capital letter, and then zero or more lower case letters. So, using our Regular Expression Tester program from the previous chapter, we will see the following:

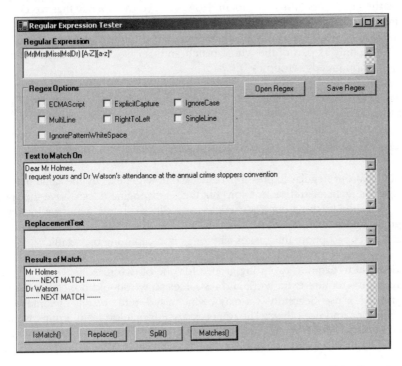

When the Matches() button is clicked, the two matching patterns will be found:

```
Mr Holmes
Dr Watson
```

Contrast this with the same regular expression *without* a group:

```
Mr|Mrs|Miss|Ms|Dr [A-Z][a-z]*
```

The problem here is this will seek to match Mr or Mrs or Miss or Ms. In addition, it will match Dr followed by the last name. Therefore, if we alter the regular expression in the Regular Expression Tester and click Matches() again, we'll get the following matches:

```
Mr
Dr Watson
```

By adding the brackets, we are telling the Regex engine to treat the alternatives as one group and therefore to match any single one of them. Notice that with the capturing groups, the pattern matched by the group becomes part of the final match. Indeed, we'll see shortly that we can access the individual matches made by a group. As you learned in the last chapter, this is referred to as a greedy match as it "hungrily" consumes the characters and stores them. However, we can specify that we don't want to capture the group. In our example, we needed to use the group so that our alternation would work; we did not have any particular interest in the results of the group as such, only as part of the whole match. In this case, we can use the non-capturing, or non-greedy, group (?:).

If we change our last name example to include a non-capturing group we will get the following:

```
(?:Mr|Mrs|Miss|Ms|Dr) [A-Z][a-z]*
```

If we test this in our Regular Expression Tester, we now get exactly the same match as we first got (Mr Holmes and Dr Watson) but the regex engine doesn't save the specific characters matched by the group for use later, as we'll see shortly when we look at getting group information. An alternative to using non-capturing groups is to set the ExplicitCapture option; this makes all groups non-capturing by default.

We would want to use non-capturing groups for one of two reasons. Firstly efficiency; capturing groups require extra work and resources so we should not capture data that we never need or use. Secondly, we may be interested in the results of some of the capturing groups and not others. The unnecessary information from groups we are not interested in just confuses matters, so it's better to make them non-capturing rather than having to alter our code to ignore them.

One final change we could make to the expression is to allow an optional period after the title, that is, "Mr." as well as "Mr", etc. Remember that the "." character has special significance in Regex syntax and means match any character, therefore we must tell the Regex parser that we mean a literal "." and not the regex syntax one. We do this as follows:

```
(?:Mr|Mrs|Miss|Ms|Dr)\.? [A-Z][a-z]*
```

The \. characters tell the Regex parser that we mean a literal "." and the "?" makes it optional, meaning that the "." should appear zero or one times.

The final group we discussed was a named capturing group – (?<name>). This allows us to reference previously matched groups using the group name. At this stage, it's not that useful, so we will leave its discussion until later in the chapter when we explain backreferences.

The Group and GroupCollection Classes

The .NET Framework allows us to access the captured characters within a group. It provides the `Group` class, which represents a single group within a match, and also the `GroupCollection` class, which contains `Group` objects, one for every group in a successful match.

To obtain a collection of all the groups in a single match, we can use the `Groups` property of the `Match` class. This returns a `GroupCollection` object, so we can obtain each of the individual groups inside each match.

Let's imagine we have the following regular expression:

```
(\d\d)\s([A-Z][A-Z])
```

This will match two digits, followed by a whitespace character, and then by two uppercased letters. We have added brackets around the two digits, giving our first capturing group, and also around the two `[A-Z]` blocks to give the second capturing group. If we have the string `"12 AB 34 CD 56 EF"` then we would get the following matches:

```
12 AB
34 CD
56 EF
```

Within each of these matches are the two groups. So, for example, in the first match the groups are `12` and `AB`. These can be accessed because each `Match` object contains the `Groups` property; this returns a `GroupCollection` object, which inherits from the `System.Text.Collection` class:

```
Dim matchGroups As GroupCollection = matchMade.Groups()
```

Now the `matchGroups` collection will hold a `Group` object for each regex group inside our regular expression. We can access each group using its index; however, note that the first group in the group collection is always the whole match. Therefore, even if no groups at all are defined, the `GroupCollection` will have at least one `Group` object in it, as demonstrated by the following code:

```
matchGroups(0).value
matchGroups(1).value
matchGroups(2).value
```

For the first match (`12 AB`), it would retrieve the following:

```
12 AB
12
AB
```

169

For the second match (34 CD) it would retrieve:

```
34 CD
34
CD
```

Remember we said earlier that we can give names to groups using the regular expression syntax (?<name>). Well, if we do that, we can access the groups using the name as well as the index. Let's change the regular expression to:

```
(?<numberGroup>\d\d)\s(?<letterGroup>[A-Z][A-Z])
```

Now, we can access the groups using their index and name:

```
matchGroups(1).Value                    ' 12
matchGroups("numberGroup").Value        ' 12
matchGroups(2).Value                    ' AB
matchGroups("letterGroup").Value        ' AB
```

> **Regular expression group names are case sensitive, so letterGroup and LetterGroup are not the same.**

Note what happens if we use a non-capturing group:

```
(?:\d\d)\s([A-Z][A-Z])
```

Now matchGroups(1).Value will be AB for the first match because the characters captured by the first group are not stored for later reference, either in code using the GroupCollection class or for backreferences or substitutions as we'll see shortly.

Let's alter our regular expression tester and add a button that when clicked shows what groups are matched in a regular expression. First, we need to open the Regular Expression Tester project, and then add a button to the form named cmdGroups. Our form should look like the following:

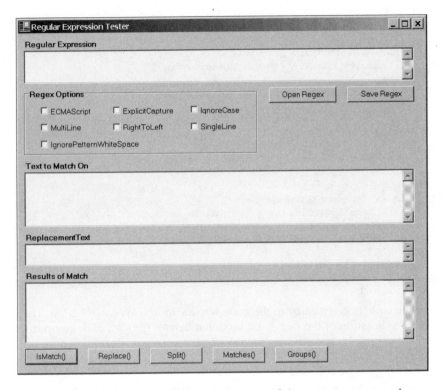

Now we need to add the code for the Click event of the new cmdGroups button:

```
Private Sub cmdGroups_Click (ByVal sender As System.Object, _
          ByVal e As System.EventArgs) Handles cmdGroups.Click

  Dim selectedRegexOptions As RegexOptions = GetSelectedRegexOptions()

  Try
    Dim matchesRegex As New Regex(Me.txtRegex.Text, _
                             selectedRegexOptions)
    Dim matchesFound As MatchCollection
    Dim matchMade As Match
    Const matchStringAs String ="-----MATCH MADE-----"
    Dim matchGroup As Group
    Dim results As New StringBuilder(64)
    Dim matchGroups As GroupCollection
    matchesFound = matchesRegex.Matches(Me.txtInputText.Text)

    ' Loop through each match made
    For Each matchMade In matchesFound
      ' Get the details of the groups within the match
      matchGroups = matchMade.Groups
```

```
            ' loop through each group within the match made and
            ' append the characters matched to the final results
            For Each matchGroup In matchGroups
               Results.Append("("& matchGroup.Value & ") ")
            Next
            Results.Append(ControlChars.NewLine & _
                           ControlChars.NewLine & _
                           MatchString & ControlChars.NewLine
         Next

         Me.txtResults.ForeColor = Drawing.Color.Black
         Me.txtResults.Text = results.ToString()

      Catch ex As ArgumentException
         Me.txtResults.ForeColor = Drawing.Color.Red
         Me.txtResults.Text = "There was an error in your regular " _
            & "expression when " & ControlChars.CrLf & ex.Message

      End Try
   End Sub
```

Much of the code is very similar to the code we saw for the Matches() button. The main
change is the insertion of the For Each loop that iterates through each group inside
a match:

```
For Each matchGroup In matchGroups
      resultsString += "(" & matchGroup.Value & ") "
   Next
```

First, we define variables to hold the details of an individual group and a collection of
groups. Then for each match made, we execute an inner For Each loop that iterates
through each group inside a match. We set matchGroups to the GroupCollection
object returned by the Groups property of the Match object. Then we loop through
each group (remember that even with no groups defined, the whole match will be the
first item in the group collection). We add the value of each group to the results string
for display in the Results of Match textbox.

Let's create a regular expression that matches title and last name, but only returns the surname as a captured group:

```
(?:Mr|Mrs|Miss|Ms|Dr) ([A-Z][a-z]*)
```

With our Regular Expression Tester, we get:

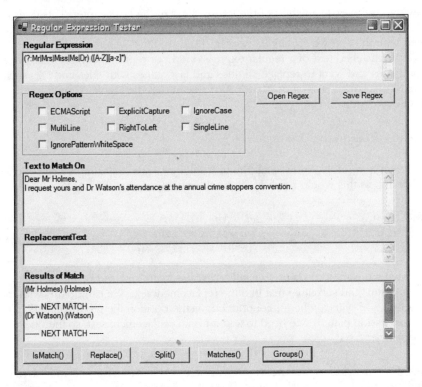

We can see from the results that the `GroupCollection` for each match contains the whole match in the first group, and then the individual group matches, just the last name in this case. We needed the title part to be in a group because of the use of the alternation characters, but we are not interested in the characters it captures, only the characters captured for the last name, which is the second group. Therefore, we made the alternation group a non-capturing group using the ?: characters after the opening bracket.

An alternative to using non-capturing groups is to specify that by default all groups should be non-capturing using the `ExplicitCapture` option. We can do this in our Regular Expression Tester by selecting the relevant checkbox and clicking the Groups() button. This time, none of the groups are matched; only the whole match is displayed. When the option `ExplicitCapture` is set, we need to specify when we want to capture a group by giving it a name. Let's do this by changing our regular expression to:

```
(Mr|Mrs|Miss|Ms|Dr) (?<lastName>[A-Z][a-z]*)
```

Now we get the results we want; the second group is captured even though the `ExplicitCapture` is set because we have explicitly told it to capture that group by naming it.

Substitutions

We saw the `Replace()` method of the `Regex` class in the last chapter. This does a global search and replace on the input string, whenever a match is made, and its text is replaced with the text we specify. However, there are times when we want to use some of the matched text of a regular expression in our replacement. Let's say we have a list of names and want to replace all titles and last names with titles and "X", such that "Mr Washington" becomes "Mr X". We've seen that the regular expression to match title and surname is:

```
(Mr|Mrs|Miss|Ms|Dr) [A-Z][a-z]*
```

The problem is we don't know what the title will be so we can't simply use code like the following, as this would result in all the titles being changed to Mr X:

```
Dim userInputString As String = "Dr Watson, Mr Holmes and Mrs Smith"
userInputString = Regex.Replace(userInputString, _
                  "(Mr|Mrs|Miss|Ms|Dr) [A-Z][a-z]*", "Mr X")
```

Clearly what we want to do is use whatever text has been captured by the first title-matching group, and substitute that into the replacement text. We can do this with the $\groupNumber syntax, where groupNumber is the position the group appears in the regular expression pattern. We need to add it to our replacement text, so the code becomes:

```
Dim userInputString As String = "Dr Watson, Mr Holmes and Mrs Smith"
userInputString = Regex.Replace(userInputString, _
                  "(Mr|Mrs|Miss|Ms|Dr) [A-Z][a-z]*", "$1 X")
```

We can use our Regular Expression Tester to demonstrate this, as shown opposite where the `Replace()` button is used:

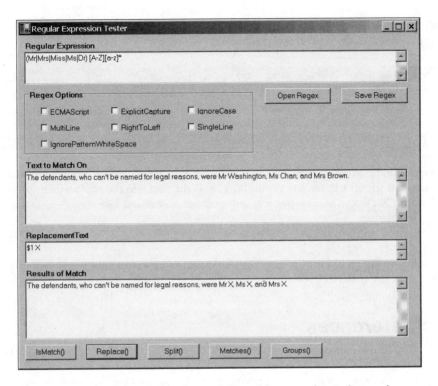

As we can see from the above screenshot, $ followed by a number indicates the group number that should be used in the replacement text, in this case the first group. There are a number of additional substitution characters available, as shown in the table below:

Character	Description
$*group*	Substitutes with the group number specified by *group*
${ *name*}	Substitutes the last substring matched by a (?<*name*>) group
$$	Substitutes a literal $ character
$&	Substitutes the entire match
$`	Substitutes all the text of the input string before the match
$'	Substitutes all the text of the input string after the match
$+	Substitutes the last group captured
$_	Substitutes the entire input string

We have already seen the `$group` used in our previous example. However, we could also have used `$+` as the last group captured, since in our example the only group captured in the match was also the first group, our title group.

An alternative to using group numbers is to give the group a name and substitute using that group name. Our regular expression could be:

```
(?<title>Mr|Mrs|Miss|Ms|Dr) [A-Z][a-z]*
```

and our replacement string would be:

```
${title} X
```

Remember that regular expressions and the replacement text are case sensitive, so if we name our group title, then using Title as the name in the replacement pattern won't work. No errors will be thrown, but we'll see something like this:

The defendants, who can't be named for legal reasons, were ${Title} X, ${Title} X, and ${Title} X.

The Regex engine could find no group called Title so instead it assumed we want to replace with the text {Title}.

Backreferences

Within our regular expression, backreferences allow us to match the same characters as a previous group. A common example is matching repeated words. The syntax for matching a previous group is \groupNumber or \k<groupName>.

Let's say we want to replace all repeated words with just the one original word. We could use the following regular expression:

```
(\b[a-zA-Z]+\b)\s\1
```

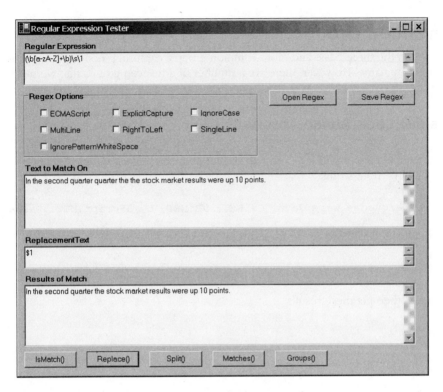

This will match one or more letters, bounded on either side by a word boundary, all of which is inside a capturing group. Then we match a whitespace character and, using a backreference, we match whatever was matched by the first group. In the Regular Expression Tester, the replacement text is simply $1; we substitute the match for the text matched for in the first group. By clicking the Replace() button, we correct the two double word problems in the sentence.

Instead of a number, we could have given the group a name and backreferenced it by name, which does the same thing in this case:

```
(?<firstWord>\b[a-zA-Z]+\b)\s\k<firstWord>
```

Something to be aware of with backreferences is how they could be confused when specifying octal numbers. \1 to \9 will always be treated as backreferences. Any number with a leading 0, for example, \040, will be treated as an octal number referring to an ASCII character, as we saw in the previous chapter. If there is no leading zero then it will be treated as a backreference, so long as there is a matching group to backreference. If we have 11 groups then \11 will match the eleventh group; if we had only 10 groups, then \11 would be treated as an octal number indicating an ASCII character.

Advanced Groups

We've seen the three basic and more common groups: capturing, non-capturing, and capturing-by-name. However, there are a number of advanced groups that we need to discuss.

Positive Look-Ahead Assertion: (?=)

This specifies that the pattern in the brackets must be found to the right of the assertion. The pattern will not form part of the final match. For example, let's consider the following input string:

```
The languages were Java, C#.NET, VB.NET, C, JScript.NET, Pascal
```

We could use the following regular expression on this input string:

```
\S+(?=\.NET)
```

We would then get these results:

```
C#
VB
JScript
```

Negative Look-Ahead Assertion: (?!)

This specifies that the pattern must not be found immediately to the right of the assertion. As before, the pattern will not form part of the final match. Let's consider the following input string:

```
123A 456 789 111C
```

We could use the following regular expression on this input string:

```
\d{3}(?![A-Z])
```

We would then get these results:

```
456
789
```

Positive Look-Behind Assertion: (?<=)

This specifies that the pattern in the brackets must be found to the left of the assertion. The pattern will not form part of the final match. Let's consider the following input string:

```
New Mexico, West Virginia, Washington, New England
```

We could use the following regular expression on this input string:

```
(?<=New )([A-Z][a-z]+)
```

We would then get these results:

```
Mexico
England
```

Negative Look-Behind Assertion: (?<!)

This specifies that the pattern must not be found immediately to the left of the assertion. As before, the pattern will not form part of the final match. Let's consider the following input string:

```
123A 456F 789C 111A
```

We could use the following regular expression on this input string:

```
(?<!1)\d{2}[A-Z]
```

We would then get these results:

```
56F
89C
```

Non-Backtracking: (?>)

This prevents the Regex engine from backtracking to attempt to match in the event of a failure, and is also known as a greedy sub-expression. Let's say we want to match all words ending in "ing". Let's use the following as our input string:

```
He was very trusting
```

To get the entire text we would use the following regular expression:

```
.*ing
```

However, if we turn off backtracking we will find no matches:

```
(?>.*)ing
```

Comparing Advanced Groups

Strictly speaking, these are assertions rather than groups; they assert (insist) that a pattern must exist at a specific place. The patterns that the assertion groups match do not form part of the final match, and so they cannot be used in backreferencing.

The first two advanced groups described match a pattern to the right of the assertion; they look ahead to see if the pattern exists. The positive look-ahead needs the existence of the pattern for the whole match to be successful. Conversely, the negative look-ahead checks to see the pattern does not exist, and if it does then no match can be made, and the whole match fails.

So, let's use our Regular Expression Tester with the following input string:

```
A1 B 2 C D3 E4
```

We can use a positive look-ahead assertion such as this:

```
[A-Z](?=\d)
```

This will produce the following matches:

```
A
D
E
```

Note that even though the assertion's pattern (here just \d) must be matched, it does not form part of the final match results. We can change the regular expression to a negative look-ahead assertion:

```
[A-Z](?!\d)
```

Now the matches will be:

```
B
C
```

In other words, a match will only be made when there is no following digit.

The next two groups are identical assertions, except they look to the immediate left of the assertion (look behind themselves) for the matching pattern. Again, a positive one asserts the pattern must exist for a successful whole match and the negative one asserts that the pattern must not exist for a successful match.

So, let's use the same input string as for the look-ahead examples, but change to a positive look-behind assertion:

```
(?<=[A-Z])\d
```

This will match any digits where they are immediately preceded by a letter in the range A to Z, producing the following matches:

180

```
1
3
4
```

The same thing but with a negative look-behind assertion is:

```
(?<![A-Z])\d
```

This says match any digit that it is not preceded by a character in the range A to Z and produces:

```
2
```

The final group is the non-backtracking group, which is perhaps the least obvious to understand. The regex engine will do its best to make a match. Let's demonstrate this with an example that has been simplified to make it easier to understand. Let's say we want to match a URL ending in .com; we could create a regular expression like this:

```
www\.(.*)\.com
```

This matches www, followed by a period character, then one or more of any characters inside a capturing group, followed by another period, and then finally by com. We can use the Regular Expression Tester to test this.

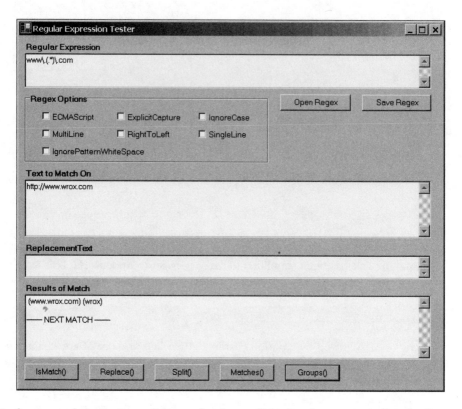

In the screenshot, the Groups() button has been clicked and we can see that the first group, containing .*, has matched wrox. Intuitively, the "." should match any character, while the "*" says match one or more of any character, so you may be interested to discover why the group has not also matched the .com part.

To make a successful match the whole regular expression has to be matched; the regex engine cannot just ignore the .com part. Like a results-only dating agency, the regex engine is very keen to make a match. Therefore, what it does is backtrack until it can make a match; let's see how it is thinking.

Its first attempt might be:

Regular Expression	Match characters	Match Made?
www.	www.	Yes
(.*)	wrox.com	Yes
.com		No

It failed on the first pass because the group (.*) has matched all the remaining characters and so .com cannot be matched. On the next pass, the Regex engine backtracks a character:

Regular Expression	Match characters	Match Made?
www.	www.	Yes
(.*)	wrox.co	Yes
.com	m	No

That's still not enough for a whole match. Now, the Regex engine keeps backtracking a character until finally it makes a match:

Regular Expression	Match characters	Match Made?
www.	www.	Yes
(.*)	wrox	Yes
.com	.com	Yes

All this backtracking is hard work and inefficient. The non-backtracking group allows us to turn off backtracking and increases efficiency. Let's change our regular expression to the non-backtracking group and try it in the Regular Expression Tester to see what happens:

```
www\.(?>.*)\.com
```

What we find now is that no matches are made. The problem is the Regex engine tests just the first option (where .* matches everything including .com) and as that fails, and backtracking is turned off for the group, then no match can be made. In this circumstance, we need to change our regular expression to:

```
www\.(?>[^.]*)\.com
```

This successfully matches because we look for any character until a period character is found. That way the .com bit isn't matched by the brackets. It's a more efficient regular expression as it removes the need for backtracking. However, it won't match sub-domains like www.domain.subdomain.com. Also, note that the non-backtracking group is also a non-capturing group – its value is not captured and made available for later use.

Making Decisions in Regular Expressions

We saw simple decision making with the alternation character | earlier in this chapter. However, regular expressions provide two further advanced decision-making instructions, as discussed now.

Expression alternations can have either of the following general syntaxes:

```
(?(expression)yes|no)
```

```
(?(?=expression)yes|no)
```

If expression is matched, then matching the yes regular expression will be attempted. Otherwise, the no regular expression is attempted. The no regular expression is optional. It is important to note that expression, the pattern that makes the decision, is zero width, which means the yes or no regexes will commence matching from the same place as expression.

Let's look at the following input string as an example:

```
1A CB 3A 5C 3B
```

Consider the following regular expression:

```
(?(\d)\dA|[A-Z]B)
```

Using this regular expression, we get these results:

```
1A
CB
3A
```

Name alternations have the following general syntax:

```
(?(name)yes|no)
```

If the name regular expression in the group is matched then matching the yes regular expression is attempted. Otherwise, matching the no regular expression is attempted. The no regular expression is optional.

Let's demonstrate this with the following input string:

```
77-77A 69-AA 57-B
```

We'll use the following regular expression:

```
(\d7)?-(?(1)\d\d[A-Z]|[A-Z][A-Z])
```

This will produce these matches:

```
77-77A
-AA
```

The decision making regular expression syntax can be quite confusing if we forget that matching of the yes or no regular expressions starts from the same place as the regex pattern that did the test. Let's take the example regex:

```
(?(\d)A|B)
```

and try it with the input string:

```
1A CB 3A 5C 3B
```

Using the Regular Expression Tester you will see the following:

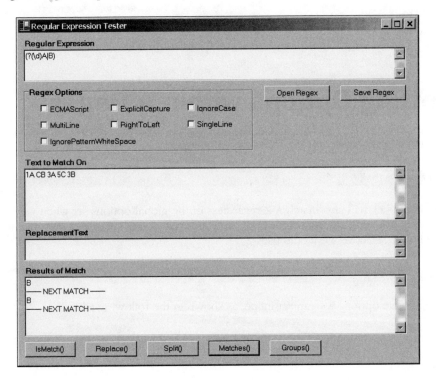

Given there are 1A and 3A, why have they not been matched? Well, the reason is that, although the pattern that decides the yes or no test (\d) is successful, our yes regular expression (here simply an actual A character) does not match. The yes test starts in the same place as the decision test, that is with the digit and, as A is clearly not a digit, the yes regex fails even though the decision making regex was successful. To make our regex work in the above example, we need to change it to this:

```
(?(\d)\dA|B)
```

Now the results are:

```
1A
B
3A
B
```

The important thing is that the yes regular expression must at least match the same pattern as the decision making regex or else it will fail. It does not have to be the same, just so long as it matches the same pattern. For example, this would work for our example too:

```
(?(\d)\wA|B)
```

This is because \w will match a word character and word characters include digits.

Setting Options within a Regex

The regex syntax allows us to change the regex options within a group. For example, let's say we want to set a group to be case insensitive:

```
(?i:[a-z])
```

Now the [a-z] will also match A-Z regardless of the global options set when we created the regex. To remove an option, we simply use the "-" sign. For example, to make it case sensitive we would use:

```
(?-i:[a-z])
```

There are five options we can set inline, as shown in the following table.

RegexOption	Flag	Description
ExplicitCapture	n	This specifies that the only valid captures are explicitly named or numbered groups of the form
IgnoreCase	i	This specifies case-insensitive matching
IgnorePatternWhitespace	x	This specifies that unescaped whitespace is excluded from the pattern and enables comments following a # sign
MultiLine	m	This specifies multiline mode, which changes the meaning of the ^ and $ characters.
SingleLine	s	This specifies that the only valid captures are explicitly named or numbered groups of the form

We can set as many of the options at once as we wish, for example:

```
(?n-i:[a-z])
```

This sets the group to ExplicitCapture and case-sensitive.

Rules of the Regex Engine

We've now covered all the regex syntax for this book. We'll finish off by looking at some rules of how the regex engine does its matching. To make life easier for us there are some basic rules to remember:

Rule 1: The regex engine will start matching as soon as possible in the input string. It will look one character at a time until it finds the start of a match.

> Input string = 123 ABC 456 DEF
>
> Regex = [A-Z]*

This will start matching at the ABC.

Rule 2: Having found the start of a match, the regex engine will continue to match until it hits a character that is not permitted by the pattern.

> Input string = 123 ABC 456 DEF
>
> Regex = [A-Z]*

The first match will start at ABC and stop when it hits the space, which is not permitted by the pattern.

Rule 3: The Regex engine is very greedy – it's looking to make as big a match as the pattern allows.

> Input String = 'Dr Watson's watch'
>
> Regex = '.*'

The match made is the whole string. The regex pattern says match a single quote, followed by any characters, and then ending with another single quote. So 'Dr Watson' also matches, there is no need for the regex engine to continue and match the other characters, it already has a pattern that matches. However, the regex engine continues (see Rule 2 – the match continues until an invalid character is hit) and finds that it can also match:

```
s watch'
```

Let's see how things change if we make the "*" a non-greedy quantifier by adding a "?" after it:

> Input String = 'Dr Watson's watch'
>
> Regex = '.*?'

Now in this case the match is only:

```
'Dr Watson'
```

The regex engine has got to the second ' and now, having sufficient characters for a match, has stopped. That is, it's non-greedy, it has enough for a match and does not try to grab any more.

Rule 4: The Regex engine is keen to find a match and will backtrack if necessary to make a match.

> Input string = 'Hello world' said K & R.
>
> Regex = '.*'

This will match:

```
'Hello World'
```

However, it wouldn't if it wasn't for backtracking. We saw in Rule 3 that the regex engine is looking for the biggest match it can make. The `.*` says match any character zero or more times. So, while the `"'"` after world is enough for a match, the Regex engine wants more and continues looking while Rule 2 does not apply (so long as a character that does not match is not found). The regex engine continues right until it hits the end of the input string in this case, as the `"."` character matches all of the characters. However, it has a problem, the pattern specifies that there must be a `"'"` character at the end of the pattern, but, as it has gobbled up all the characters with the `.*`, it means no `"'"` can be matched on. So the regex engine, ever keen to make a match, backtracks a character at a time until it gets back to the `"'"` after world; now it has its match.

We can see what happens if we disable back tracking by using a non backtracking group:

> Input string = 'Hello world' said K & R.
>
> Regex = '(?>.*)'

Now this time no match is made because the `.*` has matched all the characters right to the end, and because we have told it not to backtrack, it can't go back and make a match based on 'Hello World'.

Rule 5: The Regex engine, given a choice, will always take the first option.
When we use the `"|"` character to give alternatives, the regex engine will try to match the first one, if that doesn't match then the second, then the third, and so on.

> Input string = 1234 123 3456
>
> Regex = (\d{2}|\d{3}|\d{4})

This produces the following matches:

```
12
34
12
34
56
```

We can see that, even though it could choose to match 1234 or 123 or 3456 as complete matches, it has simply gone for the first of the alternatives and matches two digits each time.

It's handy to keep the five rules in mind, as often the regex does things that seem surprising.

Summary

In this chapter, we looked at:

- ❑ How regular expression syntax allows us to group a pattern
- ❑ How we can use groups in the .NET Framework and access their values using the `Group` class
- ❑ How groups can be used inside the substitution part of a `Replace()` method
- ❑ How we can use previously matched groups inside the regular expression itself

In the next chapter, we'll be using the regular expression syntax learned so far to create a number of useful real-world examples.

VB.NET

Text Manipulation

Handbook

7

Regular Expression Patterns

In this chapter, we'll be taking a detailed look at many practical examples of regular expression patterns. Not only will it give you a library of useful patterns, but it will also help us see how regular expressions are assembled. This should be a useful guide for learning how to construct regular expressions, as well as providing you with a set of useful regular expressions for manipulating common data.

Validating Characters

We start with some basic and commonly used regular expressions to check whether a string contains any invalid characters. Our first set of methods look at the validation of sequences of letters, numbers, and spaces:

Pattern	Description
[^a-zA-Z\d]	Check that the text does **not** contain letters of the alphabet, numbers, or spaces
[^a-zA-Z\d]	Check that the text does **not** contain letters of the alphabet or numbers
[^a-zA-Z]	Check that the text does **not** contain letters of the alphabet or spaces

These are useful where we have user input and what to make sure it only contains the characters we want. Using each of the regular expressions above is very similar; for example, to test that variable userInputString contains characters other than those of the alphabet, numbers, and spaces:

```
    If Regex.IsMatch(userInputString, "[^a-zA-Z\d ]") Then
        ' Invalid Chars found
    Else
        ' Valid chars only found
    End If
```

It is normally advisable, however, to match only on what is present, rather than on what is not. It is easier attempting to match on characters that are or should be there, than on those that are not. However, these patterns can be useful to match invalid characters if a previous match failed, for instance. In these next simple matches, we will be matching negatively as in the case used above.

Validating Numbers

In this section, we look at various methods for validating different types of number.

Numbers Only

We start with a simple regular expression to check that the passed string contains only numerical characters:

Pattern	Description
[^\d.]	Check if the string contains characters other than numbers or a decimal point

For this pattern, anything that's not a digit or decimal place is considered invalid. Note that normally the "." is a special regex character meaning match any character and if we wanted to match an actual "." we'd need to escape it like this: "\.". However, this is not necessary when using the square brackets to specify which characters to match.

We can test to see if invalid characters exist in userInputString with the following code:

```
    If Regex.IsMatch(userInputString, "[^\d.]") Then
        ' Invalid Chars found
    Else
        ' Valid chars only found
    End If
```

Integer Numbers Only

Our next regular expression checks for integers.

```
^((\+|-)\d)?\d*$
```

Unlike the simple character matching expressions we have seen previously, this one matches a specific pattern. It specifies that the string may optionally start with a "+" or "-" sign, but that if it does, then it must be then followed by at least one digit, then followed by zero or more digits. The "$" at the end ensures that no other characters are allowed after the last digit. Note that because "+" is part of the regular expression language, meaning one or more, we had to escape it in the first group, \+, to tell the regex engine that we mean an actual "+", and not the regex syntax "+".

The following would be valid:

```
+1
234
-2445234
```

Whereas, these would not:

```
++123
ABC
1.23
1234C
```

Previously if a match was found, it meant invalid characters were present. This time if a match is found it means the input string is valid. It makes more sense to check for the string being valid rather than invalid as happened previously, because we are not just checking for the existence of certain characters, but also specifying that the characters must be in a specific order, so +123 is valid but 123+ is not. The code to use the expression is therefore:

```
If Regex.IsMatch(userInputString, "^((\+|-)\d)?\d*$") Then
    ' Input string valid
Else
    ' Invalid input string
End If
```

Floating-Point Numbers

Assume we want to check for positive or negative floating-point numbers:

```
^(?:\+|-)?\d+(?:\.\d+)?$
```

As a floating-point number can be identical to an integer (1 is a valid integer and floating-point number), the regular expression will be valid for both integers and floating-point numbers.

This time the regular expression specifies that digits, minus signs, and decimal points are to be permitted. The `^(?:\+|-)?` specifies that the characters must start at beginning of the string, (our valid number can't be in the middle of other characters. It also specifies, in a non-capturing group, that we can start with a "+" or a "-". We need to put the "+" and "-" check in a group, because of the "|", which matches either the regex pattern on the left, our "+" sign, or the regex pattern on the right, our minus sign. If we don't put the "\+|-" in a group, we will get erroneous results – the pattern will look for either just a "+" sign or a "-" sign with a number following it. As we are not interested in the results of the capture, a non-capturing group has been used – an alternative is to set the `ExplictCapture` option when using the `Regex` object.

Next, we specify that one or more digits can follow using the `\d+`. This matches one or more digits before the decimal point. Finally we have `(\.\d+)?$`, the part of the regular expression that matches a decimal point and any numbers following it. It matches a literal period character; remember that this character is part of the regex language and so we need to escape it when it's the actual character we want to match. We then match one or more digits. Finally as there is a "?" after the group, it means the group must be matched zero or more times. Essentially it makes the group optional, which allows numbers with no decimal point to be matched successfully.

```
If Regex.IsMatch(userInputString, "^(?:\+|-)?\d+(?:\.\d+)?$") Then
    ' Input string valid
Else
    ' Invalid input string
End If
```

Validating a Telephone Number

So far, the data being checked has been simple. However, telephone numbers are more of a challenge to validate. The problems are:

❑   Phone numbers differ from country to country

❑   There are different ways of entering a valid number, for example adding the national or international code, or not

One way to clarify what we expect in terms of the format of the telephone number, is to split the telephone number input into separate boxes, for example one box labeled for the international dialing code, one for the area code, one for the number itself, and one for the extension number
if applicable.

Another alternative, which we look at here, is to use regular expressions to match variations of international phone numbers. We need to specify more than just the valid characters – we also need to specify the format of the data. For example, all of the following are valid:

```
+1 (123) 123 4567
+1123123 456
+44 (123) 123 4567
+44 (123) 123 4567 ext 123
+44 20 7893 4567
```

> *You can find more information on world telephone numbering systems at* http://phonebooth.interocitor.net/wtng/.

The variations that our regular expression needs to deal with (optionally separated by spaces) are:

The international number	"+" followed by 1 to 3 digits (optional)
The local area code	2 to 5 digits, sometimes in parentheses (compulsory)
The actual subscriber number	3 to 10 digits, sometimes with spaces (compulsory)
An extension number	2 to 5 digits, preceded by x, xtn, extn, pax, pbx, or extension, and sometimes in parentheses

Obviously there will be countries where this won't work, something you'd need to deal with based on where your customers and partners would be. The following regular expression is rather complex compared to the last one:

```
^(\+\d{1,3} ?)?(\(\d{1,5}\)|\d{1,5}) ?\d{3} ?\d{0,7}
( (x|xtn|ext|extn|pax|pbx|extension)?\.? ?\d{2-5})?$
```

We will need to set the case-insensitive option with this, as well as the explicit capture option. Although complex, if we break it down, it's quite straightforward. In fact, its length meant it had to be split across two lines; make sure you type it in on one line.

We'll start with the pattern that matches an international dialing code:

```
(\+\d{1,3} ?)?
```

So far, we're matching a plus sign (\+) followed by 1 to 3 digits (\d{1,3}) and an optional space (?). Remember that since the "+" character is a special character, we add a "\" character in front of it to specify that we mean an actual "+" character. The characters are wrapped inside parentheses to specify a group of characters. We allow an optional space, and match this entire group of characters zero or one times – as indicated by the "?" character after the closing parenthesis of the group.

Next, is the pattern to match an area code:

```
(\(\d{1,5}\)|\d{1,5})
```

This pattern is contained in parentheses, which designate it as a group of characters, and matches either 1 to 5 digits in parentheses (`(\d{1,5})`) or just 1 to 5 digits (`\d{1,5}`). Again, since the parenthesis characters are special characters in regular expression syntax and we want to match actual parentheses, we need the "\" character in front of them. Also note the use of the pipe symbol (`|`), which means "OR" or "match either of these two patterns".

Next, we match the subscriber number:

```
?\d{3,4} ?\d{0,7}
```

Note that there is a space before the first "?" – this space and question mark mean, "match zero or one space". This is followed by three or four digits (`\d{3}`), as although there are always three digits in the US, there are often four in the UK. Then, another "zero or one space", and finally between zero and seven digits (`\d{0,7}`).

Finally, we add the part to cope with an optional extension number:

```
( (x|xtn|ext|extn|extension)?\.? ?\d{2-5})?
```

This group is optional, since its parentheses are followed by a question mark. The group itself checks for a space, optionally followed by one of x, ext, xtn, extn, and extension, followed by zero or one periods (note the \ character, since "." is a special character in regular expression syntax), followed by zero or one space, followed by between two and five digits.

Putting these four patterns together, we can construct the entire regular expression, apart from the surrounding syntax: recall that the regular expression starts with "^" and ends with "$". The "^" character specifies that the pattern must be matched at the beginning of the string, and the "$" character specifies the pattern must be matched at the end of the string. This means that our string must match the pattern completely – it can contain no other characters before or after the pattern that is matched.

Therefore, with the regular expression explained, we can now show it in use:

```
If Regex.IsMatch(userInputString, _
                "^(\+\d{1,3} ?)?(\(\d{1,5}\)|" & _
                "\d{1,5}) ?\d{3} ?\d{0,7}" & _
                "( (x|xtn|ext|extn|extension)?" \.? ?\d{1,5})?$", _
                RegexOptions.IgnoreCase Or _
                RegexOptions.ExplicitCapture) Then
   MessageBox.Show("Valid")
Else
   MessageBox.Show("Invalid")
End If
```

Note in this case that it is important to set the `IgnoreCase` option; otherwise, our regular expression could fail to match the ext parts.

Validating a Postal Code

We just about managed to check worldwide telephone numbers, but to do the same for postal codes would be something of a major challenge. Instead, we'll create a method that only checks for US Zip codes and UK post codes. If we needed to check for other countries, then the code would need modifying. We may find that checking more than one or two postal codes in one regex begins to get unmanageable, and it may well be easier to have an individual regex for each country's postal code we need to check. For this purpose though, we will combine the regular expression for the UK and the US:

```
^(\d{5}(-\d{4})?|[a-z][a-z]?\d\d? ?\d[a-z][a-z])$
```

This is actually in two parts: the first part which checks for zip codes and the second part which checks UK post codes. We'll start by looking at the zip code part.

Zip codes can be represented in one of two formats – as five digits (12345), or five digits followed by a dash and four digits (12345-1234). The Zip code regular expression to match these is:

```
\d{5}(-\d{4})?
```

This matches five digits, followed by an optional non-capturing group that matches a dash followed by four digits.

For a regular expression that covers UK post codes, let's consider their various formats. UK postcode formats are one or two letters followed by either one or two digits, followed by an optional space, followed by a digit, and then two letters. Additionally, some central London postcodes look like this: SE2V 3ER, with a letter at the end of the first part. Currently it is only some of those starting with SE, WC, and W, but that may change. Valid examples of UK postcode include: CH3 9DR, PR29 1XX, M27 1AE, WC1V 2ER, and C27 3AH.

Based on this, our pattern is:

```
([a-z][a-z]?\d\d?|[a-z]{2}\d[a-z]) ?\d[a-z][a-z]
```

These two patterns are combined using the | character to "match one or the other" and grouped using parentheses. We then add the "^" character at the start and "$" character at the end of the pattern to be sure that the only information in the string is the postal code. Although postal codes should be upper case, it is still valid for them to be lower case, so we have also set the case-insensitive option when we use the regular expression:

```
^(\d{5}(-\d{4})?|([a-z][a-z]?\d\d?|[a-z{2}\d[a-z]) ?\d[a-z][a-z])$
```

Using the regular expression is much the same as it was with the previous examples:

```
If Regex.IsMatch(userInputString, "^(\d{5}(-\d{4})?|"([a-z][a-z]" & _
                                  "\d\d?|[a-z]{2}\d[a-z]) ?" & _
                                  "\d[a-z][a-z])$", _
                                  RegexOptions.IgnoreCase Or _
                                  RegexOptions.ExplicitCapture) Then
    MessageBox.Show("Valid")
Else
    MessageBox.Show("Invalid")
End If
```

Validating an Email Address

Before we start working on a regular expression to match email addresses, we need to look at the types of valid e-mail addresses we can have:

- ❑   someone@mailserver.com

- ❑   someone@mailserver.info

- ❑   someone.something@mailserver.com

- ❑   someone.something@subdomain.mailserver.com

- ❑   someone@mailserver.co.uk

- ❑   someone@subdomain.mailserver.co.uk

- ❑   someone.something@mailserver.co.uk

- ❑   someone@mailserver.org.uk

- ❑   some.one@subdomain.mailserver.org.uk

Also, if you examine the SMTP RFC (http://www.ietf.org/rfc/rfc0821.txt), we can have:

- ❑   someone@123.113.209.32

- ❑   """Paul Wilton"""@somedomain.com

That's quite a list and contains many variations we need to cope with. We would be best breaking it down. Firstly there are a couple of things to note about the two immediately above. The latter two versions are not often used, but are provided for. In fact, the RFC is ambiguous and suggests that the IP address version of the email should be written as: someone@[123.113.209.32]. However, the RFC also allows domain names to be provided on either side, so we shall use the more commonly used form shown above. Regarding the latter version, only a few email servers actually support this form. However, we shall cover it for completeness. We need to break up the email address into separate parts, and we will concern ourselves with the part after the "@" symbol, first.

Validating an IP Address

This is the simplest and so perhaps is the one to cover first. An email address can either have a domain name or an IP address following the "@" symbol. An IP address consists of a *dotted quad* notation of four 8-bit numbers written in decimal form, separated by dots. There are no trailing zeroes used. Regular expressions are a text pattern matching language, so we cannot test for ranges of numbers and have to specify instead exactly how they appear. As they are repeated, let's deal first with how to match just one of the numbers:

```
(1??\d{1,2}|2[0-4]\d|25[0-5])
```

The first option covers the largest number of possibilities. It defines a lazy optional 1, followed by one or two digits. This allows every number from 0 to 199. A lazy wildcard is chosen, as there are more numbers that don't begin with a 1, than those that do, so it makes sense to attempt to match against those first. Then the alternation character is reached, which defines that we can have 2, followed by any number from 0-4, followed by any number: 200-249. The last group specifies that we can have 25, followed by any number from 0-5. It is then wrapped in a group to allow us to anchor the whole expression by specifying either that it is a whole expression, or that it is surrounded by periods, which is covered now.

Making this part of an IP address is trivial. The expression looks as follows:

```
^((1??\d{1,2}|2[0-4]\d|25[0-5])\.){3}(1??\d{1,2}|2[0-4]\d|25[0-5])$
```

The first thing it does is specify the start of the string, then it adds an extra group bracket as it is going to check for a repetition of the pattern. The pattern is the same as the above, with a period following it. This matches fine. However, if you wanted to pull out the components of the IP address, then you couldn't do it. You would have to remove the repetition to do so. In addition, "\." would have to be contained within a non-capturing group. If this were part of a larger expression, the "^" and "$" would be removed.

This matches an IP address fine, but you may also want to exclude certain addresses like those starting with 10, 127, or 192.168 for private address ranges. It would depend on the nature of the application.

Validating a Domain Name

Everything has become more complicated since Unicode domain names have been allowed. However, the email RFC still doesn't allow these so we shall stick with the traditional definition of how a domain can be described using ASCII. A domain name consists of a dot-separated list of words with the last word being between 2 and 4 characters long. It was often the case that if a two letter country word was used, then there would be at least two parts to the domain name before it – a grouping domain (`.co`, `.ac`, etc.) and a specific domain name before it. However, with the advent of the `.tv` names, this is no longer the case. We could make this very specific and provide for the allowed top-level domains (TLDs), but that would make the regular expression very large and it would be more productive to perform a DNS lookup instead.

Each part of a domain name has certain rules it must follow. It can contain any letter, or number, or hyphen, but it must start with a letter. The exception is that, at any point in the domain name, you can use a #, followed by a number, which represents the ASCII code for that letter, or in Unicode, the 16-bit Unicode value. Knowing this, let's begin to build up our regular expression, firstly with the name part, assuming that we have the `IgnoreCase` option set:

```
([a-z]|#\d+)([a-z0-9-]|#\d+)*([a-z0-9]|#\d+)
```

This breaks the domain into three parts. In all parts there is the option of using the #nn notation, so we shan't mention them there. The RFC doesn't specify how many digits can be contained here, so neither shall we. The first part must only contain an ASCII letter; the second must contain zero or more of a letter, number, or hyphen, and the third must contain either a letter or number. The top-level domain has more restrictions, as shown:

```
[a-z]{2,4}
```

This restricts us to a 2, 3, or 4 letter top-level domain. So, putting it all together, with the periods:

```
^(([a-z]|#\d+?)([a-z0-9-]|#\d+?)*([a-z0-9]|#\d+?)\.)+([a-z]{2,4})$
```

Again, the domain name is anchored at the beginning and end of the string. The first thing is to add an extra group to allow one or more "name." portions, and then anchored a 2-4 letter domain name at the end in its own group. We have also made most of the wildcards lazy. Because much of the pattern is similar, it makes sense to do this as otherwise it would require too much backtracking. However, we have left the second group with a greedy wildcard, it will match as much as it can, up until it reaches a character that does not match. Then it will only backtrack one position to attempt the third group match. This is more resource-efficient than a lazy match is in this case, as it could be constantly going forward to attempt the match. One backtrack per name is an acceptable amount of extra processing.

Validating a Person's Address

Now we can attempt to validate the part before the "@" sign. The RFC specifies that it can contain any ASCII character with a code in the range from 33 to 126. We are assuming that we are matching against ASCII only, and so we can assume that there are only 128 characters that the engine will match against. This being the case, it is simpler to just exclude the required values:

```
[^<>()\[\]\\.,;:@"\x00-\x20\x7F]+
```

Using this we are saying that we allow any number of characters, as long as none of them are those contained within the square brackets. The "[", "]", and "\" characters have to be escaped. However, the RFC allows for other kinds of matches. You can escape any of the previous characters using a "\" character. This means that carriage returns are also permitted in the person's address. However, it is highly unlikely that anyone would use this version of the regular expression, so we shan't use the `SingleLine` option here. However, we do need to allow for the other excluded characters, so we need to add an OR match of:

```
\\.
```

Additionally, there is yet another form that can be used for a mailbox name, and that is a quoted string. This takes the form of any string, including spaces, surrounded by three double quote characters. The string can contain anything except carriage returns, line feeds, double quotes, or backslashes. So the regular expression looks as follows:

```
"""[^\x0A\x0D"\\]+"""
```

You can escape characters in the quoted string though by using backslash. However, as we have decided not to allow carriage returns, the only character we need to escape is "\":

```
"""([^\x0A\x0D"\\]|\\\\)+"""
```

Our full regular expression for the mailbox name would therefore be:

```
^(([^<>()\[\]\\.,;:@"\x00-\x20\x7F]|
\\.)+|("""([^\x0A\x0D"\\]|\\\\)+"""))$
```

This should obviously be all on one line, and the entire string must match.

Validating the Complete Address

Now we have seen all the previous sections, we can build up a regular expression for the entire email address. First, everything up to and including the "@" sign:

```
^(([^<>()\[\]\\.,;:@"\x00-\x20\x7F]|
\\.)+|("""([^\x0A\x0D"\\]|\\\\)+""")))@
```

That was straightforward. Now for the domain or IP address part. First the domain name:

```
^(([^<>()\[\]\\.,;:@"\x00-\x20\x7F]|\\.)+|
("""([^\x0A\x0D"\\]|\\\\)+""")))@(([a-z]|#\d+?)([a-z0-9-]|#\d+?)*
([a-z0-9]|#\d+?)\.)+([a-z]{2,4})
```

This matches the traditional style of email addresses. However, we want to allow for IP addresses as well, and this is quite easily done. If we click the ExplicitCapture option, then add the named groups as indicated below, then it will match the person and the domain name (or IP address):

```
^(?<person>([^<>()\[\]\\.,;:@"\x00-\x20\x7F]|\\.)+|
("""([^\x0A\x0D"\\]|\\\\)+""")))@(?<domain>(([a-z]|#\d+?)
([a-z0-9-]|#\d+?)*([a-z0-9]|#\d+?)\.)+([a-z]{2,4})|((1??\d{1,2}|
2[0-4]\d|25[0-5])\.){3}(1??\d{1,2}|2[0-4]\d|25[0-5]))$
```

This is a rather long expression, but it is provided as part of an enumeration in the code download. This will match against any kind of e-mail address, except those with carriage returns escaped. Test it in the Regular Expression Tester and you should see that it works fine. We have to put the choice between the domain name and the IP address in a group of its own so that either matches to the end of the string.

Analyzing an SMTP Log File

This section contains an example of analyzing a system file. In this example we are going to use regular expressions to extract information from an SMTP log file – to be more precise, from IIS's SMTP log file. For the example to work, the log file's extended properties are:

- ❑ date-time
- ❑ c-ip
- ❑ cs-username
- ❑ cs-method
- ❑ cs-uri-query
- ❑ sc-bytes
- ❑ cs-bytes
- ❑ time-taken

These properties are set from the General tab of the SMTP virtual server properties – from either IIS, or if you have Exchange 2000 installed, then from the exchange manager:

The program allows the user to select a log file and then it displays a list of the SMTP sessions and the actions taken, and highlights in red any potentially dubious sessions (attacks by a hacker, for example):

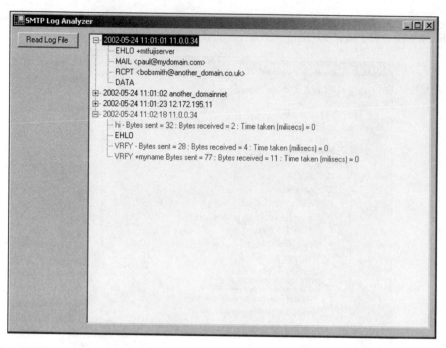

Most SMTP sessions consist of:

```
HELO or EHLO
MAIL
RCPT
DATA
QUIT
```

Therefore, those sessions are not logged in red. Those logged in red are sessions that include an SMTP command other than those, or where the time take or the bytes sent or received are of an unusual size.

Our first task is to analyze the log files ourselves and see how the information is structured; a sample from a log file is shown below:

```
#Software: Microsoft Internet Information Services 5.0
#Version: 1.0
#Date: 2002-05-24 11:01:01
#Fields: date time c-ip cs-username cs-method cs-uri-query sc-bytes
cs-bytes time-taken
2002-05-24 11:01:01 11.0.0.34 mtfujiserver EHLO +mtfujiserver 331 17
170
2002-05-24 11:01:01 11.0.0.34 mtfujiserver MAIL
+FROM:+<paul@mydomain.com> 42 30 40
2002-05-24 11:01:01 11.0.0.34 mtfujiserver RCPT
+TO:+<bobsmith@another_domain.co.uk> 32 30 0
2002-05-24 11:01:01 11.0.0.34 mtfujiserver DATA
```

```
+<000001c20312$8844cc60$0400000a@mtfujiserver> 129 501 370
2002-05-24 11:01:02 - OutboundConnectionResponse -
220+another_domainnet+Mail+Service+ESMTP+(oceanus.uk.another_domain.ne
t) 54 0 781
2002-05-24 11:01:02 another_domainnet OutboundConnectionCommand EHLO
zydec_advser.mydomain.com 4 0 781
2002-05-24 11:01:02 another_domainnet OutboundConnectionResponse -
250-oceanus.uk.another_domain.net+Hello+host113-113-204-18.in-
addr.btopenworld.com+[213.123.214.118] 92 0 821
2002-05-24 11:01:02 another_domainnet OutboundConnectionCommand MAIL
FROM:<paul@mydomain.com> 4 0 821
2002-05-24 11:01:02 another_domainnet OutboundConnectionResponse -
250+<paul@mydomain.com>+is+syntactically+correct 48 0 851
2002-05-24 11:01:02 another_domainnet OutboundConnectionCommand RCPT
TO:<bobsmith@another_domain.co.uk> 4 0 861
2002-05-24 11:01:04 11.0.0.34 mtfujiserver QUIT mtfujiserver 74 4 0
2002-05-24 11:01:23 12.172.195.11 btclick.com EHLO +btclick.com 336 16
30
2002-05-24 11:01:23 12.172.195.11 btclick.com MAIL
+FROM:<paul@mydomain.com> 42 38 0
2002-05-24 11:01:23 12.172.195.11 btclick.com RCPT
+TO:<jobs@mydomain.com> 30 27 0
2002-05-24 11:01:23 12.172.195.11 btclick.com DATA
+<000101c20312$955140a0$0400000a@mtfujiserver> 129 664 311
2002-05-24 11:01:26 12.172.195.11 btclick.com QUIT btclick.com 74 4 0
2002-05-24 11:01:43 another_domainnet OutboundConnectionResponse -
250+<bobsmith@another_domain.co.uk>+verified 34 0 41389
2002-05-24 11:01:43 another_domainnet OutboundConnectionCommand DATA -
4 0 41399
2002-05-24 11:01:43 another_domainnet OutboundConnectionResponse -
354+Enter+message,+ending+with+".".+on+a+line+by+itself 54 0 41419
2002-05-24 11:01:43 another_domainnet OutboundConnectionResponse -
250+OK+id=17BCpT-000G0E-00 26 0 41519
2002-05-24 11:01:43 another_domainnet OutboundConnectionCommand QUIT -
4 0 41529
2002-05-24 11:01:43 another_domainnet OutboundConnectionResponse -
221+oceanus.uk.another_domain.net+closing+connection 43 0 41549
2002-05-24 11:02:18 11.0.0.34 - hi - 32 2 0
2002-05-24 11:02:22 11.0.0.34 - EHLO - 331 4 0
2002-05-24 11:02:26 11.0.0.34 - VRFY - 28 4 0
2002-05-24 11:02:31 11.0.0.34 - VRFY +myname 77 11 0
2002-05-24 11:02:36 11.0.0.34 - QUIT - 77 11 4186
```

The first thing to notice is that each individual command is on a single line. Above, it doesn't look that way, but that is due to the width constraints of a book; each line starts with a date. We can also see that each element of data (date, time, client-ip, and so on) is delimited by a space. Getting the data from an individual line should be quite easy. The tricky part is making sure all the information for each session goes together – it's particularly tricky because the server, as in the log above, can have numerous concurrent sessions. This means that we don't have a nice ordering of the lines into separate sessions; for example, the top of the log starts with a standard SMTP session sending an email:

```
2002-05-24 11:01:01 11.0.0.34 mtfujiserver EHLO +mtfujiserver 331 17
170
2002-05-24 11:01:01 11.0.0.34 mtfujiserver MAIL
+FROM:+<paul@mydomain.com> 42 30 40
2002-05-24 11:01:01 11.0.0.34 mtfujiserver RCPT
+TO:+<bobsmith@another_domain.co.uk> 32 30 0
2002-05-24 11:01:01 11.0.0.34 mtfujiserver DATA
+<000001c20312$8844cc60$0400000a@mtfujiserver> 129 501 370
```

However, instead of a QUIT command line at this point, the log now contains data for
another quite separate concurrent session:

```
2002-05-24 11:01:02 - OutboundConnectionResponse -
220+another_domainnet+Mail+Service+ESMTP+(oceanus.uk.another_domain.ne
t) 54 0 781
```

This continues for a few more lines before the final line from the first session
suddenly appears:

```
2002-05-24 11:01:04 11.0.0.34 mtfujiserver QUIT mtfujiserver 74 4 0
```

This means our regular expression has to match the individual lines and data in a line,
and somehow ensure the lines of a single session are contained within one match.
Now it may well be possible to write such an expression but it would be fiendishly
complex, span a number of lines, and be very difficult to maintain. Sometimes with
regular expressions we need to know when to limit complexity – otherwise we'll end
up with two pages of regular expression so complex that it makes mapping the Human
Genome seem like a trivial task.

Instead, what we'll do is capture each line in a match and within that put each item of
data in its own group. It means we'll have to use code to put the sessions together, but
that will be much easier than using a regex – and almost certainly more efficient:

```
^(?<date>[^ #]+) (?<time>[^ ]+) (?<clientAddress>[^ -]+)
(?<clientName>[^ ]+) (?<method>[^ -]+) (?<uriQuery>[^ ]+)
(?<sentBytes>[\d]+) (?<receivedBytes>[\d]+) (?<timeTaken>[\d]+)
```

The limits of the page's width mean the single regex line has wrapped on to three
lines. We have nine groups in our regular expression, each with a name indicating the
data the group will hold. While it's not necessary to give the groups names, it will
make our code easier to create and understand later on. Note that at the end of the first
two lines there is a space character.

The regex is broken down in the table below. This table shows what happens when it
is matched against an example log line of:

```
2002-05-24 11:01:01 11.0.0.34 mtfujiserver EHLO +mtfujiserver
331 17 170
```

Regular Expression	Description	What it matches
^	We will specify the MultiLine option in our code later on; this means the ^ matches the beginning of each line. Without the option set, it only matches the beginning of the input string.	Start of each new line
(?<date>[^ #]+)	This is a capturing group, named date, whose pattern is one or more space or hash (#) characters. The "#" character denotes a remarks line in the log so our code will ignore those. The space is the delimiter between log data fields. As it's a named group, it will always capture the group even if ExplicitCapture option is set.	2002-05-24
(?<time>[^]+)	This group, named time, matches one or more characters that are not a space.	11:01:01
(?<clientAddress>[^ -]+)	The clientAddress group matches one or more characters that are not a space or "-". When there is no data, IIS inserts a "-". We are not interested in logs with no client address as this indicates information received, rather than an SMTP command.	11.0.0.34
(?<clientName>[^]+)	The clientName group matches one or more characters that are not spaces.	mtfujiserver
(?<method>[^ -]+)	The method group matches one or more characters that are not a space or a "-" sign.	EHLO
(?<uriQuery>[^]+)	The uriQuery group matches one or more characters that are not a space.	+mtfujiserver
(?<sentBytes>[\d]+)	The sentBytes group matches one or more digits.	331

Table continued on following page

Regular Expression	Description	What it matches
`(?<receivedBytes>[\d]+)`	The `receivedBytes` group matches one or more digits.	17
`(?<timeTaken>[\d]+)`	The `timeTaken` group matches one or more digits.	170

Now we have seen the regex, lets create a new Windows project that will use the regular expression to analyze the log.

Open Visual Studio .NET and create a new Windows project called `SMTPLogAnalyze`. Add a button, an open file dialog box, and a tree view control as shown below. The button is named `cmdReadLogFile`, and the open file dialog box and tree view control have their default names of `OpenFileDialog1` and `TreeView1`:

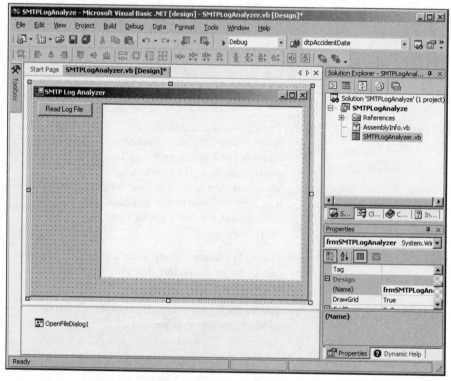

At the start, the code looks as follows:

```
Imports System.Collections
Imports System.IO
Imports System.Text.RegularExpressions
```

```
Public Class frmSMTPLogAnalyzer
   Inherits System.Windows.Forms.Form
```

Let's start examining the code proper by adding the code to the
cmdReadLogFile.Click event:

```
Private Sub cmdReadLogFile_Click(ByVal sender As System.Object, _
                        ByVal e As System.EventArgs) _
          Handles cmdReadLogFile.Click
   OpenFileDialog1.ShowDialog()
End Sub
```

This shows the open file dialog to allow the user to pick the log file to be analyzed.

Now we need to add the code for the OpenFileDialog1.FileOk event; this code
reads in the file and analyzes it. There's a lot of code so we'll examine it in stages.
We'll start with the code that reads in the log file:

```
Private Sub OpenFileDialog1_FileOk( _
              ByVal sender As System.Object, _
              ByVal e As System.ComponentModel.CancelEventArgs) _
              Handles OpenFileDialog1.FileOk
   Try
      ' Clear any pre-existing details
      TreeView1.Nodes.Clear()
      ' Create a hashtable object to hold details of sessions
      Dim ipIndex As New Hashtable()

      ' Read in the file to be analyzed
      ' We need to make a temporary copy of the file
      ' because IIS locks the latest log entry
      Dim logFileText As String
      Dim filePath As String = OpenFileDialog1.FileName
      Dim tempFile As String = Path.GetTempFileName()
      File.Copy(filePath, tempFile, True)
      Dim streamReaderRegex As StreamReader = _
         File.OpenText(tempFile)
      logFileText = streamReaderRegex.ReadToEnd()
      streamReaderRegex.Close()
      File.Delete(tempFile)
```

The code, placed inside the start of a Try...Catch statement, first clears TreeView1,
and then creates a new Hashtable object. This object will be used later to store
details of SMTP sessions and where they are located in the TreeView's nodes.

Next, we obtain the file name of the log file the user selected and we get a temporary
file name. We can't read in the IIS log file directly because if it's today's log file and IIS
is using it, then it will be locked – any attempts to open it will cause an error. The
easiest way around this, and the one chosen here, is to make a temporary copy of the
log file, read in its information, and then delete the temporary file.

We use the `File` object's shared `Copy()` method to do the copying, and we then open the temporary file using `StreamReader` and `File`. Using the `StreamReader`, we read to the end of the file, close it, and finally delete the temporary file.

We now need to create our regular expression to make the matches on each log line and capture its data in specific named groups:

```
' Get the individual log lines and data within them
Dim logLinesRegex As New Regex("^(?<date>[^ #]+) " & _
    "(?<time>[^ ]+) (?<clientAddress>[^ -]+) " & _
    "(?<clientName>[^ ]+) (?<method>[^ -]+) (?<uriQuery>[^ ]+) " & _
    "(?<sentBytes>[\d]+) (?<receivedBytes>[\d]+) " & _
    "(?<timeTaken>[\d]+)", RegexOptions.MultiLine)
Dim getEmailAddressDataRegex As New Regex("<[^>]+>", _
    RegexOptions.Compiled)
Dim logLineMatches As MatchCollection
Dim logLineMatch As Match
logLineMatches = logLinesRegex.Matches(logFileText)
Dim clientAddress As String
Dim sessionString As String
Dim method As String
Dim uriQuery As String
Dim logNode As TreeNode
Dim suspectSession As Boolean = False
```

We now have our log data, with each match containing one line from the log and each group within that match containing the data we need. What we have to do now is loop through each of these matches, extract the data, and append it to the `TreeView` control's nodes. However, this is made trickier because we want to make sure all the lines from a single session are placed under the correct node for that session. Because there can be concurrent SMTP sessions, and the lines in a log for a single session run sequentially, there may be other sessions in between. Our code needs to take account of this and does so by keeping track of each session, via the client IP address, in the `ipIndex` `Hashtable` object created earlier. Each time a new session is found, the code makes a note of the index of the node in the `TreeView` control's `Nodes` property. Then until the session ends in the log we keep adding new log lines to the same node.

Turning to the code, at the top we have the `For Each` loop that will loop through each match in the `logLinesMatches MatchCollection` object:

```
' Go through each line matched in the log
For Each logLineMatch In logLineMatches
    ' Obtain the data in uriQuery, method and clientaddress
    uriQuery = logLineMatch.Groups("uriQuery").Value
    method = logLineMatch.Groups("method").Value
    clientAddress = logLineMatch.Groups("clientAddress").Value
```

At the top of the loop, we obtain the values for the `uriQuery`, `method`, and `clientAddress` for that log line. All these details are in groups within the regex match; as we gave the groups names we can easily extract them by name, rather than having to remember which order the groups are in. This is something that is easy to get wrong when there are as many groups as there are here.

Next comes the code that attempts to pull out the abnormal SMTP sessions. It does this based on whether the SMTP session contains commands that are less common, or if the session was unusually large or took a particularly long time. The checks are fairly simple and could easily be made more sophisticated if the program was developed further:

```
' If the SMTP method is not mail, rcpt, helo,ehlo or data
' or if the time taken is more than a minute
' or the sent bytes are more than a 1mb
' or the received bytes more than a 1mb
' then this might be a suspect line
If method <> "MAIL" And _
    method <> "RCPT" And _
    method <> "HELO" And _
    method <> "EHLO" And _
    method <> "DATA" Or _
    (logLineMatch.Groups("timeTaken").Value > 60000 Or _
    logLineMatch.Groups("sentBytes").Value > 1048576 Or _
    logLineMatch.Groups("receivedBytes").Value > 1048576) Then
    uriQuery = uriQuery & _
        " Bytes sent = " & _
        logLineMatch.Groups("sentBytes").Value
    uriQuery = uriQuery & _
        " : Bytes received = " & _
        logLineMatch.Groups("receivedBytes").Value
    uriQuery = uriQuery & _
        " : Time taken (millisecs) = " & _
        logLineMatch.Groups("timeTaken").Value
    suspectSession = True
Else
    suspectSession = False
End If
```

If the session is potentially suspect, then we add additional information to the uriQuery data to help the user work out why the session was dubious. We also then set the Boolean variable suspectSession to True. Later the code will check this variable and highlight the suspect session in red.

If the line contains either a MAIL (send mail from) or RCPT (send mail to recipient) command then it would be useful to extract the e-mail address involved and display it in the analysis. This is the task for the next few lines:

```
' If the mail or rcpt methods are used then
' extract the e-mail address the mail is
' being sent to or from
If method = "MAIL" Or method = "RCPT" Then
    uriQuery = getEmailAddressDataRegex.Match(uriQuery).Value
ElseIf uriQuery = "-" Or method = "DATA" Then
    uriQuery = ""
End If
```

We have the data we need, so it is now time to add the new node to the `TreeView`. There are three possibilities for the new node:

- ❏ It's a new session

- ❏ It's the `QUIT` command of an existing session

- ❏ Its another line in an existing session

In the following `If` statement the code checks to see if there is an existing session node. If there is, then it checks for the SMTP `QUIT` command. If it is the `QUIT` command, then it doesn't need to add the log line, as all sessions must have a `QUIT` command – even if the session has timed out. Instead, we simply remove the IP address from the `ipIndex`, which contains all the open sessions so far in the log. If it wasn't a `QUIT` command then the code needs to discover the index of the top-level node for that session, then add a new node under it with the latest log line and its details. Note if the `suspectSession` variable is `True`, then we must highlight the current log line in red and the line for the session node as well. The code to do all this is shown below:

```
If ipIndex.ContainsKey(clientAddress) Then
    ' If QUIT method found, then current session has ended for
    ' that IP address and we need to remove details of its
    ' node from the session index
    If method = "QUIT" Then
        ipIndex.Remove(clientAddress)
    Else
        ' only add the line if the method was not empty
        ' IIS indicates no data with a minus sign
        If method <> "-" Then
            TreeView1.Nodes(ipIndex(clientAddress)).Nodes.Add( _
                        method & " " & uriQuery)
            ' If this is one of the lines noted as being suspect then
            ' make the line and the session line appear in red
            ' and add extra data for info
            If suspectSession Then
                TreeView1.Nodes(ipIndex( _
                            clientAddress)).LastNode.ForeColor _
                = Color.Red
                TreeView1.Nodes(ipIndex(clientAddress)).ForeColor _
                = Color.Red
            End If
        End If
    End If
Else
```

The other alternative is that this is a new session, in which case we need to add the session's IP address to the `ipIndex`, then add a new top-level node to the `TreeView` control, and then add to this the node details of the log line:

```
        ' This is a new session - create a new top level node
        ' and record session's location in tree
        logNode = New TreeNode()
        logNode.Text = logLineMatch.Groups("date").Value & " " & _
        logLineMatch.Groups("time").Value & " " & clientAddress
        logNode.Nodes.Add(method & " " & uriQuery)
        TreeView1.Nodes.Add(logNode)
        ipIndex.Add(clientAddress, TreeView1.GetNodeCount(False) - 1)

        ' Display suspect sessions in red
        If suspectSession Then
          TreeView1.Nodes(ipIndex(clientAddress)).LastNode.ForeColor _
            = Color.Red
          TreeView1.Nodes(ipIndex(clientAddress)).ForeColor _
            = Color.Red
        End If
      End If
    Next
    Catch ex As Exception
      MessageBox.Show("Error occurred - " & ex.Message)
    End Try
  End Sub
```

We also have the end of our For Each loop and the Try...Catch statement. This can be used to analyze all of your SMTP log files.

HTML Tags

In this section, you'll see how to match HTML tags. You'll start by creating a regular expression that will spot if a string contains any HTML open or close tags. This can be useful when obtaining input from a user in a web page if we want to avoid them inserting their own HTML tags, such as for images, links, or JavaScript. We may want to take it further and allow some HTML tags, for example formatting tags, but for now we'll just look for any kind of tag.

The second regular expression we'll look at is not for data validation, but instead for splitting an HTML file into its component tags and attributes. We'll be creating an example that creates a tree view of a web page's HTML.

As always with creating regular expressions, the first task is to work out what patterns and variations of patterns we will need to match; for HTML it is those shown below:

```
<tag>Text to retain</tag>
<tag>
<tag tagattribute1="somevalue">
<tag tagattribute1="somevalue" tagattribute2="somevalue">
<tag tagattribute1="somevalue">Text to retain</tag>
<tag tagattribute1=somevalue>Text to retain</tag>
<tag tagattribute1='somevalue' tagattribute2='somevalue'>
  Text to retain
</tag>
<tag></tag>
<tag attribute1="somevalue" attribute2="somevalue></tag>
```

Let's start by looking at how to match these tags inside an input string.

Removing HTML from User Input

The regular expression that will match either a start or end HTML tag is this:

```
(<[a-z]+[^>]*>)|(</[a-z\d]+>)
```

In fact, it's two regular expressions with the alternation character allowing the pattern to match one or the other pattern. The pattern on the left:

```
(<[a-z]+[^>]*>)
```

matches an HTML start tag. It looks for a "<" followed by one or more characters from a to z, then zero or more of any character so long as it's not the close tag character ">". You might be wondering why we can't have the following expression:

```
(<[^>]+>)
```

This will match any HTML start tag, however, it will also match where a less than character is used and there is no HTML, for example:

```
The value was < 22,000 but always > 10,000
```

This would provide a false match. Often with regular expressions, it's as much about defining what you don't want to match, as you do want to match. Insisting the "<" should be followed by a to z reduces the chances of a false match.

The part of the regular expression that matches the close tag is this:

```
(</[a-z\d]+>)
```

Close tags don't have attributes, so our regular expression can be simplified. It matches a "<" followed by a "/" and then a through z, or a number, occurring one or more times. Finally it matches the ">" character.

We can use the regular expression to see if there is a match, meaning that the user has inserted HTML in the input:

```
If Regex.IsMatch(userInputString, "(<[a-z]+[^>]*>)|(</[a-z\d]+>)", _
                                  RegexOptions.IgnoreCase Or _
                                  RegexOptions.ExplicitCapture) Then
    MessageBox.Show("HTML FOUND")
Else
    MessageBox.Show("HTML NOT FOUND")
End If
```

We could also use the `Replace()` method to simply remove all the offending tags and just leave the plain text.

Extracting All HTML Tags

In this section, we look at how regular expressions can help extract quite detailed information from an HTML page. In the example, we'll be building a `TreeView` control that gives a detailed overview of a web page and its tags. However, the regex itself could prove useful in any situation where we would want to analyze specific components of an HTML page.

The regular expression to extract HTML tags and their attributes is far more complex:

```
<(?<outertag>[a-z]+[\d]?)(?<attributes> [^>]*)*>
(?<innerhtml>(<(?<innertag>[a-z]+[\d]?)[^>]*>.*?</\k<innertag>>|
<[a-z]+[\d]?[^>]*>|(?>[^<]*))*(?=</\k<outertag>>))?
```

The aim of the regular expression is to split each tag and its content into a single match but within that match there is one group that matches the HTML tag type and a second one that matches the attributes of that tag, so if our HTML was this:

```
<p>
   Welcome to Wrox
</p>
<img src="ThePlane.jpg" width="149">
<hr>
<p align="left">my text</p>
```

the following matches and groups would be created:

Full Match	Group 1: outertag	Group 2: attributes	Group 3: innerhtml
`<p>` Welcome to Wrox	`p`		Welcome to Wrox
`<img src="ThePlane.jpg" width="149" height="323">`	`img`	`src="ThePlane.jpg" width="149" height="323"`	
`<hr>`	`hr`		
`<p align="left">my text`	`p`	`align="left"`	my text

One of the biggest problems we have to deal with is that of nested tags, for example:

```
<p>
    <p>some text<img src="myimg.jpg">
    <a href="somepage.htm">click here</a></p>
</p>
```

The problem we have is forcing the regular expression to work out which is the correct closing tag. In this case the closing tag for the first <p> is actually the very last </p> tag. We will need to work out a way of dealing with this. We'll see that the technique we use is to *consume* the HTML inside the outer tag; that way the regular expression engine has no choice but to match the last </p> tag as well.

We'll need to set the following options for the regular expression to work:

❏   IgnoreCase

❏   ExplicitCapture

❏   SingleLine

We are not concerned about the case of the HTML, hence the IgnoreCase option. In addition, we are only concerned with the contents of four of the groups, so for convenience and efficiency we set the ExplicitCapture option so only the named groups will have their matches stored. The SingleLine option allows the "." character to match newlines, as the HTML for one tag may well be on multiple lines.

The regular expression is very large, so let's split it down, firstly taking the regular expression pattern that matches the first opening tag:

```
<(?<outertag>[a-z]+[\d]?)(?<attributes> [^>]*)*>
```

This matches tags like <p> and <img src="ThePlane.jpg" width="149">

First, it matches the "<" of an HTML tag, then it attempts to match a group named outertag. This group will match the tag type, such as h1, p, and img. We'll be using this group for the results initially, and to match the closing tag type. Next is the attributes group; this matches any HTML tag attributes, for example src="myfile.jpg". Again, by putting it in its own group, it can easily be accessed in Visual Basic .NET code from the match results.

Some singleton tags only have an open tag, for example the <img> tag, and so the pattern matched so far is all that's needed. The majority of elements have a close tag, however, so we need the remainder of the pattern:

```
(?<innerhtml>(<(?<innertag>[a-z]+[\d]?)[^>]*>.*?</\k<innertag>>|
<[a-z]+[\d]? [^>]*>|(?>[^<]*))*(?=</\k<outertag>>))?
```

This will be analyzed shortly, but it matches any HTML open and close pairs, or any single HTML tag, or any plain text followed by a close tag, matching the outer open tag we matched above.

The outer group is the `innerHTML` group; this matches all the content inside the outer open tag and final close tag, so if our HTML were the following:

```
<p>
  <p>some text<img src="myimg.jpg">
  <a href="somepage.htm">click here</a></p>
</p>
```

Then the `innerhtml` group would match this:

```
<p>some text<img src="myimg.jpg">
<a href="somepage.htm">click here</a></p>
```

The `innerhtml` group will only perform a match if the outer close tag exists, although the outer close tag is not captured either in the group or in the match itself.

Let's break the group down. Inside the `innerhtml` group is another non-capturing group, non-capturing because we use the `ExplicitCapture` option. Inside this group are three separate patterns, each split by the "|" character, which is the regular expressions equivalent of the logical `OR`. The three groups and what they match are shown below:

Regular expression	Description	Example match
`(?<innertag>[a-z]+[\d]?)` `[^>]*>.*?</\k<innertag>>`	This matches an open HTML tag, the contents between it, and its close tag, as well as this closing HTML tag	`<p align=left>` `some text` `</p>`
`<[a-z]+[\d]?[^>]*>`	This matches a single HTML open tag with no closing tag	`<img>`
`(?>[^<]*)`	This matches anything other than HTML tags	`Some plain text`

Remember that the "|" will first try to match the expression on the left, and then, if there is no match for that, the expression on the right. We use this to our advantage because it means our pattern will first look for an HTML open tag with a subsequent close tag, such as `<p>some text</p>`. If there is no match for that, then it will look for a single HTML tag with no matching close tag, such as `<img src="image.gif">`. If there is still no match, then it simply looks for anything, matching plain text or newline characters.

Lets start with the first regular expression in the table:

```
(?<innertag>[a-z]+[\d]?)[^>]*>.*?</\k<innertag>>
```

This is very similar to the regular expression that matches the outer HTML tag. First, we create an explicitly capturing group called `innertag`; `innertag` will capture the start tag, we'll use it later in the pattern to match a close tag of the same type.

Then, as we have seen before, we match one or more letters from a through z, followed by an optional number, so that tags like `h1` and `h2` are matched. Following the `innertag` group, we have a non-greedy match, that will look for zero or more characters of any type, including the newline character, because we have the `SingleLine` option set. We're using a non-greedy version of "*" because we want to limit what the regular expression engine matches. There's a danger it will match everything it can, including things we don't want it to, such as the rest of the string, when there are more HTML tags to match separately.

Finally, at the end we match a close tag of the same type as the open tag:

```
</\k<innertag>>
```

The next item in the table, described here, is the regular expression that matches a single open tag:

```
<[a-z]+[\d]?[^>]*>
```

This is almost identical to the pattern for the `innertag` group we saw above, except we don't need to capture any further groups, as there is no close tag to match.

The final regular expression in the table is as follow:

```
(?>[^<]*)
```

This simply matches anything the previous matches didn't match, except a "<" character. This will capture any text in between the tags.

We've looked at the `innerhtml` group; all that's left is this:

```
)*(?=</\k<outertag>>))?
```

After the `innerhtml` group is an "*", which will tell the regex engine to match the contents of the group zero or more times. So if our HTML was this:

```
<p>
  <h1><img>some text<p>more text</p></h1>
</p>
```

the first <p> tag is matched by the outer tag matching pattern, and all of the innerhtml; the <h1> tag, the <img> tag, the text, the inner <p> tag, and its text, will all be matched by the innerhtml group. Without the "*", only the <h1> tag would be matched.

At the very end of our regular expression is the pattern to match the close tag of the same type as the outer HTML tag:

```
<(?<outertag>[a-z]+[\d]?)(?<attributes> [^>]*)*>
(?<innerhtml>(<(?<innertag>[a-z]+[\d]?)[^>]*>.*?</\k<innertag>>|
<[a-z]+[\d]?[^>]*>|(?>[^<]*))*(?=</\k<outertag>>))?
```

In the next section, we turn this regular expression into a useful example of Visual Basic .NET code.

HTML Extraction Example

We're going to create a new application in .NET so that we can use some of these new concepts just covered. We'll be loading an HTML page and then using the regular expression above to split the HTML up into its individual tags and display the results in a TreeView.

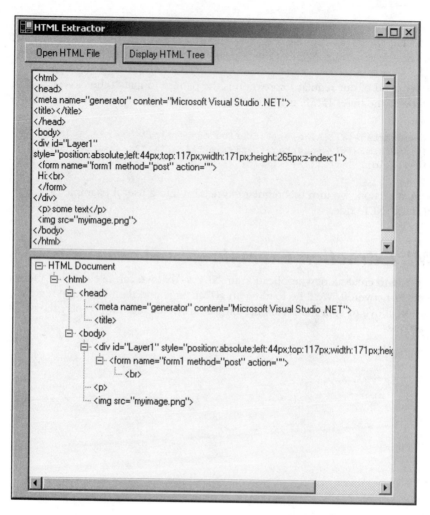

Start up Visual Studio .NET and start a new Windows application called HTMLExtractor. We need to create a form with the controls as shown overleaf:

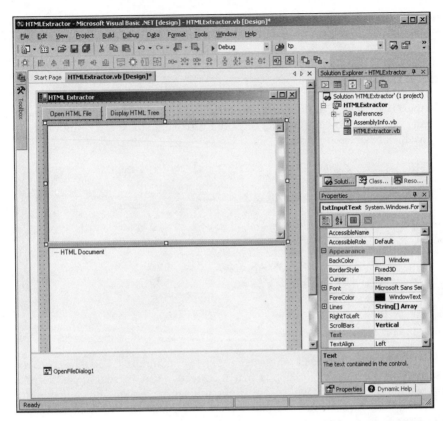

The relevant properties for the individual controls are shown in the table below:

Control Type	Properties
Button	Name = cmdOpenHTML
	Text = Open HTML File
Button	Name = cmdDisplayHTML
	Text = Display HTML Tree
Form	Name = frmHTMLExtractor
OpenFileDialog	Name=OpenFileDialog1
	Filter = Web Pages|*.htm;*.html;
TextBox	Name=txtInputText
	MultiLine= True
	ScrollBars = Vertical
TreeView	Name = HTMLTreeView

Firstly, at the top of the form class we need to inform the compiler that we'll be using the `System.Text.RegularExpressions`, and `System.IO` namespaces:

```
Imports System.Text.RegularExpressions
Imports System.IO
```

Within the `frmHTMLExtractor` class, we now need to declare two variables; the first containing our `Regex` object, and the second a variable that keeps a count of how many matches have been made:

```
Public Class frmHTMLExtractor
    ...
    Private extractHTMLRegex As _
        New Regex("<(?<outertag>[a-z]+[\d]?)(?<attributes> [^>]*)*>" & _
            "(?<innerhtml>(<(?<innertag>[a-z]+[\d]?)[^>]" & _
            "*>.*?</\k<innertag>>|<[a-z]+[\d]?[^>]*>|" & _
            "(?>[^<]*))*(?=</\k<outertag>>))?", _
        RegexOptions.IgnoreCase Or _
        RegexOptions.Compiled Or _
        RegexOptions.ExplicitCapture Or _
        RegexOptions.SingleLine)

    Private MatchesMade As Integer
```

We have set the three options `IgnoreCase`, `ExplicitCapture`, and `SingleLine` necessary for the regular expression to match correctly. Also, by setting the `Compiled` option, we tell the regex engine to convert the regular expression into something more approaching how the computer uses the pattern, as opposed to the more 'human friendly' syntax. If you remove the `Compiled` option, you'll see a noticeable increase (about 50%) in the time taken to analyze a web page.

Let's now add the code to read in an HTML file; first the button-click code:

```
Private Sub cmdOpenHTML_Click(ByVal sender As System.Object, _
                            ByVal e As System.EventArgs) _
            Handles cmdOpenHTML.Click
    OpenFileDialog1.ShowDialog()
End Sub
```

Using the `OpenFileDialog1.ShowDialog()` method, the code obtains the name of the HTML file to be analyzed. Now the code for the `OpenFileDialog1.FileOk` event:

```
Private Sub OpenFileDialog1_FileOk(ByVal sender As System.Object, _
            ByVal e As System.ComponentModel.CancelEventArgs) _
            Handles OpenFileDialog1.FileOk
    Dim filePath As String = OpenFileDialog1.FileName
    Dim streamReaderRegex As StreamReader = File.OpenText(filePath)
    Me.txtInputText.Text = streamReaderRegex.ReadToEnd()
    streamReaderRegex.Close()
End Sub
```

This uses the `System.IO.StreamReader` class to read in the selected file and sets the `Text` property of the `txtInputText` box to the contents of the file. Next, we need to add code to the `cmdDisplayHTML` button's click event; this event starts the matching and tree creation:

```
Private Sub cmdDisplayHTML_Click(ByVal sender As System.Object, _
                        ByVal e As System.EventArgs) _
                        Handles cmdDisplayHTML.Click
   MatchesMade = 0
   HTMLTreeView.Nodes.Clear()
   HTMLTreeView.Nodes.Add(populateTagNode(Me.txtInputText.Text, _
    "HTML Document"))
   HTMLTreeView.ExpandAll()
   MessageBox.Show("Completed " & MatchesMade & " matches")
End Sub
```

We reset the `MatchesMade` variable, which counts how many HTML tags have been found, and then clear the `TreeView` control ready for the new HTML. We then add a new tree node to the tree, a value that is returned by the `populateTagNode()` method, which is shown below:

```
Private Function populateTagNode(ByVal inputString As String, _
                        ByVal titleText As String) _
                As TreeNode
  Try
    Dim matchesFound As MatchCollection
    Dim matchMade As Match
    Dim htmlTagNode As TreeNode
    Dim htmlSubTagNode As TreeNode
    Dim tag As String
    matchesFound = extractHTMLRegex.Matches(inputString)

    htmlTagNode = New TreeNode()
    htmlTagNode.Text = titleText
    For Each matchMade In matchesFound
      MatchesMade += 1
      tag = "<" & matchMade.Groups(1).Value() & _
        matchMade.Groups(2).Value() & ">"
      htmlSubTagNode = _
        populateTagNode(matchMade.Groups(3).Value, tag)
      htmlTagNode.Nodes.Add(htmlSubTagNode)
    Next
    Return htmlTagNode
  Catch ex As ArgumentException
    MessageBox.Show("The following error occurred " _
      & ControlChars.CrLf & ex.Message)
  End Try
  End Function
End Class
```

The method is a recursive one; it keeps extracting nested HTML tags by obtaining the outer tags, and then keeps calling itself to obtain the inner tags. The easiest way to understand the code is with an example:

```
<html>
<body>
  <p>some text</p>
  <img src="myimage.png">
</body>
</html>
```

When the above HTML is matched there will be only one match, the whole HTML. However in the first group will be the `<html>` tag, the second its attributes, if it had any, and the third group will contain the entire HTML between the opening and closing `<html>` tags. The function creates a `TreeNode` with the title of `html`.

Next, the method calls itself, but this time passing not the whole HTML input string, but only the HTML in the third group – the HTML between the outer start and close tags. This will be split, and this time there is again just one match, the body tag. Again, a `TreeNode` is created and the `populateTagNode()` method is called again, but with just the HTML inside the `<body>` tag. This time there are two matches, the `<p>` tag, and the `<img>` tag. If the nesting were deeper, then the `populateTagNode()` method would be called repeatedly until the entire HTML has been extracted, and a node created for each tag. The application is currently very simple, but it could be expanded for other uses. For example, it could check for missing close tags, or it could be used for displaying poorly formatted HTML.

Summary

In this chapter, we have used all the knowledge gained in the previous two chapters and put it into practice. You have seen a range of regular expressions, from simple ones for data validation, to more complex ones for validating email addresses, to multi-line expressions that can analyze log files or an HTML page.

You've seen that the way to approach regular expressions is to first look at the data against which we are planning to match. Often when you look at some data, you can instantly spot the pattern; for example, you can guess what person@somedomain.com is without much further instruction. With regexes, you need to replicate how you spot the pattern by working out how you see it, and then by working out what information you use to inform how you then recognize it. Having worked this out, you then need to work out all of the combinations of valid patterns, and importantly, which patterns you don't want to match. We've seen that if we do this preparation, and then construct the regular expression in stages, they are not as difficult as they might first appear.

Throughout the entire book, you have learned both how text is stored, and how various tools can be used to assist in the construction, matching, appending, and replacing of strings. You should now be knowledgeable enough to manipulate text confidently in all your applications. The following appendices provide a quick reference to the methods of the `String` and `StringBuilder` classes, as well as for the various characters used in regex patterns. In the code download for this book, much of the code used throughout this book has been wrapped in an assembly and namespace that you can use for your applications. We hope you find this book useful in your future projects.

VB.NET

Text Manipulation

Handbook

Appendix A

The String Class

This appendix contains all the methods, properties, and constructors of the String class. You can find more details in Chapter 2.

Constructors

Here you can see the various overloads for the construction of a new String object instance:

Constructor	Description
String(Char charArray())	Creates a new string with the contents of a character array charArray.
String(Char x, Integer count)	Creates a new string consisting of the specified character x repeated count number of times.

String(Char charArray(),
       Integer pos,
       Integer count)
	Creates a new string consisting of a sub string defined within character string charArray, defined by starting position pos and count number of characters.

Properties

Below are the properties for this class:

Property	Description
String.Empty	Read-only shared constant representing the empty string.
Chars(Integer index)	Returns the character within the string at position index.
Length	Returns the number of characters in the string.

Methods

This table contains all the methods and overloads of these methods for the String class. The table also indicates whether the method is an instance method, or Shared:

Method	Access Level	Description
Clone()	Instance	Returns a reference to the String object. This is counter to how Clone() is normally implemented on objects, but is appropriate as System.String is immutable and so doesn't need a copy made.
Compare(String str1, String str2)	Shared	Performs a case-sensitive comparison of the two given strings according to the current culture.
Compare(String str1, String str2, Boolean ignoreCase)	Shared	Performs a comparison of the two given strings according to the current culture. If ignoreCase is True, a case-insensitive comparison is performed.
Compare(String str1, String str2, Boolean ignoreCase, CultureInfo culture)	Shared	Performs a comparison of the two given strings according to the provided culture settings. If ignoreCase is true, a case-insensitive comparison is performed.

Method	Access Level	Description

Compare(String str1,
        Integer index1,
        String str2,
        Integer index2,
        Integer length)
	Shared	Performs a case-sensitive comparison of two sub-strings defined by the given parameters.

Compare(String str1,
        Integer index1,
        String str2,
        Integer index2,
        Integer length,
        Boolean ignoreCase)
	Shared	Performs a comparison of two sub-strings defined by the given parameters. If ignoreCase is True, a case-insensitive comparison is performed.

Compare(String str1,
        Integer index1,
        String str2,
        Integer index2,
        Integer length,
        Boolean ignoreCase,
        CultureInfo culture)
	Shared	Performs a comparison of two sub-strings defined by the given parameters and according to the provided culture settings. If ignoreCase is True, a case-insensitive comparison is performed.

CompareOrdinal(String str1, String str2)	Shared	Performs a comparison of the two given strings without regard to their cultures.

CompareOrdinal(String str1,
   Integer index1,
   String str2,
   Integer index2,
   Integer length)
	Shared	Compares the two given sub-strings without regard to their cultures.

CompareTo(Object obj)	Instance	Performs a case-sensitive, culturally aware comparison of the given object with the instance string.
CompareTo(String str)	Instance	Performs a case-sensitive, culturally aware comparison of the given string with the instance string.

Table continued on following page

Method	Access Level	Description
`Concat(Object obj)`	Shared	Creates a string representation of the given object.
`Concat(ParamArray objects())`	Shared	Creates a string based on the concatenation of the objects in the given array.
`Concat(ParamArray strings())`	Shared	Creates a string based on the concatenation of the strings in the given array.
`Concat(Object obj1, Object obj2)`	Shared	Creates a string based on the concatenation of the two given objects.
`Concat(String str1, String str2)`	Shared	Creates a string based on the concatenation of the two given strings.
`Concat(Object obj1, Object obj2, Object obj3)`	Shared	Creates a string based on the concatenation of the three given objects.
`Concat(String str1, String str2, String str3)`	Shared	Creates a string based on the concatenation of the three given strings.
`Concat(String str1, String str2, String str3, String str4)`	Shared	Creates a string based on the concatenation of the four given strings.
`Copy(String str)`	Shared	Returns a new string with the same value as the given string.
`CopyTo(Integer sourceIndex, Char dest(), Integer destIndex, Integer count)`	Instance	Copies a sub-string from the instance string to the given destination string.
`EndsWith(String str)`	Instance	Returns `True` if the instance string ends with the given string.
`Equals(String str)`	Instance	Returns `True` if the instance string has the same value as the given object.

Method	Access Level	Description
Equals(String str1, String str2)	Shared	Returns True if the two provided strings have the same value.
Format(String format, Object arg)	Shared	Returns a string consisting of the format specification replaced by the given argument.
Format(String format, ParamArray args())	Instance	Returns a string consisting of the format specification replaced by the argument array.
Format(IFormatProvider provider, String format, ParamArray args())	Instance	Returns a string consisting of the format specification replaced by the argument array according to the given format provider.
Format(String format, Object arg1, Object arg2)	Instance	Returns a string consisting of the format specification replaced by the given two arguments.
Format(String format, Object arg1, Object arg2, Object arg3)	Shared	Returns a string consisting of the format specification replaced by the given three arguments.
GetEnumerator()	Instance	Returns an object that can be used to iterate through the characters in the string.
GetHashCode()	Instance	Returns the unique hash code for the string instance.
GetType()	Instance	Returns the type of the string instance.
GetTypeCode()	Instance	Returns the type code for the string class.
IndexOf(Char x)	Instance	Returns the index of the first occurrence of the given character.
IndexOf(String str)	Instance	Returns the index of the first occurrence of the given string.

Table continued on following page

Method	Access Level	Description
IndexOf(Char x, Integer startPos)	Instance	Returns the index of the first occurrence of the given character starting at the given position.
IndexOf(String str, Integer startPos)	Instance	Returns the index of the first occurrence of the given string starting at the given position.

IndexOf(Char x,
    Integer startPos,
    Integer count)
	Instance	Returns the index of the first occurrence of the given character starting at the given position and searching for count characters.

IndexOf(String str,
    Integer startPos,
    Integer count)
	Instance	Returns the index of the first occurrence of the given string starting at the given position and searching for count characters.

IndexOfAny(Char chars())	Instance	Returns the index of the first occurrence of any character in the given array.
IndexOfAny(Char chars(), Integer startPos)	Instance	Returns the index of the first occurrence of any character in the given array starting at the given position.

IndexOfAny(Char chars(),
    Integer startPos,
    Integer count)
	Instance	Returns the index of the first occurrence of any character in the given array starting at the given position and searching for count characters.

Insert(Integer startPos, String str)	Instance	Inserts the given string into the instance string at the given position.
Intern(String str)	Instance	Returns a reference to the given string. If the string is not interned, this method will intern it.
IsInterned(String str)	Instance	Returns a reference to the given string if it is in the intern pool. Otherwise Nothing.

Method	Access Level	Description
`Join(String separator,` `        String arrStr())`	Instance	Returns a string consisting of the strings in the given array concatenated together and with the given separator between each element.

`Join(String separator,`
`        String arrStr(),`
`        Integer startIndex,`
`        Integer count)`
	Instance	Returns a string consisting of the strings in the given array concatenated together and with the given separator between each element. Only a number of count array elements are used and first string to use is startIndex.

`LastIndexOf(Char x)`	Instance	Returns the index of the last occurrence of the given character.
`LastIndexOf(String str)`	Instance	Returns the index of the last occurrence of the given string.
`LastIndexOf(Char x,` `    Integer startPos)`	Instance	Returns the index of the last occurrence of the given character starting at the given position.
`LastIndexOf(String str,` `    Integer startPos)`	Instance	Returns the index of the last occurrence of the given string starting at the given position.

`LastIndexOf(Char x,`
`        Integer startPos,`
`    Integer count)`
	Instance	Returns the index of the last occurrence of the given character starting at the given position and searching for count characters.

`LastIndexOf(String str,`
`        Integer startPos,`
`    Integer count)`
	Instance	Returns the index of the last occurrence of the given string starting at the given position and searching for count characters.

`LastIndexOfAny(Char chars())`	Instance	Returns the index of the last occurrence of any character in the given array.

`LastIndexOfAny(Char`
`            chars(),`
`        Integer`
`            startPos)`
	Instance	Returns the index of the last occurrence of any character in the given array starting at the given position.

Table continued on following page

Method	Access Level	Description
LastIndexOfAny(Char chars(), Integer startPos, Integer count)	Instance	Returns the index of the last occurrence of any character in the given array starting at the given position and searching for count characters.
PadLeft(Integer totalWidth)	Instance	Adds to the left the required number of spaces to the instance string to make it totalWidth.
PadLeft(Integer totalWidth, Char x)	Instance	Adds to the left the required number of the given character to the instance string to make it totalWidth.
PadRight(Integer totalWidth)	Instance	Adds to the right the required number of spaces to the instance string to make it totalWidth.
PadRight(Integer totalWidth, Char x)	Instance	Adds to the right the required number of the given character to the instance string to make it totalWidth.
Remove(Integer startPos, Integer count)	Instance	Starting at startPos, removes count characters.
Replace(Char oldChar, Char newChar)	Instance	Replaces all occurrences of oldChar with newChar in the instance string.
Replace(String oldString, String newString)	Instance	Replaces all occurrences of oldString with newString in the instance string.
Split(ParamArray separators())	Instance	Splits the instance string according to the given character separators.
Split(ParamArray separators (), Integer maxElements)	Instance	Splits the instance string according to the given character separators. Returns up to maxElements.
StartsWith(String str)	Instance	Returns True if the instance string starts with the given string.
SubString(Integer startPos)	Instance	Returns a sub-string starting at the given position.

Method	Access Level	Description
SubString(Integer startPos, Integer length)	Instance	Returns a sub-string starting at the given position and for given length.
ToCharArray()	Instance	Returns a character array with the character values in the string instance.
ToCharArray(Integer startPos, Integer length)	Instance	Returns a character array with the character values in the string instance starting from startPos of length characters.
ToLower()	Instance	Returns a lowercase copy of the instance string.
ToLower(CultureInfo culture)	Instance	Returns a lowercase copy of the instance string according to the given culture settings.
ToString()	Instance	Returns a reference to the instance string.
ToString(IFormatProvider format)	Instance	Returns a reference to the instance string.
ToUpper()	Instance	Returns an uppercase copy of the instance string.
ToUpper(CultureInfo culture)	Instance	Returns an uppercase copy of the instance string, according to the given culture settings.
Trim()	Instance	Removes all leading and trailing white space characters in the string instance.
Trim(ParamArray chars())	Instance	Removes all leading and trailing specified characters in the string instance.
TrimEnd(ParamArray chars())	Instance	Removes all trailing specified characters in the string instance. If none are specified, whitespace characters are removed.
TrimStart(ParamArray chars())	Instance	Removes all leading specified characters in the string instance. If none are specified, white space characters are removed.

VB.NET

Text Manipulation

Handbook

Appendix B

The StringBuilder Class

In this appendix are listed all of the methods, properties, and constructors for the StringBuilder class. More details can be found in Chapter 2.

Constructors

Below are the constructors invoked on creation of a new StringBuilder object:

Constructor	Description
StringBuilder()	Creates a new StringBuilder object with an initial length of zero characters and default capacity of 16 characters.
StringBuilder(Integer capacity)	Creates a new StringBuilder object with an initial length of zero characters and given initial capacity.
StringBuilder(String strValue)	Creates a new StringBuilder object with string value of strValue.

StringBuilder(
  Integer capacity,
  Integer maxCapacity)
	Creates a new StringBuilder object with an initial length of zero characters and given initial capacity. The capacity is defined to not grow larger than maxCapacity.

Table continued on following page

Constructor	Description

StringBuilder(
   String strValue,
   Integer capacity)
	Creates a new StringBuilder object with string value of strValue, and given initial capacity.

StringBuilder(
   String strValue,
   Integer startPos,
   Integer length,
   Integer capacity)
	Creates a new StringBuilder object with a value of the given sub-string of strValue defined by startPos and length.

Properties

Here are the properties of any StringBuilder instance:

Property	Description
Capacity	The number of characters currently allocated for the instance. Not necessarily the same value as the Length property.
Chars(Integer index)	Gets or sets the character within the string at the position: index.
Length	The number of characters in the string. Can be set smaller than the current string value to truncate it.
MaxCapacity	The maximum number of characters that can be allocated for this instance.

Methods

Below are all the methods of a StringBuilder instance. There are no Shared methods:

Method	Description
Append(<type>)	Appends the string representation of the given value. There is an overload for each .NET primitive type. For brevity, they are not all listed here.

Method	Description
Append(Char value, Integer count)	Appends the given character value count times.
Append(Char charArray(), Integer startPos, Integer count)	Appends a sub-string of a Char() array, defined by the given parameters.
Append(String strValue, Integer startPos, Integer count)	Appends a sub-string of strValue, defined by the given parameters.
AppendFormat(String specification, Object value)	Appends a formatted string defined by the given specification and value.
AppendFormat(String specification, ParamArray values())	Appends a formatted string defined by the given specification and value.
AppendFormat(IFormatProvider provider, String specification, Object value)	Appends a formatted string defined by the given specification and value and according to the given format provider.
AppendFormat(String specification, Object value1, Object value2)	Appends a formatted string defined by the given specification and values.
AppendFormat(String specification, Object value1, Object value2, Object value3)	Appends a formatted string defined by the given specification and values.
EnsureCapacity(Integer capacity)	If the current capacity is less than the given capacity, memory is allocated to increase memory to the given capacity.
Equals(StringBuilder sb)	Returns True if current instance and given StringBuilder have the same value.

Table continued on following page

Method	Description
GetHashCode()	Returns a unique hash code for the StringBuilder instance.
GetType()	Returns the type of the StringBuilder instance.
Insert(Integer position, \<type>)	Inserts at the given position the value provided as the second parameter. There is an overload for each .NET primitive type. For brevity, they are not all listed here.

Insert(Integer position,
  String strValue,
  Integer count)
	Inserts strValue at the given position, count number of times.

Insert(Integer position,
  Char charArray(),
  Integer startPos,
  Integer count)
	Inserts a sub-string of the given Char array, defined by the given parameters, at the given position.

Remove(Integer startPos, Integer count)	Removes count characters starting at startPos.
Replace(Char oldChar, Char newChar)	Replaces all occurrences of oldChar with newChar in the instance string.
Replace(String oldString, String newString)	Replaces all occurrences of oldString with newString in the instance string.

Replace(Char oldChar,
  Char newChar,
  Integer startPos,
  Integer count)
	Replaces all occurrences of oldChar with newChar in the instance string between positions startPos and count − 1.

Replace(String oldString,
  String newString,
  Integer startPos,
  Integer count)
	Replaces all occurrences of oldString with newString in the instance string between positions startPos and count − 1.

ToString()	Returns a reference to a String object whose value is the same as that contained within the StringBuilder instance.
ToString(Integer startPos, Integer count)	Returns a reference to a String object whose value is the sub-string of StringBuilder defined by the given parameters.

VB.NET

Text Manipulation

Handbook

Appendix C

C

Regular Expression Syntax

In this appendix we include details of the various characters that can be used inside a regular expression to match text. This can be used as a quick reference if you need to decipher an existing regular expression.

Matching Characters

Character Class	Characters it Matches	Example
\d	Any digit from 0 to 9	\d\d matches 72, but not aa or 7a.
\D	Any character that is not a numerical digit	\D\D\D matches abc, but not 123.
\w	Any word character, as in A-Z, a-z, 0-9, and the underscore character _	\w\w\w\w matches Ab_2, but not £$%* or Ab_@.
\W	Any non-word character	\W matches @, but not the letter a.
\s	Any whitespace character, includes tab, newline, carriage return, form feed and vertical tab	Matches all traditional whitespace characters, as defined in HTML, XML, and other standards.
\S	Any non-whitespace character	Every character bar whitespace: A%&g3:, etc.

Table continued on following page

Character Class	Characters it Matches	Example
.	Any character	". " matches any single character, except a newline character (unless the MultiLine option has been set).
[...]	Any one of the characters between the brackets	[abc] will match a single character a, or b, or c, but nothing else.
		[a-z] will match any character in the range a to z.
[^...]	Any character, but not one of those inside the brackets	[^abc] will match any character except a or b or c, but A or B or C could be matched by this pattern.
		[^a-z] will match any character which is not in the range a to z, but all uppercase letters could be matched by this pattern.

Repetition Characters

Below, you can see the repetition characters.

Repetition Character	Meaning	Example
{n}	Match n of the previous item	x{2} matches xx, but not x or xxx
{n,}	Match n or more of the previous item	x{2,} matches two or more xs, that is xx, xxx, xxxx, xxxxx, ...
{n,m}	Match at least n and at most m of the preceding item; if n is 0, that makes the character optional	x{2,4} matches xx, xxx, and xxxx, but not x or xxxxx
?	Match the previous item zero or one times, essentially making it optional	x? matches x or zero x

Repetition Character	Meaning	Example
+	Match the previous item one or more times	x+ matches x, or xx, or any number of x greater than zero
*	Match the previous item zero or more times	x* matches zero x, x, xx, or any number of x

Positional Characters

Below are the various positional characters. These apply to the character or group to the immediate left or right.

Position Character	Description
^	The following pattern must be at the start of the string, or if it's a multi-line string, at the beginning of a line. For multi-line text, (a string that contains carriage returns) we need to set the multi-line flag.
$	The preceding pattern must be at the end of the string, or if it is a multi-line string then at the end of a line.
\A	The preceeding pattern must be at the start of the string; the multi-line flag is ignored.
\z	The preceding pattern must be at the end of the string; the multi-line flag is ignored.
\Z	The preceeding pattern must be at the end of the string or before a newline at the end of a string.
\b	This matches a word boundary, essentially the point between a word character and a non-word character. Remember a word character is any of [a-zA-Z0-9_]. The start of a word.
\B	This matches a position that is not a word boundary; not the start of a word.

Grouping Characters

Below you can find the various grouping characters that can be used to collect together specific matches and which allow you to retrieve these specific matches.

Grouping Character	Definition	Example
( )	This groups together the characters matched by the pattern inside the brackets. It's a capturing group; this means the characters matched by the pattern become part of the final match, unless the ExplicitCapture option is set – which would mean that by default, the characters are not part of the match.	With input string: `ABC1 DEF2 XY` The regular expression that matches three characters A to Z and then one digit: `([A-Z]{3})\d` will produce two matches: `Match 1 = ABC1` `Match 2 = DEF2` with each match having one group: `Match 1's first group = ABC` `Match 2's first group = DEF` With backreferencing we can access the group via its number within the regular expression and also via VB.Net and the Group and GroupCollection classes. If the ExplicitCapture option is set then the contents captured by the groups will not be available.
(?:)	This groups together the characters matched by the pattern inside the brackets. It's a non-capturing group, this means the characters matched by the pattern will not be captured as a group, though it will form part of the final match results. It's basically exactly the same as the group type above but as if the ExplicitCapture option was set.	With input string: `1A BB SA 1 C` the regular expression that matches a digit or a letter from A - Z, followed by any word character is: `(?:\d|[A-Z])\w` and this will produce three matches: `First Match = 1A` `Second Match = BB` `Third  Match = SA` but there will be no groups captured.

Grouping Character	Definition	Example

(?<name>)	This groups together the characters matched by the pattern inside the brackets, and gives the group a name, as specified between the angle brackets. Within the regular expression we can use the name for back referencing, instead of having to use a number. It's a capturing group, even if the ExplicitCapture option is set; this means the characters matched within the group are available for back referencing or via access from the Group class, as we'll see shortly.	With the input string:
		
		`Characters in Sienfeld included Jerry Seinfeld, Elaine Benes, Cosmo Kramer and George Costanza`
		
		the regular expression to match their first and last names and capture the last name in a group called lastName is:
		
		`\b[A-Z][a-z]+ (?<lastName>[A-Z][a-z]+)\b`
		
		This produces four matches:
		
		`First Match = Jerry Seinfeld`
		`Second Match = Elaine Benes`
		`Third Match = Cosmo Kramer`
		`Fourth Match = George Costanza`
		
		There is one group in each match, the lastName group:
		
		`First Match:`
		`  lastName group = Seinfeld`
		`Second Match:`
		`  lastName group = Benes`
		`Third Match:`
		`  lastName group = Kramer`
		`Fourth Match:`
		`  lastName group = Costanza`
		
		The groups will be captured regardless of whether the ExplictCapture option is set.

(?=)	Positive look-ahead assertion. To the right of the assertion must be the specified pattern in brackets. This pattern will not form part of the final match.	`\S+(?=.NET)`
		
		used with the input string:
		
		`"The languages were Java, C#.NET, VB.NET, C, JScript.NET, Pascal"`
		
		would produce the following matches:
		
		`C#`
		`VB`
		`JScript`

Table continued on following page

Grouping Character	Definition	Example

(?!)	Negative look-ahead assertion. This specifies that the pattern must not be found immediately to the right of the assertion. The pattern will not form part of the final match.	`\d{3}(?![A-Z])`
		
		used with the input string:
		
		`"123A 456 789 111C"`
		
		would produce the matches:
		
		`456`
		`789`

(?<=)	Positive look-behind assertion. To the left of the assertion must be the specified pattern in brackets. This pattern will not form part of the final match.	`(?<=New )([A-Z][a-z]+)`
		
		used with the input string:
		
		`"The following states, New Mexico, West Virginia, Washington, New England"`
		
		would produce the matches:
		
		`Mexico`
		`England`

(?<!)	Negative look-behind assertion. To the left of the assertion must not be the specified pattern in brackets. The pattern will not form part of the final match.	`(?<!1)\d{2}[A-Z]`
		
		used with the input string:
		
		`"123A 456F 789C 111A"`
		
		will produce the following matches:
		
		`56F`
		`89C`

Grouping Character	Definition	Example

(?>)	Non-backtracking group. Prevents the Regex engine from going back and trying to make a match.	Let's say we want to match all words ending in "ing". With the input string:
		
		`He was very trusting`
		
		the regular expression:
		
		`.*ing`
		
		will find a match – the word `trusting`. The "." matches any character but unfortunately that also includes the "ing" that the expression needs to be successful. So the Regex engine back tracks a bit and stops at the second "t" and then matches the "ing" as the pattern specifies.
		
		However if we turn off backtracking:
		
		`(?>.*)ing`
		
		and use this we will find no match – the "." consumes all the characters including the "ing" – this means the "ing" at the end of our pattern can't be matched and so the match is unsuccessful.

Decision Making Characters

Below are those characters that force the processor to make an Or decision:

Character	Description	Example

(? (*regex*) *yes_regex*| *no_ regex*)	If *regex* is matched, then matching the *yes* regular expression will be attempted. Otherwise, the *no* regular expression is attempted. The *no* regular expression is optional. It is important to note that *Regex*, the pattern that makes the decision, is zero width. This means the *yes* or *no* regexs will commence matching from the same place as the *regex* expression.	`(?(\d)\dA|[A-Z]B)`
		
		with input string
		
		`"1A CB 3A 5C 3B"`
		
		will match:
		
		1A
		CB
		3A

Table continued on following page

Grouping Character	Definition	Example
(? (*group name or number*) *yes_regex*| *no_regex*)	If the regular expression in the group is matched then the *yes* regular expression match is attempted. Otherwise, the *no* regular expression is attempted. The *no* regular expression is optional	`(\d7)?-` `(?(1)\d\d[A-Z]|[A-Z][A-Z])` with input string: `77-77A 69-AA 57-B` will produce the matches: `77-77A` `-AA`

Substitution Characters

Below are the various characters that can be entered as part of a substitution string.

Character	Description
$*group*	Substitutes with the group number specified by *group*
${*name*}	Substitutes the last substring matched by a (?<*name*>) group
$$	Substitutes a literal $
$&	Substitutes the entire match
$`	Substitutes all the text of the input string before the match
$'	Substitutes all the text of the input string after the match
$+	Substitutes the last group captured
$_	Substitutes the entire input string

Escape Sequences

Below are the escape characters that may be needed in your regular expression.

Escape Sequence	Description
\\	Matches actual "\"
\.	Matches "." character
*	Matches "*" character
\+	Matches "+" character

Escape Sequence	Description
\?	Matches "?" character
|	Matches "|" character
\(	Matches "(" character
\)	Matches ")" character
\{	Matches "{" character
\}	Matches "}" character
\^	Matches "^" character
\$	Matches "$" character
\n	Matches newline
\r	Matches carriage return
\t	Matches tab
\v	Matches vertical tab
\f	Matches form feed
\nnn	Matches an ASCII character specified by octal number nnn. So \103 matches an uppercase C
\xnn	Matches an ASCII character specified by hexadecimal number nn; so \x43 matches C.
\unnnn	Matches the Unicode character specified by the four hexadecimal digits represented by nnnn
\cV	Matches a control character; for example \cV matches *Ctrl-V*

Option Flags

Following are the regular expression options that can be set in the pattern itself:

Option Flag	Name
i	IgnoreCase
m	Multiline
n	ExplicitCapture
s	Singleline
x	IgnorePatternWhitespace

Table continued on following page

253

The Options themselves mean the following:

Flag	Description
IgnoreCase	Makes the pattern matching case insensitive. The default is that matches are case sensitive.
RightToLeft	Searches input string from right to left. The default is from left to right which suits languages like English that read from left to right but not languages like Arabic or Hebrew where its from right to left.
None	Sets no flags. This is the default.
MultiLine	Specifies that ^ and $ can match the beginning and the end of lines as well as the beginning and end of the string. This means that you can get different matches for each line, separated with a newline character. However, the "." character will still not match newline characters.
SingleLine	Specifies that the "." special character matches any character, not any character except a newline. Default is that the "." special character does not match a newline. This is often used with the MultiLine option.
ECMAScript	ECMA (European Computer Manufacturer's Association) have defined how regular expressions *should* be implemented and so they have been implemented this way in the ECMAScript specification, which is a standards-based JavaScript. This option can only be used with the IgnoreCase and MultiLine flags set. Using the ECMAScript flag with any other flags results in an exception being thrown.
IgnorePatternWhiteSpace	This removes all unescaped whitespace characters from the regular expression pattern used. This allows for the expression to span multiple lines, although you will have to ensure that you do escape all whitespace in the pattern. You can also comment your regular expression using "#" characters if this option is set.
Compiled	This compiles the regular expression into something more closely resembling machine code. This makes it faster, but also doesn't allow for any changes to be made to it.

VB.NET

Text Manipulation

Handbook

Appendix D

D

Support, Errata, and Code Download

We always value hearing from our readers, and we want to know what you think about this book and series: what you liked, what you didn't like, and what you think we can do better next time. You can send us your comments either by returning the reply card in the back of the book, or by e-mailing us at feedback@wrox.com. Please be sure to mention the book title in your message.

How to Download the Sample Code for the Book

When you log on to the Wrox site, http://www.wrox.com/, simply locate the title through our Search facility or by using one of the title lists. Click on Download Code on the book's detail page.

The files that are available for download from our site have been archived using WinZip. When you have saved the attachments to a folder on your hard-drive, you will need to extract the files using WinZip, or a compatible tool. Inside the Zip file will be a folder structure and an HTML file that explains the structure and gives you further information, including links to e-mail support, and suggested further reading.

Errata

We've made every effort to ensure that there are no errors in the text or in the code. However, no one is perfect and mistakes can occur. If you find an error in this book, like a spelling mistake or a faulty piece of code, we would be very grateful for feedback. By sending in errata, you may save another reader hours of frustration, and of course, you will be helping us to provide even higher quality information. Simply e-mail the information to support@wrox.com; your information will be checked and if correct, posted to the Errata page for that title.

To find errata, locate this book on the Wrox web site (http://www.wrox.com/ACON1.asp?ISBN=1861007302), and click on the Book Errata link on the book's detail page:

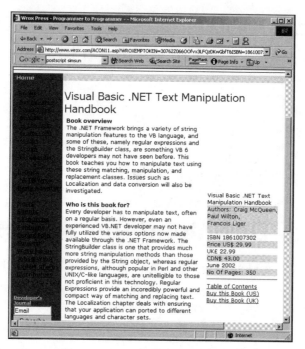

E-Mail Support

If you wish to query a problem in the book with an expert who knows the book in detail then e-mail support@wrox.com, with the title of the book, and the last four numbers of the ISBN in the subject field of the e-mail. A typical e-mail should include the following:

❑   The name, last four digits of the ISBN (7302), and page number of the problem, in the Subject field

❏ Your name, contact information, and the problem, in the body of the message

We won't send you junk mail. We need the details to save your time and ours. When you send an e-mail message, it will go through the following chain of support:

❏ **Customer Support**

Your message is delivered to our customer support staff. They have files on most frequently asked questions and will answer anything general about the book or the web site immediately.

❏ **Editorial**

More in-depth queries are forwarded to the technical editor responsible for that book. They have experience with the programming language or particular product, and are able to answer detailed technical questions on the subject. Once an issue has been resolved, the editor can post the errata to the web site.

❏ **The Authors**

Finally, in the unlikely event that the editor cannot answer your problem, they will forward the request to the author. We do try to protect the author from any distractions to their writing (or programming); but we are quite happy to forward specific requests to them. All Wrox authors help with the support on their books. They will e-mail the customer and the editor with their response, and again all readers should benefit

The Wrox support process can only offer support for issues that are directly pertinent to the content of our published title. Support for questions that fall outside the scope of normal book support, is provided via our P2P community lists – http://p2p.wrox.com/forum.

p2p.wrox.com

For author and peer discussion, join the P2P mailing lists. Our unique system provides Programmer to Programmer™ contact on mailing lists, forums, and newsgroups, all in addition to our one-to-one e-mail support system. Be confident that the many Wrox authors and other industry experts who are present on our mailing lists are examining any queries posted. At http://p2p.wrox.com/, you will find a number of different lists that will help you, not only while you read this book, but also as you develop your own applications.

To subscribe to a mailing list follow this these steps:

❏ Go to http://p2p.wrox.com/

❏ Choose the appropriate category from the left menu bar

❏ Click on the mailing list you wish to join

❑   Follow the instructions to subscribe and fill in your e-mail address and password

❑   Reply to the confirmation e-mail you receive

❑   Use the subscription manager to join more lists and set your mail preferences

VB.NET
Text Manipulation
Handbook

Index

Index

A Guide to the Index

The index is arranged alphabetically in word-by-word order (so that New York would appear before Newark), with symbols preceding the letter A. Unmodified headings indicate the principal treatment of a topic, the ~ symbol represents repeated beginnings and acronyms have been preferred to their expansions as main entries on the grounds that they are generally easier to recall.

E

F

G

MSIL (Microsoft Intermediate Language)
(continued)
code corresponding to string initializing
instructions, 47
code corresponding to string storing strings
as arrays, 24, 25
MSIL Disassembler see **Ildasm.exe tool.**
MUI (Multilingual User Interface), 109
Multiline flag, RegexOptions, 131
matching whole lines, 158
regular expression position characters and, 151
setting options inline, 187
musical symbols, 119

N

name alternations, 184
named groups
backreferences and, 177
ExplicitCapture option and, 173
names
access to regex groups through, 170
negative look-ahead assertion, 178, 180
negative look-behind assertion, 179, 181
nested HTML tags, 217, 226
.NET Framework
class library, 10
classes for manipulating strings, 39
introduced, with its components, 8
resource files, creating, 35
support for UTF encoding formats, 101
encoding classes, 102
text architecture, 41
neutral cultures, 106, 108
NextMatch() method, Match class, 136
MatchCollection class alternative, 137
non-backtracking regular expressions, 179,
181, 189
non-capturing groups, regular expressions,
165, 168
title and surname example, 173
non-greedy quantifiers, 188
non-standard characters
escaping in regular expressions, 159
nothing, assigning to a reference type, 42
NumberFormat property, CultureInfo class, 83
NumberFormatInfo class, System.Globalization,
64, 83
numbers
formatting as strings, 80
validating with regular expression patterns, 194
floating point numbers, 195
integers, 194
NumberStyles enumeration, 90
numeric formatting, 63
converting strings to numbers, 90
currency, 64

O

Object class, System namespace
ToString method, 63
inheritance from79
octal numbers
backreferences and, 177
specifying ASCII characters as, 160
option flags and options, regexes
quick reference guide, 253
Ordinal option, CompareInfo class, 117

P

p2p.wrox.com mailing list, 259
PadLeft() method, String class, 236
PadRight() method, String class, 236
parentheses
grouping characters in regular expressions, 164
Parse() method, DateTime class, 90, 93
ParseCombiningCharacters() method,
StringInfo class, 125
ParseExact() method, DateTime class, 90, 94
parsing strings, 32
parsing XML, 33
Pascal strings, 18
pattern matching see **regular expressions.**
percentages
string formatting as, 64
performance
concatenation using interning and
StringBuilder compared, 57
greedy and lazy instructions, 159
String and StringBuilder classes compared, 74
String class methods compared, 59
string operations, optimizing, 77
concatenation, 26
encouraging string caching, 20
interning, 21
using ASCII characters, 23
using tries, 21
PerfTest module
string operations, 75
Pi constant
System.Math class, 63
plus sign (+)
indicating possibly repeated character
matches, 151, 157
position characters, regexes
quick reference guide, 247
tabulated, 150
positive look-ahead assertion, 178, 180
positive look-behind assertion, 178, 180
postal codes
validation with regular expression patterns, 199
pre-composed characters, 123
primitive data types, 12

Q

question mark (?)
  indicating optional character match, 151
quotation marks
  strings assignments and, 49

R

recursive functions, 226
reference data types
  introduced, 12
Regex class, System.Text.RegularExpressions, 130
  constructors, 132
  IsMatch() method, 132
  Match() method, 135
  Matches() method, 137
  public non-shared methods, 135
  Replace() method, 133
    removing HTML tags from user inupt, 217
  Split() method, 134
Regex Tester example, 138
  modified to illustrate assertions, 180
  modified to illustrate expression alternations, 185
  modified to illustrate matched groups, 170
  modified to illustrate substitutions, 174
**RegexOptions enumeration,
  System.Text.RegularExpressions**
  Compiled option, 224
  ExplicitCapture option, 196, 204, 218
    effect on capturing groups, 165, 168, 173
  flags tabulated, 131
  IgnoreCase option
    email address validation example, 202
    HTML analysis example, 218
    telephone number matching example, 198
  Multiline flag, 131
    matching whole lines, 158
    regular expression position characters and, 151
    setting options inline, 186, 187
  Singleline option
    HTML analysis example, 218
RegexTester Windows Application, 140
  expressions using groups, 167
Regional Options, Windows Control Panel, 86
regular expression patterns, 193
  analyzing an SMTP log file, 204
    identifying suspect sessions, 213
  analyzing HTML tags, 215, 217
    HTML extraction Visual Basic .NET example, 221
  validating characters, 193
  validating email addresses, 200
  validating numbers, 194
  validating postal codes, 199
  validating telephone numbers, 196
Regular Expression Validator, 129

regular expressions
  see also **regular expression patterns and
    Regex Tester.**
  advanced groups, 178
    comparing, 179
  advanced regex syntax, 163
  backreferences, 176
  deciphering, quick reference guide, 245
  decision making, 184
  fundamental syntax, 147
  greedy and lazy quantifiers, 153
  introduced, 129
  limiting complexity, 208
  match position, 149
  matching character classes, 148
  Regex Tester example, 138
  rules of the Regex engine, 187
  setting options within, 186
  special characters and escaping, 159
  specifying a complete string match, 198
  specifying alternatives, 159
  specifying repetition, 151
  String and StringBuilder alternatives, 73
  substitution characters, 175
  syntax (Appendix), 245
  System.Text.RegularExpressions namespace, 130
Remove() method, ArrayList class, 96
Remove() method, String class, 74, 236
Remove() method, StringBuilder class, 74, 242
RemoveAt() method, ArrayList class, 96
removing text from strings, 74
repetition characters, regexes, 151
  greedy and non-greedy, 157
  need for, introduced, 149
  quick reference guide, 246
  special repetition characters, 152
  use of ?, 152
Replace() method, Regex class, 130, 133
  removing HTML from user input, 217
  substitutions and, 174
  using with the Regex Tester example, 139
    coding for the Replace() button Click event, 145
Replace() method, String class, 44, 74, 236
Replace() method, StringBuilder class, 51, 74, 242
replacing text in strings, 74
  see also **substitutions, regexes.**
Resgen.exe utility, 35
resource files, .NET, 35
  XML version, 35
Result() method, Match class, 137
Reverse() method, Array class, 26, 72
RightToLeft flag, RegexOptions, 131
Rotor tool see shared source CLI.

S

WROX
Programmer to Programmer™

WROX PRESS INC.

Wrox writes books for you. Any suggestions, or ideas
about how you want information given in your
ideal book will be studied by our team.
Your comments are always valued at Wrox.

Free phone in USA 800-USE-WROX
Fax (312) 893 8001

UK Tel. (0121) 687 4100   Fax (0121) 687 4101

NB. If you post the bounce back card below in the UK, please send it to:
Wrox Press Ltd., Arden House, 1102 Warwick Road, Acocks Green, Birmingham. B27 9BH. UK.

Registration Code : 73026Y3J1D5VOHA01

VB.NET Text Manipulation Handbook - Registration Card

Name

Address

City _____ State/Region

Country _____ Postcode/Zip

E-mail

Occupation

How did you hear about this book?

☐ Book review (name)
☐ Advertisement (name)
☐ Recommendation
☐ Catalog
☐ Other

Where did you buy this book?

☐ Bookstore (name) _____ City
☐ Computer Store (name)
☐ Mail Order
☐ Other

What influenced you in the
purchase of this book?

☐ Cover Design
☐ Contents
☐ Other (please specify)

How did you rate the overall
contents of this book?

☐ Excellent   ☐ Good
☐ Average   ☐ Poor

What did you find most useful about this book?

What did you find least useful about this book?

Please add any additional comments.

What other subjects will you buy a computer
book on soon?

What is the best computer book you have used this year?

*Note: This information will only be used to keep you updated
about new Wrox Press titles and will not be used for any other
purpose or passed to any other third party.*

Check here if you **DO NOT** want to receive further support for this book. ▮

7302

7302

wrox
PROGRAMMER TO PROGRAMMER™